Cool Infographics

Effective Communication with Data Visualization and Design

Randy Krum

WILEY

Cool Infographics: Effective Communication with Data Visualization and Design

Published by
John Wiley & Sons, Inc.
10475 Crosspoint Boulevard
Indianapolis, IN 46256
www.wiley.com

Copyright © 2014 by John Wiley & Sons, Inc., Indianapolis, Indiana
Published simultaneously in Canada

ISBN: 978-1-118-58230-5
ISBN: 978-1-118-58228-2 (ebk)
ISBN: 978-1-118-83715-3 (ebk)

Manufactured in the United States of America

SKY10078182_070124

For general information on our other products and services please contact our Customer Care Department within the United States at (877) 762-2974, outside the United States at (317) 572-3993 or fax (317) 572-4002.

Wiley publishes in a variety of print and electronic formats and by print-on-demand. Some material included with standard print versions of this book may not be included in e-books or in print-on-demand. If this book refers to media such as a CD or DVD that is not included in the version you purchased, you may download this material at http://booksupport.wiley.com. For more information about Wiley products, visit www.wiley.com.

Library of Congress Control Number: 2013948016

For Dale, in whose eyes my company is at least as important as Google...but maybe not as big a deal as Apple. Within a week of opening my company, he asked a random hairdresser, "My dad has his own company, InfoNewt. Have you heard of it?"

You're the reason I keep dreaming big.

About the Author

Randy Krum is the founder and president of InfoNewt (www.infonewt .com), a data visualization and infographics design company. In 2007, he started the Cool Infographics blog (www.coolinfographics.com) as a hobby, which has since grown into one of the world's most popular websites focused on infographics.

Randy is a designer of data visualizations and infographics for both online and internal use for clients. He is also a frequent speaker at conferences, professional organizations, MBA classes, corporate meetings, and government agencies. He was honored to be selected as the 2012 Central Intelligence Agency speaker series presenter. With a degree in mechanical engineering rather than graphic design and 15 years of prior experience working for consumer product companies, Randy focuses on telling visual stories with data.

Acknowledgments

I must first thank Carol Long from John Wiley & Sons whose first question, "Have you considered writing a book?" led ultimately to the one you are holding. I might have put it off indefinitely if not for Carol's confidence in me.

At John Wiley & Sons I especially thank Adaobi Obi Tulton, my project editor, for her patience with this first-time author and her enthusiasm for the project. Thanks also to Nancy Gage (www.coroflot.com/n-gage), Ashley Zurcher, San Dee Phillips, Christine Mugnolo, Katie Wisor, and the many other people involved in bringing this book together.

Heartfelt appreciation to my good friend Penny Sansbury for acting as my personal editor. Penny not only brought her technical writing background to the table, but she's the kind of friend from whom I am guaranteed to get honest feedback.

Thanks to designer Ray Vella for adapting one of his infographics for use as the cover design.

Special thanks to all the companies and designers of the data visualizations and infographic designs included in this book. Your generosity helps us all learn to be better designers.

I owe a debt of gratitude to the thousands of visitors and subscribers to the Cool Infographics blog and to all the readers that have contributed comments and submitted infographics, and everyone that contacted me over the years to share their support.

I offer both thanks and encouragement for the thousands of infographic designers throughout the world. Your work has taught me, inspired me, and convinces me we will be doing this work for a long time to come.

I must also thank my parents, Sue and Bill, for always encouraging me to explore my interests and teaching me not to be afraid of going my own way.

Finally, I offer the most credit to my wife Mary Kaye, my biggest and most steadfast supporter. I can never thank her enough for encouraging me to follow my passion when I started the blog, started my own company, and eventually started writing this book. I can count on her to continually remind me—without subtlety—to get back to writing.

Contents

3 INFOGRAPHICS AND SEO　113

4 INFOGRAPHIC RESUMES　173

5 INTERNAL CONFIDENTIAL INFOGRAPHICS — 233

6 DESIGNING INFOGRAPHICS — 271

Introduction

I have always loved data.

The data could be huge spreadsheets of numbers, quantitative research data, business processes, demographics, financial results, map locations, or web statistics. It didn't matter—I loved it all.

After hours of working with a data set in a spreadsheet or database, I could see patterns and make interesting discoveries from the numbers. However, nobody else wanted to review the spreadsheet in that detail. They didn't want to see the data; they just wanted to understand the conclusions. That's when I embraced data visualization and infographics design.

If I could put a large number of data points onto one page, I could make it easier for the audience to understand how they all compared. People could look at one data point and understand how it fit into the context of the whole data set. Much later, I learned about studies and research that support the power of data visualization, but at the time I saw for myself that for most audiences, seeing is believing. If I could visualize the data, audiences could understand the information.

Working in marketing and product development departments for several consumer product companies, I was mining these visualizations as inspiration to create visual designs with my own data. I needed to walk the audience through a sequence of information so that it would understand how I was reaching my conclusions; I needed to tell a story with the data. I also determined that it needed to be visually distinctive for it to be memorable.

Internal graphic design departments never had enough time available to help with presentations. They were busy with product packaging, websites, and advertisement designs. My degree in mechanical engineering—not graphic design—meant I had to learn information design on my own. I came to infographics from the data side and learned design along the way.

Over time, my designs got better and visualizing the data conveyed a strong sense of understanding and credibility. I practiced and learned what resonated with audiences. I might not have started out with the intent to become an infographics designer, but that is where I ended up.

In 2007, I started the Cool Infographics blog (coolinfographics.com) as an experiment. I was already collecting good infographic designs I liked and hanging them on the walls of my office, so those became the first infographics I posted about on the blog. Privately, I didn't think the blog would last more than year because I was afraid I would run out of material. Fortunately, the awareness and popularity of infographics exploded online, and now there are more good infographics than I will ever be able to post.

What's in This Book

This is a book for everyone, but different people use infographics for different purposes. The chapters have been written so they can each be read independently, and even though I think you should read every word, you don't need to read this book cover to cover to understand the content.

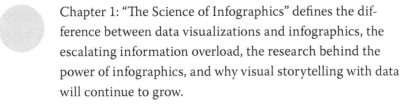 Chapter 1: "The Science of Infographics" defines the difference between data visualizations and infographics, the escalating information overload, the research behind the power of infographics, and why visual storytelling with data will continue to grow.

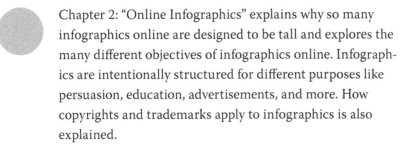 Chapter 2: "Online Infographics" explains why so many infographics online are designed to be tall and explores the many different objectives of infographics online. Infographics are intentionally structured for different purposes like persuasion, education, advertisements, and more. How copyrights and trademarks apply to infographics is also explained.

Chapter 3: "Infographics and SEO" delves into why publishing infographics is so valuable to online marketing campaigns, and how you can get the most value from launching infographics online. Relevance and online lifespan are key components to successfully launching an infographic. A complete strategy for releasing infographics online is described in detail.

 Chapter 4: "Infographic Resumes" takes a close look at the growing phenomenon of visualizing data in personal resumes. These resumes have benefits and risks that every job seeker should understand. Also, various publishing strategies for successful infographic resumes are explained, and a number of design tools are introduced.

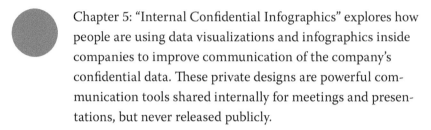

Chapter 5: "Internal Confidential Infographics" explores how people are using data visualizations and infographics inside companies to improve communication of the company's confidential data. These private designs are powerful communication tools shared internally for meetings and presentations, but never released publicly.

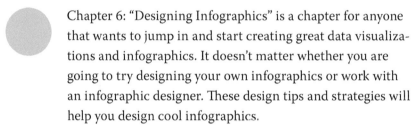

Chapter 6: "Designing Infographics" is a chapter for anyone that wants to jump in and start creating great data visualizations and infographics. It doesn't matter whether you are going to try designing your own infographics or work with an infographic designer. These design tips and strategies will help you design cool infographics.

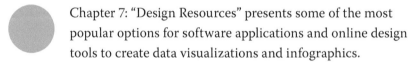

Chapter 7: "Design Resources" presents some of the most popular options for software applications and online design tools to create data visualizations and infographics.

The edge of the book is color-coded as a simple visual way to find the chapter you want.

Jump in anywhere and enjoy!

What Makes an Infographic Cool?

I've been asked by a lot of different people, "What makes an infographic cool?" Over the years, I've selected hundreds of designs to post on the Cool Infographics site, out of the thousands of infographics published online. Is there some magic formula for what makes an infographic cool? How does one infographic design get chosen as "cool" when others don't?

Like anything judged to be "cool," the criteria are a moving target and the topic of much debate. Opinions about what makes an infographic cool are quite varied. In 2013, I invited a number of experts in data visualization and infographics design to weigh in on this question with guest posts on CoolInfographics.com. Here's what a few of them said:

What makes infographics cool is that they can be extremely effective at explaining every conceivable topic in any industry for any reason.

>—KARL GUDE, spearheads the first information graphics program at Michigan State University's School of Journalism and is the former Director of Information Graphics at Newsweek magazine and The Associated Press

"Cool" infographics effectively build links, drive social shares, and create buzz in a unique way.

>—MATT SILTALA, President of Avalaunch Media

To create a powerful infographic, save the big graphics and clever images. Dig into the information and find the story that means something to us all.

>—DEAN MEYERS, Visual Problem-Solver

An infographic is "cool" when it presents an important and complex story and does so with integrity and good looks.

>—NATHANIEL PEARLMAN, Founder of Graphicacy and Timeplots

You can find the complete guest posts and much more at:
coolinfographics.com/blog/tag/cool

My own short answer is, "I know it when I see it."

My long answer is that a cool design will be a combination of the following aspects:

- Engaging topic
- New, surprising information
- Visually appealing and distinctive
- Simple, focused message
- Quick and easy to read

- ▸ Easy to share

- ▸ Clear, easy to understand data visualizations

- ▸ Credible data sources

This book shares more than 100 examples of cool infographics from designers all over the world that got many of these aspects right. These designs were chosen to be representative of the thousands of cool infographics available online.

Viewing the Infographics

Most of the infographic designs I've included in the book are actually better when viewed online. Many of them had to be reduced in size to fit on these pages, because it's important for you to see the scale of the entire infographic designs instead of just pieces. I have created a close-up portion of many of the designs to demonstrate a particular point or to make some of the text readable.

For all the example designs that are available online, I have included a link to the original source so that you can see the full-size original version online, the way the designer intended. However, many of the URLs are long and difficult to type into your browser.

The other challenge I faced is that over time links break. Sites go down or move to new domain names, but when the URLs are printed in the book, they are permanent. I wanted to ensure that many years from now you could still view the full-size versions online. So I have created a shortcut URL for each of the online examples that I control. If any of the websites move the infographics to a new link address, I will change the destination of this shortcut URL to redirect to the new address.

For each of the figures available online, there are four ways you can get to the original infographics:

- ▸ The complete original URLs for online infographics are listed at the end of each chapter.

- ▸ I have created a simple shortcut URL for each online infographic using the coolinfographics.com domain that will take you to the original page online.

- ▸ All the links are listed by chapter on a page at www.wiley.com/go/ coolinfographics. From that page, you can simply click the links instead of typing them in.

- ▸ All the clickable links are also listed by chapter on a page at coolinfographics.com/figures.

Join the Conversation

The ideas and strategies behind data visualizations and infographics are continuing to evolve and change every day. Cool infographics from three years ago might not be considered "cool" today. As new tools and technologies become available to designers, you can expect to see new innovations in infographics design and distribution.

I encourage you to follow along and add your voice.

Cool Infographics blog: CoolInfographics.com

Twitter: @rtkrum (twitter.com/rtkrum)

Facebook: facebook.com/rtkrum

Google+: gplus.to/rtkrum

LinkedIn: linkedin.com/in/rtkrum/

InfoNewt: InfoNewt.com

Vision trumps all other senses. We learn and remember best through pictures, not through written or spoken words.

—John Medina, *Brain Rules*

The Science of Infographics

Why do people love infographics?

Humans have been drawing pictures to communicate with each other for thousands of years—from pictograms on cave walls to Egyptian hieroglyphics to ideograms on modern signs (Figure 1-1). People love using pictures to communicate and tell stories because it's hardwired into the human brain.

Infographics and data visualizations are all around us. We are surrounded by visual representations of information—charts, maps, icons, progress bars, signs, posters, diagrams, and online visuals (Figure 1-2). These are all examples of visual communication, but these are not all infographics.

FIGURE 1-1
Altamira bison
cave painting,
ancient Egyptian
hieroglyphics, and
modern signs.

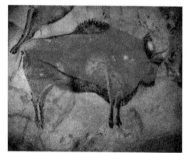

The word *infographic* is used by people to mean many different things. In many cases infographics and *data visualizations* are considered synonymous, but in the world of an infographic designer they mean different things.

Data visualizations are the visual representations of numerical values. Charts and graphs are data visualizations and create a picture from a given set of data. Figure 1-3 shows the price chart of the S&P 500, the NASDAQ, and the Dow Jones Industrial Average since 1950. The reader can easily see the overall upward trend and the comparison between the three data sets. Including the volume chart beneath the price chart, this data visualization creates a picture using at least 80,000 data points.

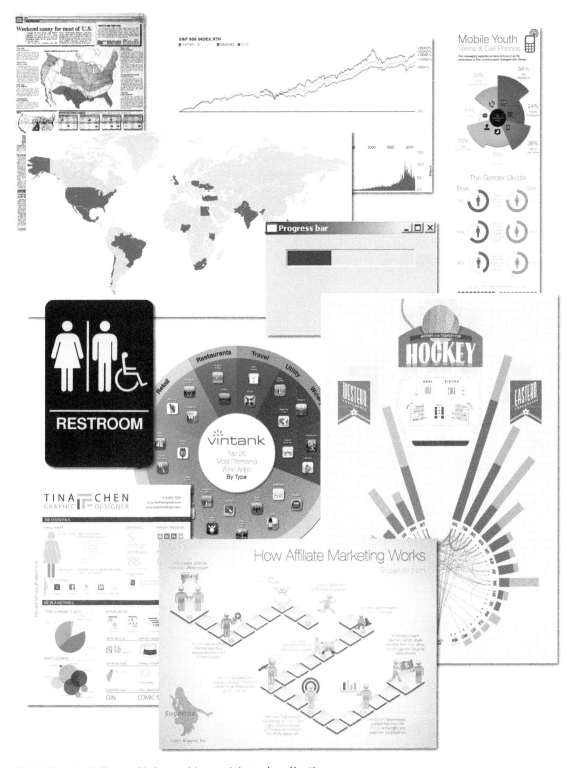

FIGURE 1-2: Collage of infographics and data visualizations

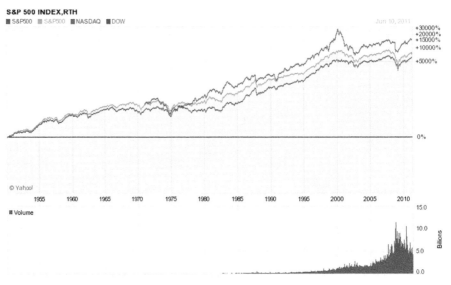

S&P 500 INDEX,RTH
■ S&P500 ■ S&P500 ■ NASDAQ ■ DOW

Jun 10, 2011

+30000%
+20000%
+15000%
+10000%

+5000%

© Yahoo!

0%

1955   1960   1965   1970   1975   1980   1985   1990   1995   2000   2005   2010

15.0

■ Volume

10.0

Billions

5.0

0.0

Stock price chart

It takes us only seconds to understand the long-term trend, to see the close relationship between the three indices, and to see the significant spikes and falls in the stock market. This visualization easily fits on one piece of paper, a computer screen without scrolling, or a presentation slide. Seeing the entire data set on one page, we can understand the data quickly and with little effort.

This is an efficient way to communicate data. Data visualizations can be very space efficient by visualizing a large set of numbers in a small space. By designing a visualization that displays all of the data within the readers' field of view, this enables us to see the entire data set with minimal eye movement without scrolling or flipping between pages.

If we looked at a spreadsheet with 80,000 values instead, how long would it take us to get a general understanding of the market?

In 2001, Dr. Edward R. Tufte, one of the pioneers of modern data visualization and professor emeritus of political science, statistics, and computer science from Yale University, clearly explained this phenomenon when he stated, "Of all methods for analyzing and communicating statistical information, well-designed data graphics are usually the simplest and at the same time the most powerful."[1]

This screen shot (Figure 1-4) from the StockTouch app on an iPad is another example of a good data visualization design. The top 100 largest U.S. stocks are shown from nine different market sectors. In this view, the companies from each market segment are organized in a spiral pattern from largest (in the center) to smallest. Each stock is color coded based on its stock price performance over the prior 12 months, but the time period is adjustable with the slider on the right. The shades of green show stock prices that have increased, and shades of red show prices that have decreased.

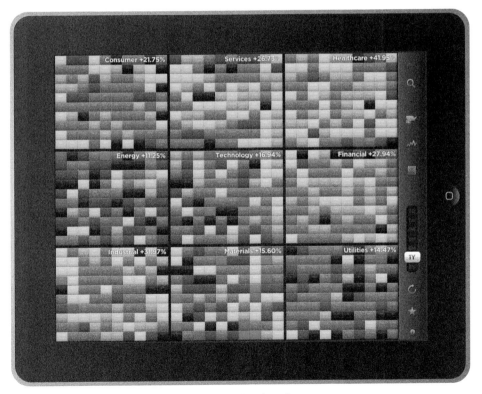

FIGURE 1-4: Heatmap visualization of stock price changes

coolinfographics.com/Figure-1-4

Source: StockTouch iOS app, Visible Market, Inc.

Whether it's a new definition or an additional definition of the term *infographics*, its use now implies much more than just a data visualization. Up until recently, a common definition for infographics was simply "a visual representation of data"; however, that definition is outdated and is more indicative of data visualizations. Originally derived from the phrase *information graphics*, infographics was a term used in the production of graphics for newspapers and magazines.

Today, the use of the word infographics has evolved to include a new definition that means a larger graphic design that combines data visualizations, illustrations, text, and images together into a format that tells a complete story. In this use of the word, data visualizations by themselves are no longer considered to be complete infographics but are a powerful tool that designers often use to help tell their story visually in an infographic.

This new definition of infographics is used consistently throughout this book. and data visualizations are meant as a separate design element used within the design of infographics. The art of data visualization is a huge topic about which many books have been written and is taught in many university classes. For the purposes of this book, they are not synonymous.

As shown in Figure 1-5, charts were the primary design element used to create the infographic, *Could You Be a Failure?* The designer, Jess Bachman (byjess.net), combined data visualizations (line charts), along with text, illustrations, and a photo of a Sharpie marker into this complete infographic design. The overall design is considered to be one infographic that uses many data visualizations in its design.

However, the best infographics tell complete stories. Infographics have become more like articles or speeches than charts. Their purpose can be categorized into the same three objectives as public speaking: to inform, entertain, or persuade the audience. They have introductions to get readers' attention, so the readers know why they should take the time to read the infographic. They end with conclusions and calls to action, so the readers have some indication of what they should do with the information they have just learned.

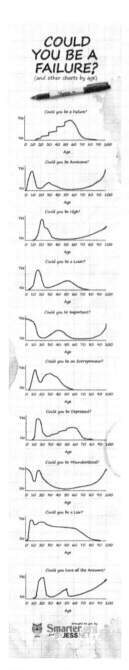

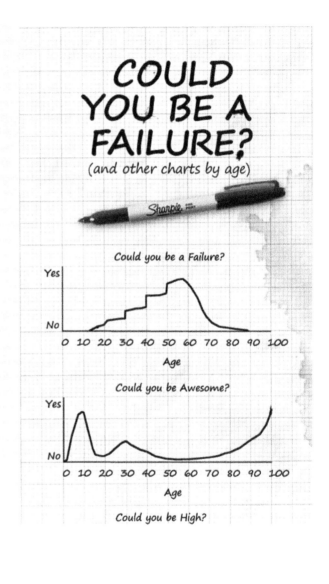

FIGURE 1-5: Infographic design made from 10 data visualizations

coolinfographics.com/Figure-1-5

Source: Could you be a Failure? *from Jess.net and Smarter.org*

This is how many would-be designers end up designing bad infographics. Many designs simply put a bunch of data visualizations on the same page without a cohesive story. They include all the data available, instead of choosing only the data relevant to a central storyline. The process of good infographic design is about storytelling and not about just making your data visualization pretty or eye-catching.

The term infographics is also becoming mainstream. Thirty years ago, the word was only used by art directors and print publications, but the Internet has changed that. Figure 1-6 (based on data from Google Insights for Search) shows that the last 3 years (2010–2012) has seen extraordinary growth in people searching for the term *infographic*. The Internet is turning infographics into a household word.

FIGURE 1-6:

Growth of search
for the term
infographic

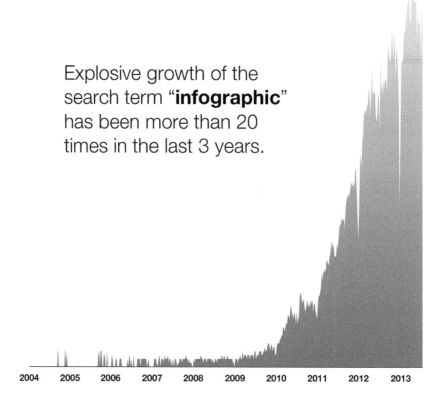

Explosive growth of the search term "**infographic**" has been more than 20 times in the last 3 years.

2004   2005   2006   2007   2008   2009   2010   2011   2012   2013

Information Overload

We are all confronted with an immense amount of data and information every day—news, advertisements, e-mail, conversations, text messages, tweets, books, billboards, signs, videos, and of course the entire Internet. The challenge we face is to filter out the junk, focus on the relevant information, and remember the important stuff.

It's a push-pull problem. We are actively seeking information, and at the same time, companies and advertisers are pushing their information at us.

The Rise of the Informavore

The first part of this problem is that people are constantly looking to find new information. In a real sense, we are our own enemy. We are confronted by most of the information because we look for it. The simplified reason for this is that we want to be better informed so we can make better decisions.

In 1983, George A Miller[2], one of the founders of the field of cognitive psychology, coined the term *informavore* to describe the behavior of humans to gather and consume information (Figure 1-7). It was later popularized by philosopher Daniel Dennett[3] and by cognitive scientist Steven Pinker[4]. Miller states, "Just as the body survives by ingesting negative entropy, so the mind survives by ingesting information. In a very general sense, *all higher organisms are informavores.*"

In 2000, technology writer Rachel Chalmers[5] wrote, "We're all informavores now, hunting down and consuming data as our ancestors once sought woolly mammoths and witchetty grubs." She wrote that description as part of her article on how researchers at Xerox's Palo Alto Research Center in California were investigating how people find information on the Internet by using anthropology to compare them to the foraging habits of early humans. Here's the condensed version: The results were that the two behaviors were similar.

FIGURE 1-7: The evolution of the informavore

This behavior of hunting for information is not new. Humans have been driven to gather new information since before recorded history. It's a major reason that humans have not only survived, but also have developed the advanced civilization that exists today. How to grow better crops, how to build better weapons, and how to survive the winter, successfully hunting for more food, killing invading enemies, and so on. Our species thrives because we are constantly learning and improving.

There is also an immense amount of pressure to make better decisions. Why do people still make poor choices when this massive library of human knowledge is available? For example, people are pressured to research products before making purchase decisions because price comparisons, promotional offers, star ratings, customer reviews, expert recommendations, feature comparisons, and third-party testing results are easily available.

Part of this behavior is that people want to be perceived by others as having made good, well-informed decisions. It might take days to decide which is the best, new microwave to buy because we respond to this pressure by doing more research. We need more data, so we go looking for it.

The Rise of Big Data

We live in the Information Age. People have more information at their fingertips than at any time in history, and this problem is going to get worse (or better, depending on your point of view). It's like putting a starving man in a Las Vegas buffet restaurant. We see this growth in data all around us; however, it's hard to quantify how much information we see every day.

On average, we are exposed to the information equivalent of 174 newspapers every day (assuming an 85-page newspaper). This research by Dr. Martin Hilbert[6] at the University of Southern California looked at the state of information capacity in 2007, and the results represented an incredible growth when compared to the information equivalent of only 40 newspapers per day in 1986 (Figure 1-8).

Another way we can estimate the sheer magnitude of information is by measuring the amount of data that moves across the Internet. First, here's a quick reminder of how data is measured. In Figure 1-9, the tiny yellow square in the bottom-left corner represents 1 gigabyte of data (a single pixel on the computer screen). The larger, blue square represents 1 terabyte of data, and the big, purple square represents 1 petabyte. Each square is 1,024 times larger than the previous square.

Estimates from 2008 are that Google was processing 24 petabytes of data each day[7] and that the entire written works of mankind, from the beginning of recorded history, in all languages would be a total of 50 petabytes.[8]

With the size of a petabyte in perspective, the Cisco Visual Networking Index[9] makes more sense. Figure 1-10 shows you the historical Internet traffic that has been measured and leads up to the future projection of more than 120,000 petabytes per month by 2017.

FIGURE 1-8:

We are exposed to the information equivalent of 174 newspapers of information every day

Information equivalent of 174 newspapers per day

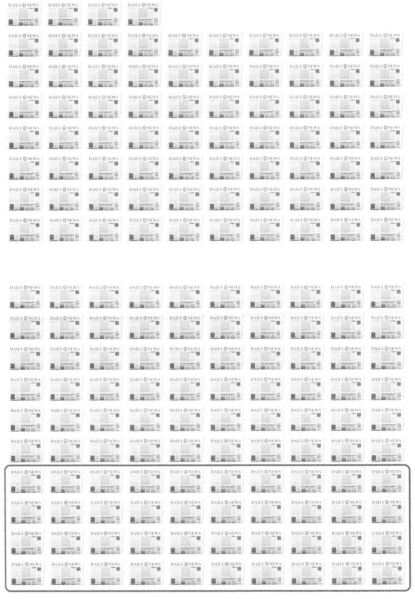

Up from only 40 newspapers in 1986

FIGURE 1-9: The size of a petabyte

FIGURE 1-10:
Global Internet traffic growth

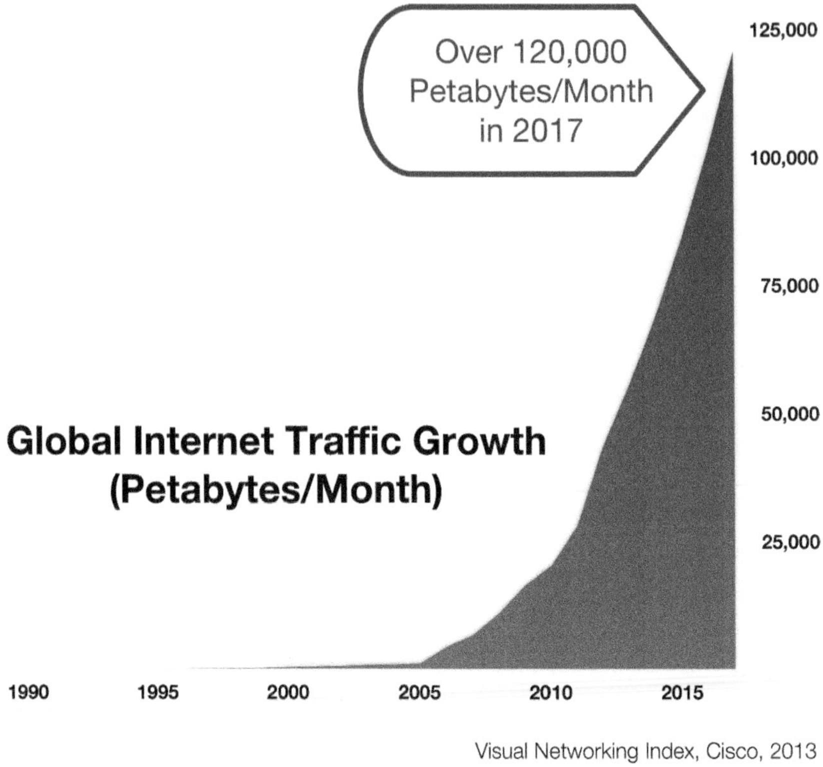

Over 120,000 Petabytes/Month in 2017
Global Internet Traffic Growth (Petabytes/Month)
125,000
100,000
75,000
50,000
25,000
1990
1995
2000
2005
2010
2015
Visual Networking Index, Cisco, 2013

The amount of data available in the modern world can be measured in many ways, but they all indicate that it will continue to increase.

Why Infographics Work

So, how can we cope?

There are a number of reasons why visual information is a more effective form of communication for humans. The main reason is that vision is the strongest form of input that we use to perceive the world around us. In his book *Brain Rules,* developmental molecular biologist John Medina states, "Vision is by far our most dominant sense, taking up half of our brain's resources."[10]

Studies estimate that between 50–80 percent of the human brain is dedicated to forms of visual processing,[11][12] such as vision, visual memory, colors, shapes, movement, patterns, spatial awareness, and image recollection.

Pattern Recognition

Humans are pattern recognition machines. Yes, this comes from the evolution of a survival instinct. To survive, humans needed to see a situation and react appropriately in mere seconds. We can see the scene from the photo in Figure 1-11, recognize the lion hiding in the grass, understand the mortal danger we may be in, and start running away in a fraction of second.

FIGURE 1-11: Lion hiding in the grass

Visualizing data taps into this pattern recognition ability and significantly accelerates the understanding of the data.[13] You can look at a chart of data presented and understand it quickly by seeing the patterns and trends. This is a much faster way to comprehend information compared to reading numbers, comprehending the math, and then imagining in your mind how the numbers relate to each other.

The human ability to see patterns and trends quickly is the major reason why data visualizations are so powerful as components of infographic design.

The Language of Context

Data visualization is the language of context, which is all about showing multiple values in comparison to each other to provide context for the reader. If we see a number in text by itself, we don't know how to understand it.

Figure 1-12 shows a numeric value in text by itself. In isolation, the brain doesn't know how to comprehend this value. Is it big or small, good or bad, increasing or decreasing? You don't know. If no context is provided, your brain tries to provide context from your own experiences. You may think: *"There are a lot of digits, so it looks like it might be a big number. I know there are about 500 kids in my son's school, so this number sounds very big in comparison!"*

This is the baggage that an audience brings with them. If the designer doesn't provide context to help understand the value, the audience will make up their own. Chances are good that it won't be how the designer intended the audience to interpret that data. To communicate clearly, the context needs to be provided to them.

We can't effectively visualize a number all by itself. The bar chart in Figure 1-13 has only one bar and it doesn't provide context to the readers either.

There are approximately

2,267,233,742

global Internet users

InternetWorldStats.com
Dec 31, 2011

FIGURE 1-12: A text number by itself has no context. [14] [15]

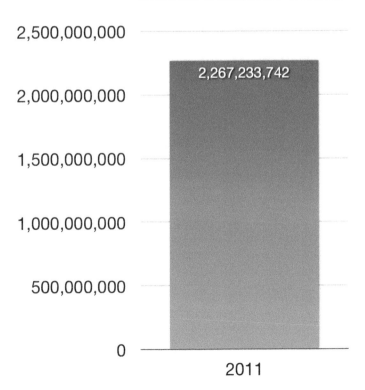

Global Internet Users

FIGURE 1-13:
A bar chart with
only one bar doesn't
provide context.

Adding a second value for comparison puts the original value into context for the reader. It provides a frame of reference to give the reader a way to understand the magnitude of the original number. Figure 1-14, includes the population of the United States for comparison, using circles to visualize both values.

Now the readers have a way to comprehend the original number by comparing it to something they might be familiar with. They might think: *"The number of global Internet users is more than seven times larger than the total population of the United States. That's a lot of Internet users!"*

There are approximately

2,267,233,742

global Internet users

InternetWorldStats.com
Dec 31, 2011

Approximately

311,591,917

Total people in the U.S.

US Census Bureau (USCB)
July 2012

By providing the second number as a comparison, the designer can control the context that the audience uses to understand the data. Visualizing the two numbers taps into the pattern recognition of the brain, and even if the audience doesn't already know the population of the United States, they can see the comparison between the two values. Context is a powerful tool for the designer.

However, with great power comes great responsibility. *All data visualization is biased.* This upsets a lot of people that want data visualizations to be objective and "true to the data." By putting numbers into context for readers, the designer is shaping the perception of the values. This introduces bias into the data visualization.

The choices a designer makes bring bias to the design. Just by choosing which numbers to include in the visualization for comparison creates some bias in the design. What numbers are left out? How far back in time should data be used to show a trend? How recently was the data collected? All of these choices introduce small and large elements of bias to the design.

Figure 1-15 changes the reference value used to create context to be the estimated total population of Earth.[15] Now the original value appears smaller in comparison because only approximately one-third of the world population has access to the Internet. This changes the reader's perception and understanding of the original value.

Notice the data visualization style is changed between the two examples. In the first visualization, not everyone in the United States has access to the Internet, so they display as two separate circles. In the second visualization, all Internet users are part of the total population of the planet, so the reader can visualize them as a portion of the total in a pie chart.

Designers need to balance two conflicting demands—the need to communicate a message and the need to minimize bias in the design. Designers struggle with this challenge every day.

FIGURE 1-15:
Providing a differ-
ent second value for
context

There are approximately

2,267,233,742

global Internet users

InternetWorldStats.com
Dec 31, 2011

Approximately

7,009,000,000

Total people on Earth

US Census Bureau (USCB)
July 2012

The Picture Superiority Effect

Probably the strongest way that visual systems can benefit us is in
memory retention. People remember pictures better than words,
especially over longer periods of time. This phenomenon is called the
Picture Superiority Effect.

Even without understanding the science behind the concept, advertisers
have known this intuitively for many years. Even in simple applications such as the *Yellow Pages*, listings that include pictures are more

successful. People are more likely to remember the company advertised if there was an image included in the listing.

This is also the primary reason why companies design logos for themselves, as seen in Figure 1-16. People are more likely to remember the company logo, an illustration representing the company, than the actual name of the company. When it comes to purchase decisions, consumers are more likely to buy products from familiar companies. When buyers are in a store looking at products on the shelf, they are more likely to choose the products from companies they recognize, and logos are more likely to be remembered. Companies know this, and are very careful to design their product packaging to clearly show the company or brand logo.

 Starbucks Corporation

 Apple, Inc.

 The Coca-Cola Company

 Nike, Inc.

 The Home Depot U.S.A. Inc.

 Budwiser, Anheuser-Busch

 FedEx Corporation

FIGURE 1-16:
Consumers are more likely to remember a company's logo than the text of the company name

Based on research into the Picture Superiority Effect (Figure 1-17), when we read text alone, we are likely to remember only 10 percent of the information 3 days later. If that information is presented to us as text combined with a relevant image, we are likely to remember 65 percent of the information 3 days later![10]

Combining relevant images with your text dramatically increases how much your audience remembers by 650 percent!

However, it's not just any image. It needs to be an image relevant to the content, which reinforces the message from your data. This works in advertisements, presentation slides, posters, brochures, websites, billboards, and, of course, infographics. A simple text message combined with a relevant image can make a lasting, memorable impression on your audience (Figure 1-18).

FIGURE 1-17:
Picture Superiority
Effect

Picture Superiority Effect
Memory retention after 3 days

10%
Text or Audio Only

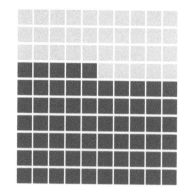

65%
Text + Picture

Getting information off the
Internet is like taking a
drink from a fire hydrant.

Mitchell Kapor

FIGURE 1-18:
**Getting information
from the Internet**
coolinfographics
.com/Figure-1-18

Source: The Information
Hydrant, *Will Lion, 2008*

In 1917, artist and illustrator James Montgomery Flagg designed the still-famous "I Want YOU for U.S. Army" poster (Figure 1-19) that combines a simple text message with a dramatic image depicting Uncle Sam.[16] This poster is still recognizable and remembered almost 100 years later because of the Picture Superiority Effect. Without the image portion, no one would remember these posters at all.

In infographic design, the Picture Superiority Effect is extended to include charts, graphs, and data visualizations. Infographic designers use data visualizations and illustrations as the visual component of a design to trigger the Picture Superiority Effect, which can have incredible success getting the audience to remember the information presented.

FIGURE 1-19: "I Want YOU" poster from World War I, designed by James Montgomery Flagg

The secret is that the visualization needs to stand out. Just because you include a chart doesn't make a design interesting or memorable. The visualization must be unique and impactful, or it won't be memorable to the audience. Just as seeing a presentation full of similar bar charts can put an audience to sleep, if an infographic designer uses the same chart style over and over again, the audience won't remember the difference between multiple designs. Designers can spend a lot of time working on the design of one data visualization to find a new style or visualization method. This long amount of time focused on one chart design can contribute to why many people mistakenly think that infographic design is just about making charts pretty.

In 2010, Sam Loman designed the infographic *Underskin*, shown in Figure 1-20. The design maps eight different systems within the body (Digestive, Respiratory, Arterial, and more) and highlights the major connection points using the visualization style of a subway map. The design was unique and stood out because it wasn't a text list or a bunch of callouts on an image of an actual human body. Even though the subway map design style was well known, it had never been applied to this medical topic before, and the design stood out dramatically compared to other medical information sources. Even though it was intended for a medical audience, the design went viral with the general public online on many nonmedical sites such as Gizmodo, Behance, Vizworld, Information Aesthetics, Neatorama, Flickr, and Cool Infographics.

Loman effectively applied an existing design style to a new set of information to create a visualization that was new and different. The resulting design is definitely unique and memorable.

Underskin

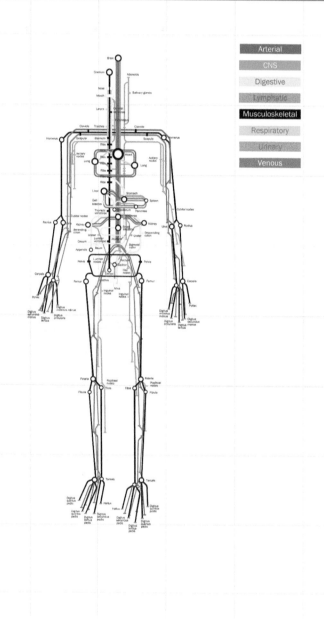

© Transport for body

Created by: Sam Loman
www.just-sam.com

FIGURE 1-20: *Underskin* by Sam Loman

coolinfographics.com/Figure-1-20

Source: Underskin *by Sam Loman*

Good infographic design is about storytelling by combining data visualization design and graphic design. Many of the good infographics follow a simple three-part story format: introduction, key message, and conclusion, as shown in Figure 1-21.

FIGURE 1-21: The three-part story format

Introduction/Foundation

The introduction needs to introduce the reader to the topic of the infographic. What is the infographic about and why should the reader care? This is usually some combination of the title and a brief paragraph of text. This is the designer's chance to tell the target audience that this infographic is intended for them and contains something they will find interesting.

This section also needs to lay the foundation for the information—anything the readers need to understand clearly before they are ready to grasp the main event. Introductions may include a couple data visualizations that help lay the groundwork. Maybe it's a visualization of an entire industry before getting into the details, which helps prepare the reader to be ready to learn something new.

Ah-Ha! The Main Event

For an infographic to be remarkable to the audience, it needs to contain some new, previously unknown piece of information. This is the main event and usually the dominant visual portion of the infographic.

This section is the infographic's entire reason for existence. The information contained here is why someone went to the trouble of designing the infographic. Usually, a large illustration or data visualization is used in this section to trigger the Picture Superiority Effect with the readers. If the audience only remembers one thing from the infographic, the designer wants it to be this main point of information.

Conclusion/Call-to-action

Infographic designs need to have some closure at the bottom where the designer wraps up the message for the reader—just like ending a good speech.

If appropriate, this is where a call-to-action should be included if there is some type of follow-up the designer would like the readers to take after learning this amazing piece of information. Should they visit a website, sign a petition, buy a product, start eating healthier, write a letter to their congressman, or call their mother?

The design should not leave it to chance that they will act appropriately, but should tell the readers explicitly what to do with the nugget of wisdom just bestowed upon them.

Figure 1-22 is an infographic from RothIRA.com that targets a young audience with information about saving for retirement. There is a brief introduction that introduces the character Tom. Some basic assumptions are outlined as foundation information, such as saving $1.00 per day up until age 70.

The main event is the visualization of the tower of stacked beer cases that Tom would be able to afford if he starts saving at age 25. This stack of beer is shown in comparison to two smaller objects: the Statue of Liberty and, the world's tallest building, the Burj Khalifa Tower. By choosing two recognizable objects that are smaller than the Tower of Beer, the design highlights how impressively tall this stack would be.

The explicit call-to-action is the deceptively simple statement: "Learn more at RothIRA.com." The subtle call-to-action is for the reader to start saving for retirement right now.

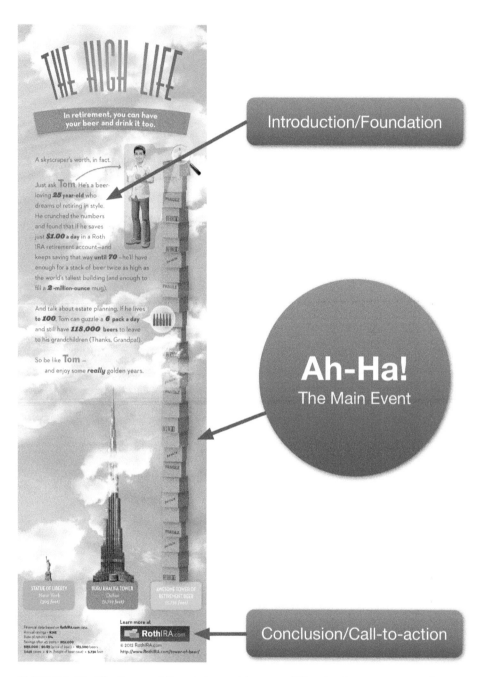

FIGURE 1-22: The Tower of Beer infographic exemplifies the three-part story format

coolinfographics.com/Figure-1-22

Source: The High Life, Tower of Beer, *RothIRA.com, 2012*

Six different media formats of infographics are available to designers, as shown in Figure 1-23. Even though the majority of the infographics we see online are static images, many designers have begun to utilize storytelling and data visualization in different ways. The choice between these hinges on the overall objectives of the design.

Static Infographics

Static infographics are the simplest and most common form of infographics design. The final design is saved as an image file for easy distribution online and to print on paper. Most software applications have the capability to save the final design as a static image file (JPG, PNG, GIF, and such) for easy viewing in a browser or as a PDF file.

Figure 1-24 is a good example of a static infographic design. *Voice is King* from Nuance Communications uses data visualizations and illustrations to tell a compelling message. The design fits easily into website and blog posts, and the static image can be easily shared as a PDF file by e-mail.

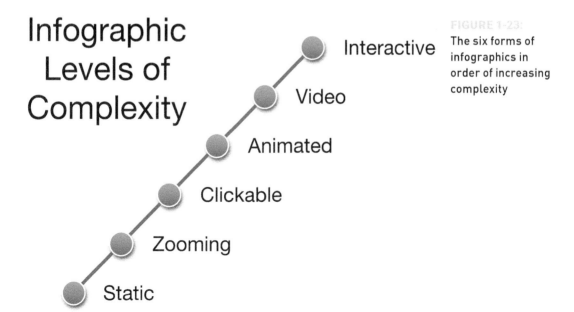

FIGURE 1-23:
The six forms of infographics in order of increasing complexity

FIGURE 1-24: *Voice is King,* Static infographic example

coolinfographics.com/Figure-1-24

Source: Voice is King, *Nuance Communications, 2012*

Static infographics are also the easiest format to share online. No special applications or browser add-on extensions are required. Static images have a long history as part of web design and are easy to post and control in web design packages. After a static infographic image is published online, it becomes available for most readers to share online using the built-in function on social media sites to share images.

The major social media sites (Twitter, Facebook, Google+, Pinterest, Tumblr, and LinkedIn) have the capability to share static images built into the existing status update function (Figure 1-25).

FIGURE 1-25:
Facebook upload photo image interface

A smaller, thumbnail image of the infographic becomes embedded in the status update and appears to all of the followers as part of the stream of status updates, as seen in Figure 1-26.

FIGURE 1-26:
Infographic image shown in Facebook News Feed

Zooming Infographics

Zooming infographics add an interactive layer to large, static infographics online and enable the readers to easily zoom in closer to read the details. These are normally used for large designs and posters because the small space available in a computer's browser window makes the text too small to read. A large design is reduced in size so that the entire design can be viewed all at once on the screen, and the zooming controls are made available to allow the reader to view the small details clearly.

Figure 1-27 shows a zooming interface being used to view *The Genealogy of Pop/Rock Music* infographic poster from HistoryShots. This is a very popular design, but the large format makes it difficult to view online. The zooming viewer allows the reader to zoom into the details, but keeps a thumbnail of the overall design in the top left corner. This thumbnail shows the reader which portion of the design is being shown, and allows them to easily navigate to other parts of the design.

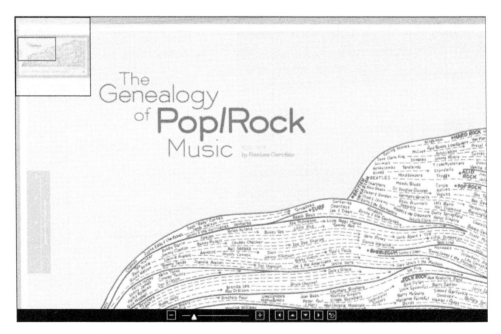

FIGURE 1-27: **Zooming interface example**

coolinfographics.com/Figure-1-27

Source: Genealogy of Pop & Rock Music, Reebee Garofalo, HistoryShots

A zooming interface is usually created by starting with a large image file of a static design and then adding the interface controls as part of the web page. Custom web page code such as HTML5 and JavaScript can create the user interface, but online services such as Zoom.it (zoom.it/) from Microsoft enable anyone to create an interactive, zoomable image interface using the link to an available image online.

Figure 1-28 shows the huge infographic design, Ownership of Beer Brands and Varieties 2010 by Associate Professor Phillip H. Howard from Michigan State University and his wife Ginger Ogilvie. The design is a large visualization of the many varieties of beers owned by the various parent companies. Viewed as a whole on the screen or page, most of the text is unreadable.

FIGURE 1-28: Large poster-sized info-graphic designs are perfect for zooming interfaces

coolinfographics .com/Figure-1-28

Source: Ownership of Beer Brands and Varieties 2010, *Phillip H. Howard and Ginger Ogilvie*

However, by using the Zoom.it tool, they were able to create the zooming interface you see in Figure 1-29. The reader can navigate the design using the mouse or the controls in the lower right-corner. The design with the zooming interface can be seen in all browsers and even embedded into other websites to share.

A major advantage to using a zooming interface is that it enables readers to see the entire design on the screen without any scrolling before delving deep into details. By starting with the big picture, the readers gain a better understanding and context of how the details fit into the overall story.

FIGURE 1-29: Beer Ownership info-graphic as seen in the Zoom.it inter-face tool

coolinfographics .com/Figure-1-29

Source: Ownership of Beer Brands and Variet-ies 2010, *Phillip H. How-ard and Ginger Ogilvie*

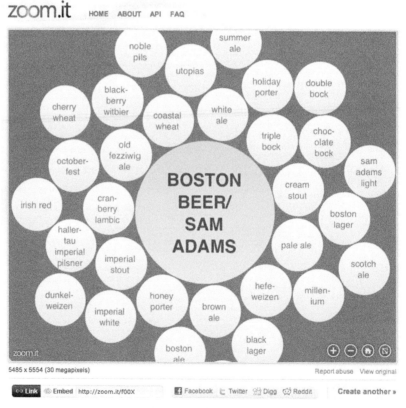

Clickable Infographics

Clickable infographics also add a user interface layer to static infographic designs by making specific regions of the design clickable with HTML links. This interface is often created as an HTML Image Map, which is interpreted by the web browser to identify specific regions of the static image by their pixel locations as clickable to a URL address. Designers use the advantage of clickable designs to remove secondary information and additional details from the primary infographic design.

The designer can use clickable infographics as a method to keep the original infographic clean and simple to read. Readers who want more information can dig deeper by clicking the links, but the main infographic remains simple and easy to understand.

It's a little difficult to show how this works on a printed page, as shown in Figure 1-30. In this design from 2011, the list of the *Top 26 Most Promising Wine Apps* from VinTank is shown within a visualization that groups them by category. Each of the iOS app icons takes the reader to the appropriate page in the iTunes App Store when clicked. This kept the design clean and simple by removing the need to spell out all the URL addresses in the text.

A variation of this type of design style is a pop-up infographic style. Instead of the reader clicking different areas of the infographic to access additional information, the secondary information appears as the reader hovers their mouse pointer over different regions of the design.

FIGURE 1-30:

Each icon in this infographic is a separate HTML link

coolinfographics
.com/Figure-1-30

Source: VinTank App Spectrum

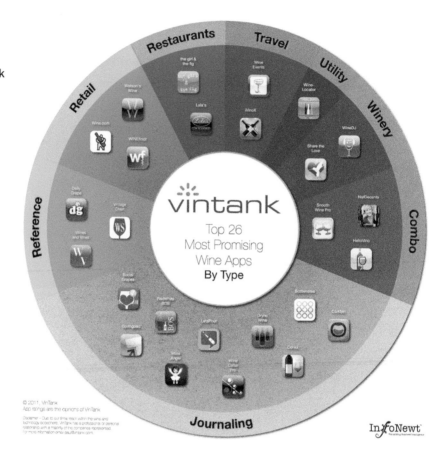

A Raw Chocolate History is an infographic timeline. The main design in Figure 1-31 is a simple, circular timeline with illustrations, but when the reader hovers over any of the illustrations, secondary information specific to that time period appears (Figure 1-32) providing additional information to the reader without cluttering the original design.

Both the clickable and pop-up design style share one major drawback. The additional functionality of the clickable regions and pop-up information is only functional when viewed on the original landing page that includes all the extra HTML code. Whenever a reader shares the infographic image on another site, only the static image file of the original infographic is shared.

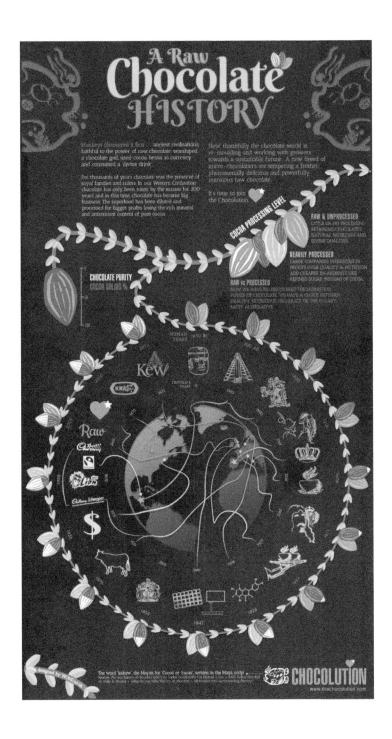

FIGURE 1-31:

Using pop-up information can keep the original design clean

coolinfographics.com/Figure-1-31

Source: The Raw Chocolate History, *The Chocolution.com*

FIGURE 1-32:

Additional Informa-
tion pop-up window
close-up

300-900 A.D. : The Mayans
The first true chocolate lovers, treasuring cacao as a restorative, mood-enhancing tonic. It became an integral part of their society, used in ceremonies, given as gifts and incorporated into their mythologies.

Another variation of this style is that many programs that have the capability to create the HTML Image Map files can also export the file into PDF format and maintain the clickable functionality. That means a designer can save the clickable infographic into a clickable PDF file. The resulting PDF file is then easy to send through e-mail or make available for download.

The clickable PDF file is not only fully functional when viewed on the reader's computer, but also when viewed on portable devices such as tablets and smartphones; all the clickable regions in the PDF file still function correctly and bring up the target URL addresses in the default web browser on the device.

My Visual Mapping Blogroll designed by Claude Aschenbrenner (`SerialMapper.com`) in 2008 is an infographic design in the style of a subway map. It's a PDF file available to view or download from the SerialMapper site (`serialmapper.com/archive/2008/09/25/mise-en-seine-de-blogs.html`) and each blog listed at a node is a clickable link that takes the reader to the URL address of each blog (Figure 1-33).

FIGURE 1-33: *The Visual Mapping Blogroll*

coolinfographics.com/Figure-1-33

Source: My Visual Mapping Blogroll, *by Claude Aschenbrenner*

Animated Infographics

Animated infographics create some motion or change to the design as the reader watches. It might be the bars in a bar chart growing, a color change, or an animated character. These are differentiated from the video infographics (next) because these are not video files. These are animated with HTML code or an image file format to create the animation but can exist as an object on the web page.

In the *Cheetah* infographic (Figure 1-34) by Jacob O'Neal, the cheetah is animated as running in the infographic, along with some other smaller animations in the charts. You'll have to follow the URL link to see the animation online. This is accomplished by using the animated GIF file format that displays a sequence of static images in a repeating loop. The result is a constantly moving animation that makes this design clearly stand out and get noticed.

The use of the animated GIF image file format has a significant additional advantage. Because the animation is completely contained within the image file, the animation will function when posted on other sites and blogs. This is in contrast to other designs using code to create an animated infographic, which is much harder to share.

How Far is it to Mars? shown in Figure 1-35 is an animated infographic design built into a webpage. Created by David Paliwoda and Jesse Williams, the design visualizes the distance between Earth and Mars at a scale that makes planet Earth a diameter of 100 pixels on screen. Clicking on the arrow at the bottom of the screen begins the animation of scrolling the page to the orbit of the Moon and eventually to the planet Mars. The visual motion of the star field and the amount of time it takes before Mars appears on the screen gives the audience a clear understanding of how far apart the planets truly are.

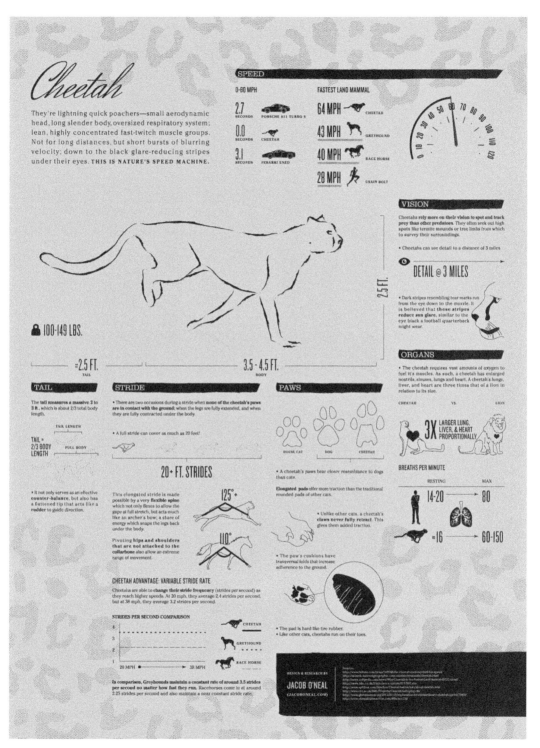

FIGURE 1-34: Animated GIF image file used to create an animated infographic

coolinfographics.com/Figure-1-34

Source: Cheetah, *Jacob O'Neal jacoboneal.com/cheetah)*

Media Formats of Infographics   43

FIGURE 1-35: Animated infographic begins when clicked by the viewer

coolinfographics.com/Figure-1-35

Source: David Paliwoda and Jesse Williams

Video Infographics

Video infographics are still fairly new but quickly gaining momentum online because of the ease of usability on video sharing sites such as YouTube and Vimeo. The ability to embed fully playable videos from these sites into blogs and social media posts has caused a tremendous increase in the traffic and value of video infographics to marketers.

The first video infographic I posted about on Cool Infographics in 2007 was the music video for "Remind Me," by Royksopp (`youtube.com/watch?v=eo4u4JJAPGk`). The video is a story about a day in the life of a young woman living in London. The data visualizations in the video are about the details behind modern life that surround her, like showing how the plumbing system in her apartment works while she is shown brushing her teeth. This video set a high standard for the video infographic designs that followed (Figure 1-36).

Other video infographics are not made with high-end animation software applications. Many of the most popular video infographics online have been made using readily available presentation software applications such as Microsoft PowerPoint, Apple Keynote, and Prezi. Using the animated slide transitions and careful timing steps to automate the entire presentation, a presentation can be exported as a video file for distribution.

The "Did You Know? Shift Happens" video infographic by Karl Fisch, Scott McLeod, and Jeff Brenman (`youtube.com/watch?v=ljbI-363A2Q`) started out as a PowerPoint presentation to the faculty at Arapahoe High School in Centennial, Colorado in August 2006. The initial video was remixed to remove the school-specific information and uploaded to YouTube in 2008. It quickly went viral, and that one infographic video had more than 5.6 million views by the end of 2012 (Figure 1-37).

FIGURE 1-36:

"Remind Me" by
Royksopp video
infographic

coolinfographics
.com/Figure-1-36

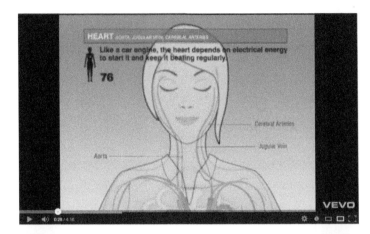

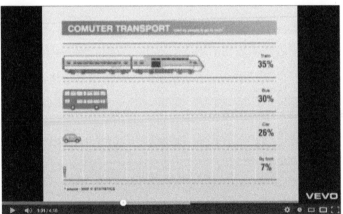

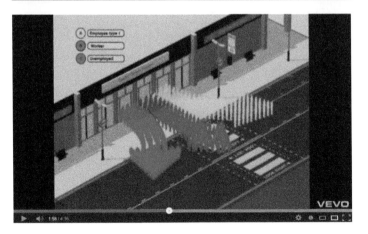

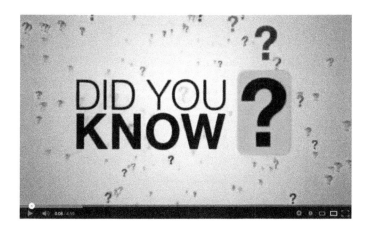

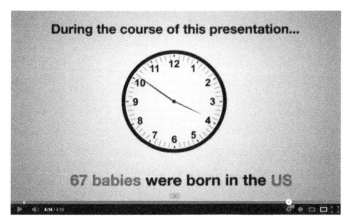

FIGURE 1-37:
"Did You Know? 3.0"
Infographic video
coolinfographics
.com/Figure-1-37

These videos didn't use many data visualizations (most of the data was shown in text only), but it did a good job of putting the numbers into context for the audience. That initial video has spawned a series of updates over the subsequent years and has grown to become probably the most successful video infographic campaign to date. Over the last 5 years, it has become a series of videos with the help of design firm XPLANE (xplane.com) and began using more advanced animation software tools. By the end of 2012, the entire series of videos had more than 33 million views online. A complete wiki site has been created around the history of the video series at shifthappens.wikispaces.com/.

Interactive Infographics

Interactive infographics are designs that give readers some control over the data or the visualization displayed. They are also popular because they keep the readers engaged with the data for a much longer period of time than static infographics. Some of these sites are standalone data visualizations, and others are built into a larger infographic design.

The New York Times website has become recognized by many as the world leader in interactive infographics and data visualizations. Figure 1-38 shows a map of results from the 2012 U.S. Presidential election. Each county in the country is colored a shade of red or blue depending on the final tally of votes. I would call this an interactive data visualization, but because of the historical use of the word infographics within the newspaper design industry, many people refer to this as an interactive infographic.

In this case, the data was being updated in real-time as the election results were officially released. Users could see the map evolve as additional results were reported. The user had the ability to zoom in to specific states, view the numeric data from each country or change the display based on the choices along the left-hand side.

FIGURE 1-38: *The New York Times* 2012 Election interactive infographics

coolinfographics.com/Figure-1-38

Some companies design and provide interactive data visualization tools for others to use. Tableau Software is one of the leaders in this area and makes its Tableau Public version of their product available to users for free. The tool enables us to use our own data to create interactive visualizations and then embed the visualizations into our websites (Figure 1-39).

FIGURE 1-39:

Tableau Public

coolinfographics
.com/Figure-1-39

Source: Tale of 100
Entrepreneurs, Tableau
Software.

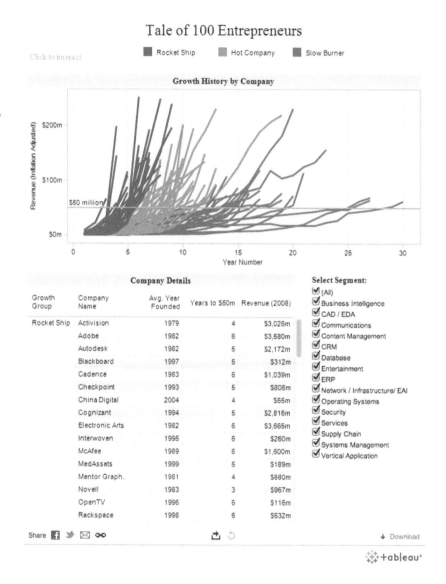

A few complete infographics have been designed using Tableau as a design tool to include interactive data visualizations within a larger infographic design. *Inside Super PACs* (Figure 1-40) was designed by Jess Bachman at Visually, Inc., using Tableau visualization modules as the charts within the design. As a result, all the charts are interactive, and the reader can adjust any of them by clicking to highlight different information.

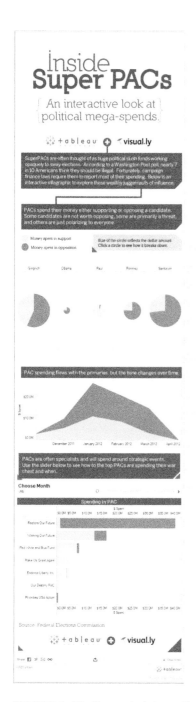

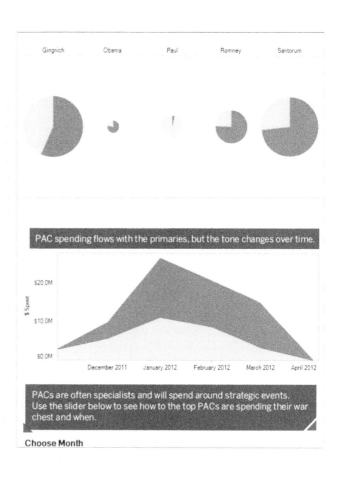

Separate interactive charts were put together to create the complete infographic

coolinfographics.com/Figure-1-40

Source: Inside Super PACs, *Visually, Inc.*

Final Thoughts

Infographics have exploded in popularity in just a few years. Their formats will undoubtedly evolve into new types of media, but the use of data visualization and design to tell stories with data will only continue to grow. We will never have less data available than we do today. The amount of data we have to filter through and understand will continue to grow, and infographic designs are one of the best tools we have to share and communicate the things we can learn from that information.

References

1. Edward R. Tufte, *The Visual Display of Quantitative Information* (Cheshire, CT: Graphics Press LLC, 2001). http://www.edwardtufte.com/

2. George A. Miller, "Informavores," in *The Study of Information: Interdisciplinary Messages*, ed. Fritz Machlup and Una Mansfield, (New York: Wiley-Interscience, 1983), 111–113

3. Daniel Dennett, *Kinds of Minds: Toward an Understanding of Consciousness*, (New York: Basic Books, 1997).

4. Steven Pinker, *How the Mind Works*, (New York: Norton, 1997).

5. Rachel Chalmers, "Surf like a Bushman," *NewScientist*, no. 2264, (November 11, 2000).

6. Dr. Martin Hilbert, "Mapping the dimensions and characteristics of the world's technological communication capacity during the period of digitization (1986–2007/2010)," presented at the 9th World Telecommunication/ICT Indicators Meeting (WTIM-11), International Telecommunication Union (ITU), (Mauritius, December 7–9, 2011).

7. Kevin Kelly, "Scan This Book," *New York Times*, May 14, 2006: `http://www.nytimes.com/2006/05/14/magazine/14publishing.html?pagewanted=all&_r=0`.

8. Jeffrey Dean and Sanjay Ghemawat, "MapReduce: Simplified Data Processing on Large Clusters," *Communications of the ACM* 51, no. 1, (January 2008), 107–113. `http://static.usenix.org/event/osdi04/tech/full_papers/dean/dean.pdf`.

9. Cisco Visual Networking Index, 2013: `http://www.cisco.com/en/US/netsol/ns827/networking_solutions_sub_solution.html`.

10. John Medina, *Brain Rules: 12 Principles for Surviving and Thriving at Work, Home, and School*, (Seattle: Pear Press, 2009).

11. Michael Weliky, "Under the Surface, the Brain Seethes With Undiscovered Activity", University of Rochester Newsroom, October 6, 2004, `http://www.rochester.edu/news/show.php?id=1898`.

12. MIT Research—Brain Processing of Visual Information, *MIT News*, December 19, 1996, `http://web.mit.edu/newsoffice/1996/visualprocessing.html`.

13. J. Heer, M. Bostock, and V. Ogievetskey, "A Tour through the Visualization Zoo," *Communications of the ACM* 53, no.6 (June 2010), 59–67. `http://queue.acm.org/detail.cfm?id=1805128`.

14. Internet World Stats: `http://internetworldstats.com/stats.htm`

15. U.S. Census Bureau, "World POPClock Projection": `http://www.census.gov/population/popclockworld.html`.

16. James Montgomery Flagg, `http://en.wikipedia.org/wiki/James_Montgomery_Flagg`.

Links

Many of the images in this chapter can be viewed by using the following links or going to www.wiley.com/go/coolinfographics.

1. StockTouch iOS app, Visible Market, Inc.:
   https://itunes.apple.com/us/app/stocktouch/id445170859?mt=8

2. *Could you be a Failure?* From Jess.net and Smarter.org:
   http://www.smarter.org/research/fail-charts/

3. *The Information Hydrant,* Will Lion, 2008:
   http://www.flickr.com/photos/will-lion/2595497078/

4. *Underskin,* Sam Loman:
   http://www.just-sam.com

5. The High Life, Tower of Beer, RothIRA.com, 2012:
   http://www.rothira.com/tower-of-beer

6. *Voice is King,* Nuance Communications, 2012:
   http://enterprisecontent.nuance.com/mobile-app-feature-adoption.html

7. *Genealogy of Pop & Rock Music,* Reebee Garofalo, HistoryShots:
   http://www.historyshots.com/Rockmusic/index.cfm

8. *Ownership of Beer Brands and Varieties 2010,* Phillip H. Howard and Ginger Ogilvie: https://www.msu.edu/~howardp/beerownership.html

9. *VinTank App Spectrum*: http://www.vintank.com/2011iphoneapps/

10. *The Raw Chocolate History,* The Chocolution.com:
    http://thechocolution.com/raw-chocolate-history-interactive-infographic-dark-version/

11. *My Visual Mapping Blogroll,* Claude Aschenbrenner:
    http://www.serialmapper.com/archive/2008/09/25/mise-en-seine-de-blogs.html

12. *Cheetah,* animated infographic:
    http://jacoboneal.com/cheetah/

13. *How Far is it to Mars?* by David Paliwoda and Jesse Williams:
    http://www.distancetomars.com; http://www.davepaliwoda.com,
    Twitter @davepaliwoda
    http://www.iamjessewilliams.com, Twitter @jesse_lauren

14. *Remind Me,* infographic music video, Royksopp:
    http://www.youtube.com/watch?v=eo4u4JJAPGk

15. *Did You Know?* Original video, 2006:
    http://www.youtube.com/watch?v=ljbI-363A2Q

16. *Did You Know?* Wiki page with links to all videos:
    http://shifthappens.wikispaces.com/

17. *The New York Times* 2012 interactive election maps:
    http://elections.nytimes.com/2012/results/president

18. Tableau Public:
    http://www.tableausoftware.com/public

19. Visualizing Super PAC Spending:
    http://blog.visual.ly/visualizing-super-pac-spending/

Competition for your audience's attention is fierce. The fact that infographics are unique allows organizations an opportunity to make the content they are publishing stand out and get noticed.

—MARK SMICIKLAS, *THE POWER OF INFOGRAPHICS*

Online Infographics

Infographics published and shared online are the driving force behind the explosion in the public awareness of infographics. The term *infographics* was mostly confined to newspaper designers and was a behind-the-scenes term used in the print production process of art departments. As mentioned in Chapter 1, these more recent online infographics are quickly turning even the term infographic into a household word.

Of course, infographics aren't actually new. There are many historical examples of infographics and data visualization designs from the last 200 years. Traditionally, infographics have been defined as anything that qualified as "information graphics," or any visual representation of data or information. Charts, graphs, data visualizations, maps, diagrams, and tables were all considered infographics.

The online revolution has created a new, additional definition of the word infographics for the Internet age. Mostly used for the marketing purposes of companies, online designs have become a new definition of what is an infographic. These new infographics are a complete story or article designed into a single image by combining text, images, illustrations, and data visualizations. Published as standalone images, they provide a visually engaging story in a self-contained package, usually an image file. The tools to share photos and images online were already strong, and these new infographics have taken full advantage of those tools to make sharing easy and popular.

In the last two years, the Internet has matured to a point at which people are now using it every day as their primary source of news and information. Photos, illustrations, and charts have always improved the readership of stories in print publications by adding a visual element, and that phenomenon is even stronger online. At the same time, online tools such as Tumblr, Flickr, Blogger, and WordPress have helped personal publishing become mainstream. People using these online publishing tools to create their own sites and blogs have quickly learned the same lesson: Visuals help drive traffic and engagement, and infographics are often more effective than images alone.

Vertical Versus Horizontal Layouts

The tall infographic format shown in Figure 2-1 is a perfect example of this new type of online infographic. The *Mobile Youth: Teens & Cell Phones* design was published online by PrepaidPhones.com and is laid out in a sequential order that leads the reader through the information from top to bottom in five sections. This creates a tall design, and most infographics online follow this same format.

This design format is referred to in a number of different ways, such as a tall, long, or tower infographic design. From a design and web interface perspective, the aspect ratio of the tall format has some distinct advantages. The technology built into a computer mouse makes it easier for the computer user to scroll up and down with a simple flick of the finger, but more difficult to scroll side to side.

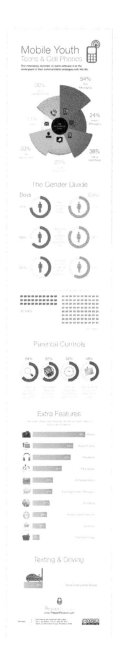

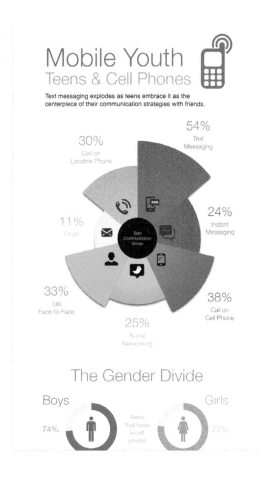

FIGURE 2-1: An example of a tall format infographic

coolinfographics.com/Figure-2-1

Source: Teens & Cell Phones, *PrepaidPhones.com*

More important, most site layouts are designed to allow easy vertical scrolling, but not horizontal. Websites generally fit the width of a browser window without the need for scrolling sideways and have content that runs down past the bottom of the window. Users already expect downward scrolling to reveal the rest of the site content. Images that are too tall to display on the screen disappear off the bottom of the browser window, and users know they can scroll down to see the rest of the image.

As a general rule of thumb, the original full-size version of an infographic is published online at an image size that is 800 pixels wide and as long as necessary to tell the story. This size allows an infographic to display on the company website at full resolution and fits within the window width of most web browsers and screen resolutions.

However, when the infographic is shared and reposted on other sites, the image size is normally reduced to a smaller thumbnail image to fit the width of the content space of a blog or website layout. Most of the layout templates available on blog design platforms (such as WordPress) have a content space that is only 600 pixels wide to allow for additional site content in a sidebar. A vertical, tall format design is usually still somewhat readable when reduced to fit the smaller content width, but a horizontal format would be reduced so dramatically that it would become a tiny, unreadable thumbnail.

For example, Figure 2-2 shows an infographic design from Hotels.com called *What Guests Want.* The original infographic design was published as an 800 × 4,000 pixel JPG image file. People who repost the infographic on their own blog would probably shrink that image file down to 500 × 2,500 pixels. A reduction in width of 37.5 percent, but a reduction in overall size (area of the design) of 61 percent.

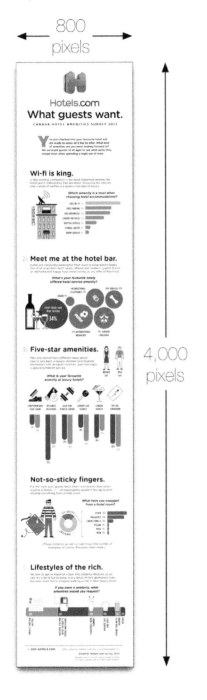

800 pixels

4,000 pixels

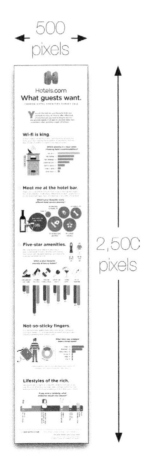

500 pixels

2,500 pixels

FIGURE 2-2:

Vertical infographic size comparison

coolinfographics .com/Figure-2-2

Source: What Guests Want, Hotels.com

By contrast, if we consider this fun design, in *The History of Swimwear* infographic from BackyardOcean.com in Figure 2-3, the story is different. The original infographic design is a wide 4,000 × 800 pixel horizontal format design, and the viewers are required to scroll side to side to see all the content. Side scrolling is not ideal, but the implementation on the BackyardOcean.com site is easy for the audience to scroll through the design. However, to fit within a standard blog format, the 4,000 pixel width would have to be reduced to 500 pixels wide. A reduction in width of 87.5 percent, but the overall size reduction is 98.4 percent—too small for viewers to read.

NOTE Width is the size-limiting factor when posting infographics online.

4,000 pixels

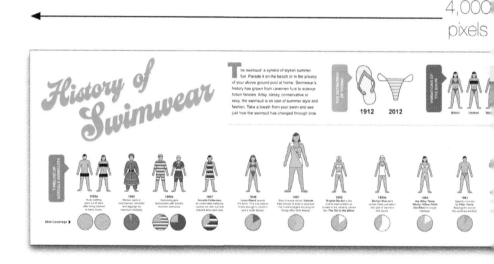

500 pixels

100 pixels

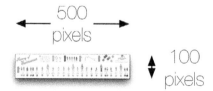

FIGURE 2-3: Horizontal infographic size comparison

coolinfographics.com/Figure-2-3

Source: History of Swimwear, *BackyardOcean.com*

Image-sharing sites such as Pinterest use a vertical, scrolling interface to browse images with variable lengths. This allows for tall format designs to display in their entirety. Although it wasn't intended for this purpose, it resulted in an ideal display for a gallery of tall format infographics. In Figure 2-4, you can see how all the infographic image sizes are condensed to fit the fixed width columns. The tall format designs are much easier for the reader to view, but horizontal format infographics are reduced to a very small size.

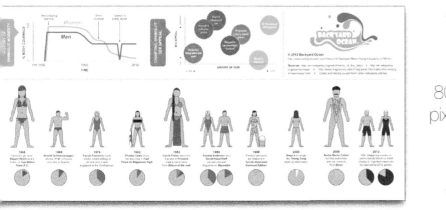

800
pixels

FIGURE 2-4: Pinterest vertical display format

coolinfographics.com/Figure-2-4

Although tall format infographic designs are ideally suited for online distribution, they are only effective if online is the only place you are going to publish the infographic. The tall format designs are particularly difficult to use in presentation slides or printed out for physical distribution. For both presentation slides and printing, the limiting dimension changes to height, not width.

Tall format designs that are printed out on standard letter-size or A4 paper or pasted into presentation slides are scaled down to make their height fit the size of the page. This creates images that are usually too small to read or understand.

The *Our Amazing Planet: Top to Bottom* infographic (Figure 2-5) is a cool infographic by designer Karl Tate that illustrates the scale of altitude and depth from 35,000 feet above Earth, down to 35,000 feet below sea level. The design places all the height and depth examples correctly on a visual scale. The original design (far left) created an incredibly tall format infographic, sized at 800 × 15,000 pixels, but when shrunk down to fit on a printed page, it becomes too small to read.

This infographic was specifically designed for the online viewing experience. The tall format reinforces the huge scale of distance represented by making the audience spend a lot of effort scrolling the page to view the entire design. A second version (middle) was created as a better aspect ratio for printing as a custom poster, but even this version must be significantly reduced in size to print on a standard page size.

In this case, this works very well because the primary experience is online. However, designers need to carefully consider their publication strategy for any infographic design. If it's primarily going to be viewed online, tall formats are optimal. If you intend to print the infographic as a handout or use the infographic in presentations, consider limiting the overall design to fit within the size of a single piece of paper, or designing it in sections that can be easily printed on separate pages.

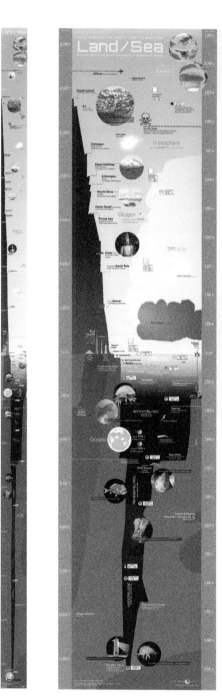

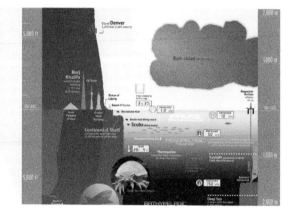

Original Size   Poster Size

FIGURE 2-5: Tall format is great for viewing online, but can be a poor choice for printing.

coolinfographics.com/Figure-2-5

Source: Our Amazing Planet, *Karl Tate, LiveScience.com*

Types of Online Infographics

One of the biggest challenges for any marketing function within a company is to communicate directly to the end user of its product or service. Many companies sell to an intermediary company, like a retailer or service provider, and don't have many opportunities to send their message to the end users of their product or service. In addition, consumers generally don't thoroughly read the packaging or the manual that comes with the products they buy.

However, companies have some great stories to tell about their products or services.

- What consumer problems do they solve?

- What unique advantages or value propositions do they offer?

- How do they differ from other products?

- What benefits to the consumer have been designed into the product?

- Why were specific design choices made?

- How have they addressed environmental or sustainable concerns?

How do they get the consumers to listen to stories about why their products are better than the competition or how to use the products effectively? Infographics have become a fantastic format to reach consumers directly. Cool, fun, and engaging infographics published online can reach the target end users directly and grab the consumer's attention.

Figure 2-6 is a great example of this from Extra Space Storage. The *Solar Savings: A Solar Innovation Story* infographic is a design meant to share additional information with both customers and shareholders. The infographic provides some transparency into the data behind the decisions that are driving the business, and helps establish Extra Space Storage as a market leader in self storage.

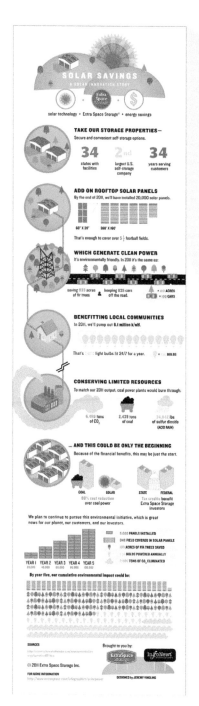

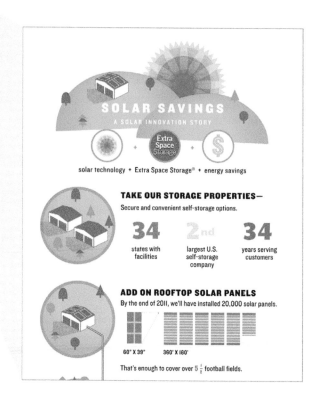

FIGURE 2-6: Using an infographic to inform consumers and shareholders about the company

coolinfographics.com/Figure-2-6

Source: Solar Savings: A Solar Innovation Story, *Extra Space Storage Inc.*

Informative Infographics

Informative infographics are the dominant type of design you see online. The underlying theory is that online audiences are more willing to read and share valuable information instead of advertisements. If companies can provide valuable information to readers without a blatant sales pitch, those infographics have a significantly higher chance to be shared with friends and family and potentially go viral online.

After publishing infographics online for a number of years, I am completely convinced of this theory. If the goal of the design project is to maximize the number of views, visitors, and backlinks to the hosting site, informative infographics are more successful than all other types of designs.

Consider this example from S.B. Lattin Design in Figure 2-7, *The Common Cook's How-Many Guide to Kitchen Conversions*. The design is beautiful, and the topic is a purely informative summary of common kitchen measurement conversions shown in a visual form. Nowhere in this design does it tell you what the company does or pitch its services to the reader. You know it comes from S.B. Lattin Design because it clearly shows its logo in the footer at the bottom of the design.

The information presented is common knowledge, available publicly to anyone that wants to compile it (people can figure out the conversion rates from most cookbooks), but the designer took the time to gather the data and present it in a visually compelling way to reach its audience. The design continues to be shared heavily online, generates sales as a printed poster, and puts S.B. Lattin Design into the mindshare of its target customers.

FIGURE 2-7:

**Informative info-
graphic design**

coolinfographics
.com/Figure-2-7

Source: The Common
Cook's How-Many
Guide to Kitchen Con-
versions, *S.B. Lattin
Design*

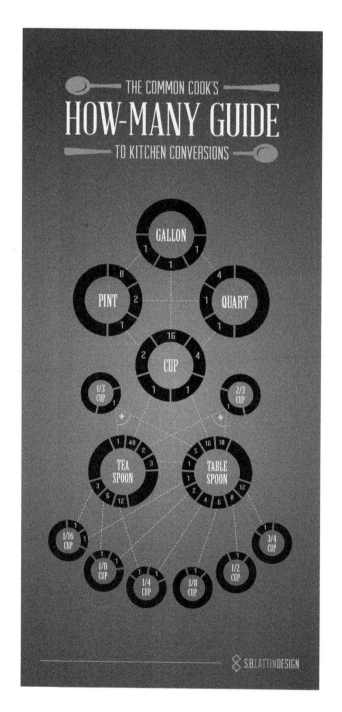

The best designs focus on a topic directly related to the company business or brand, and this creates the relevance that search engines are looking for. The infographic in Figure 2-8 is *The Lifespan of Storage Media* published by CrashPlan, an online backup company. Of course the company wants to sell its backup services to new customers, but the infographic isn't a sales pitch. Based on its extensive research, the infographic uses data visualizations to show the readers why an online, cloud-based backup is better than storing their data, music, videos, or photos onto their own devices.

The overall message is that all storage devices are at risk of failure over time, but an online storage solution offers a backup that has the additional benefits of being expandable, redundant, and offsite. Notice that the message is meant to be independent and objective. "Any" online cloud-based storage solution could provide those same basic benefits, but by publishing the informative infographic, Crash-Plan establishes itself as a credible market leader in the minds of the readers.

The link to the company brand could be blatantly obvious or subtle, but the objective of informative infographics is to tie the value of the information presented to the value of the brand. This creates a positive perception of the brand.

Persuasive Infographics

Persuasive infographics take a slightly different approach. These infographic designs lead the readers to a clear call to action and they attempt to convince the audience to do something after seeing the infographic.

FIGURE 2-8:

Informative info-
graphic about data
storage, not an
advertisement or a
sales pitch

coolinfographics
.com/Figure-2-8

Source: The Lifespan
of Storage Media,
CrashPlan

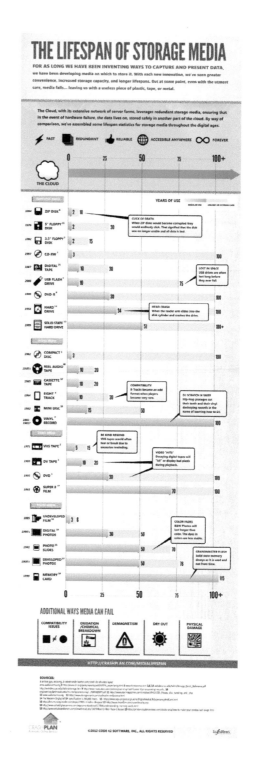

The visualizations and information in persuasive designs are all intended to lead the reader to a predetermined conclusion and then provide a specific action that the reader should take. This type of design can make readers skeptical and resistant to the message. They know the company or designer behind the infographic is pushing a specific agenda, but that doesn't mean these designs mislead the audience.

It's worth stating the obvious: "Readers should be skeptical of any infographic information." Everyone should check the sources and make sure they understand the context of the information being presented, but they often don't.

There is a portion of the population (probably a large portion) that is not good at critical thinking. Over the years, information presented in an official-looking form is often perceived to be credible and has been often mocked:

I read it in the newspaper, so it must be true.

I heard it on the radio, so it must be true.

I saw it on television, so it must be true.

I found it on the Internet, so it must be true.

I learned it from an infographic, so it must be true.

Readers might not question the authenticity or validity of information being shared with them, and data visualizations can be especially compelling to audiences. Even if the audience doesn't understand the detailed data, the mere presence of data visualizations implies a scientific, quantitative credibility that appears to be objective. They imply that the information is a fact, not an opinion, even though that may not be reality.

As mentioned in Chapter 1, all data visualizations have some bias. The designer chooses what data to include in a visualization design. If the goal of the infographic is to persuade, of course the designer wants to present the information in a compelling way.

Millions of different reasons motivate people to choose their actions every day, and good storytelling is an effective way to convince people that they should join a particular effort. The actions that these designs try to convince the audience to take could be anything. Often these try to convince you to do good things to help yourself, your local community, or the world at large.

- Start exercising.

- Vote for a candidate, party, or referendum.

- Travel to a new destination.

- Visit a website.

- Improve the environment.

- Donate to a charitable organization.

- Join a community.

- Contact an elected official.

- Sign a petition.

- Buy a product.

- Give time to a worthy cause.

- Participate in an event.

Figure 2-9 shows the *Most Polluted Cities in United States 2012* infographic based on data gathered and published by the American Lung Association. The organization gathers air quality data from thousands of air sensors across the country and is an organization dedicated to improving health. The data is published in a 200-page report for anyone that wants to dig into the detailed information, but a series of infographics effectively shares the key findings with the general population.

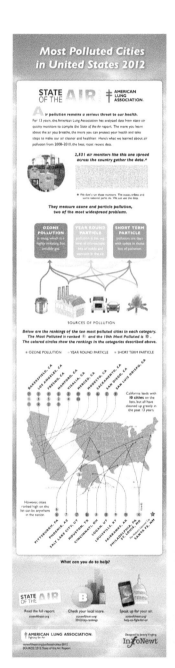

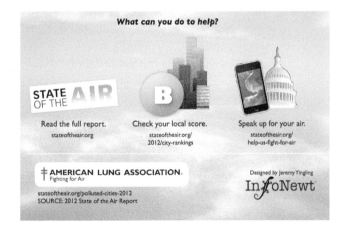

FIGURE 2-9: Persuasive infographic leading the reader to the suggested actions at the bottom

coolinfographics.com/Figure-2-9

Source: Most Polluted Cities in United States 2012, *American Lung Association*

There's nothing subtle about this design, and that's the point. It's obviously from the American Lung Association, a well-recognized organization, and the title "Most Polluted Cities... " immediately tells the readers that this infographic is about to tell them how bad the situation is.

After the readers have looked through the information, the design assumes they are now convinced to act and offers three clear potential actions at the bottom of the design:

- ▷ Read the full report.

- ▷ Check local air quality score.

- ▷ Send a message to a congressional representative.

Another persuasive infographic is *Cancer* from MesotheliomaHelp.net, shown in Figure 2-10. This design includes data visualizations using several statistics gathered about the types of cancer, different locations across the country, and the mortality rate of cancer victims. At the end of the design is one clear call to action: Click to Donate, which takes the reader to a specific page on its website that lists many different cancer charities that the reader should contribute to. This design does a great job of laying out the scope of the problem and presenting a specific action that the reader can take to help the fight against cancer.

Now break down a persuasive design. The *Can Soap Make You Sick?* infographic from GOJO Industries in Figure 2-11 is a great example and demonstrates a structure similar to *Monroe's Motivated Sequence*[1], a classic technique for organizing persuasive speeches. As you read through the infographic from top to bottom, the story told to the audience is a series of carefully structured facts with a powerful effect.

1. **The key message.** "1 in 4 bulk soap dispensers are contaminated with bacteria." This grabs the audience's attention, and even if they don't read the rest of the infographic, they can understand the main point of the design.

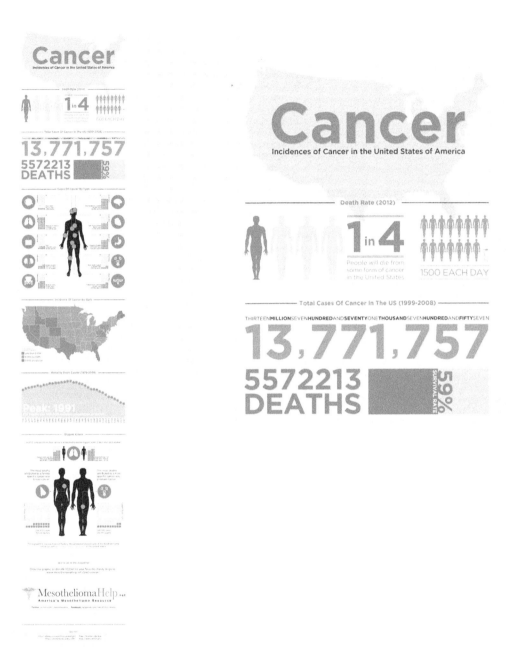

FIGURE 2-10: Persuasive infographic design with one clear call to action: Donate

coolinfographics.com/Figure-2-10

Source: Cancer: Incidences of Cancer in the United States of America, *MesotheliomaHelp.net*

2. **What's the problem?** This section builds credibility of the Key Message by explaining how easy it is to get bacteria into a bulk soap dispenser.

3. **What's the danger?** This section tells the readers specifically the risks they can face and makes the information more meaningful to individual readers. It explains how the problem can affect the readers personally.

4. **What's the solution?** Now that the audience understands the underlying problem, it can understand the solution presented and what problems it solves.

5. **What can I do?** The design finishes with two clear calls to action that the reader should take. Forward this information to a facility manager (which implies that the reader is concerned about the issue), or sign an online petition to help raise awareness of the issue.

Notice that this is not an advertisement. The call to action is not to purchase a product, but to help inform others of the potential health risk. The design does not explicitly try to sell a GOJO soap dispenser, but the design is clearly from GOJO. By raising awareness of a potential health risk, GOJO raises its brand authority, and a persuaded facility manager is likely to contact GOJO to help replace its current soap dispensers with safer products.

Visual Explanations

Many infographic designs do not try to visualize a bunch of statistics, numbers, or data sets. Instead, they try to explain an idea, a process, relationships, or a complex concept to the audience. These visual explanation designs use illustrations, diagrams, and icons (and occasionally data visualizations) to explain their topic to the audience.

The Key Message

What's the problem?

What's the danger?

What's the solution?

What can I do?

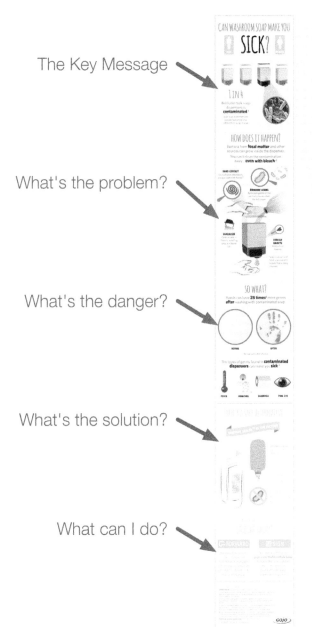

FIGURE 2-11: Persuasive structure that leads the reader through the sequence of information

coolinfographics.com/Figure-2-11

Source: Can Soap Make You Sick?, *GOJO Industries*

How Our Laws Are Made (Figure 2-12) is an award-winning design by Mike Wirth and Dr. Suzanne Cooper Guasco, PhD. The infographic is a visualization of the step-by-step process that takes a bill to a law at the federal level in the United States. Notice that there are no charts or data visualizations. It's an infographic design that uses illustrations and text to explain a process to the audience.

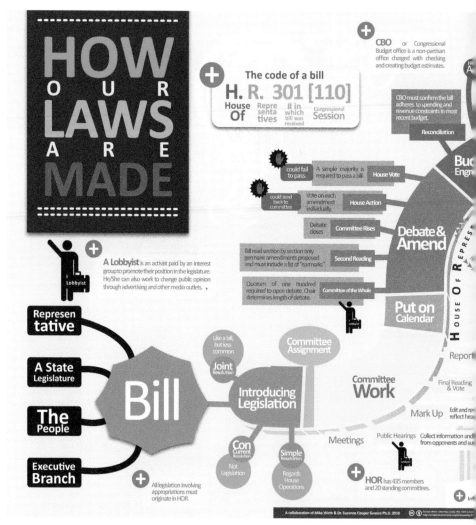

FIGURE 2-12: Visual explanation of the process to pass a new law in the United States

coolinfographics.com/Figure-2-12

Source: How Our Laws Are Made, Mike Wirth and Dr. Suzanne Cooper Guasco, PhD.

Visual explanations are an effective way for companies to demonstrate their authority and competence in an industry. These infographics often become a design that readers keep or print out for future reference, which from a marketing sense is terrific because it provides ongoing exposure to the company. Of course, for the exposure to the brand to be meaningful, the topic has to be relevant to the company's business.

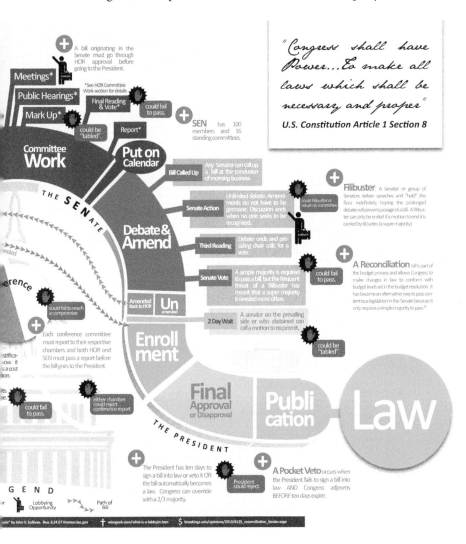

Figure 2-13 is a visual explanation of *How Affiliate Marketing Works* from Sugarrae.com. There is no numerical data in the design. The design visualizes the process by using three color-coded characters on a path to show the sequence of events that occur. This could have been a simple 10-item text bullet list in a blog post, but turning the process into an infographic design, made it incredibly popular. The infographic went viral online and further established Rae Hoffman as one of the top authorities in the country on Affiliate Marketing.

FIGURE 2-13: A 10-step process designed as a visual explanation infographic

coolinfographics.com/Figure-2-13

Source: How Affiliate Marketing Works, *Rae Hoffman, Sugarrae.com*

Infographic Advertisements

Infographic advertisements are a specific form of persuasive infographics, in that they obviously attempt to motivate the audience to take action. In this case, the call to action is usually intended to convince readers to purchase specific products or services.

In general terms, readers are less likely to share an infographic advertisement than a purely informative one. This is true for any form of content, not just infographics. People are less likely to share obvious advertisements with friends because it can feel like a sales pitch instead of forwarding something valuable.

However, data visualizations and infographics are a fantastic way for companies to show customers their product benefits. The goals of these designs are different.

For an infographic advertisement, the quality of readers is more important than the quantity of readers.

NOTE

The goal of an infographic advertisement is to educate the potential customers about the product instead of building links and traffic to the web page. They can be used to effectively share the often-complex information about a product.

- Comparing competitive products

- Assembly or usage directions

- Product benefits

- Product specifications

- Consulting or service processes

Figure 2-14 is *How to Pair Wine with the Bright, Bold Flavors of Southeast Asia,* an infographic advertisement from the P.F. Chang's restaurant chain. This is an advertisement for its new promotional menu items. The design visually ties unique cooking ingredients with the new dishes and presents wine pairing suggestions. The call to action is for the reader to go to a P.F. Chang's restaurant location and try the new menu items.

The company is obviously trying to sell their food, and that's perfectly acceptable. My impression is that the design is meant to appeal specifically to repeat restaurant guests by giving them a reason to come back to try something new.

This infographic advertisement is one content piece of a larger marketing campaign that includes a dedicated web page, print advertisements, an interactive PDF available for download, online videos, and the infographic.

Every product and service has a complex story to tell customers why the company made specific design decisions that shaped a product idea into an actual product on the store shelf. People work hard on these projects at companies and become passionate about them. They are often disappointed when the customers they expected to buy these products or services aren't as excited and passionate as they were.

The main difference is that the company's employees get to see all the stories behind the product. Consumers see only what's on the product packaging or in the advertisements, and they often don't take the time to completely read either of them. A company's opportunity to catch a consumer's interest long enough to tell their stories is rare.

FIGURE 2-14:

**P.F. Chang's
new menu items
infographic
advertisement**

coolinfographics
.com/Figure-2-14

Source: How to Pair
Wine with the Bright,
Bold Flavors of South-
east Asia, *P.F. Chang's
China Bistro, Inc.*

The use of infographics to tell the product's message can be a convincing form of advertisement. There are many specific reasons a company's products have been designed to its unique specifications, including:

- Unmet consumer needs
- Differentiation from competitors
- Unique benefits
- Lower price points
- Color selection
- Design style or fashion trends
- Ergonomic design
- Ease of use
- Environmental impact

The Picture Superiority Effect (refer to Chapter 1) can be used to make visual information 650 percent more likely to be remembered by the audience, and this is a major reason that companies have logos. A potential customer is more likely to remember a visual logo than the name of the company alone, and that memory carries over into purchasing behavior in stores. Customers tend to buy products from brands they recognize.

Infographics provide an opportunity for companies to tell the unique stories about their products and services in a compelling way that makes the complex stories easy for consumers to understand, share, and remember. By making the stories about their products visual, companies can increase the amount of information potential customers will remember when they stand in a store making a purchase decision.

Making an Organic Choice from SoNice in Canada (Figure 2-15) is an infographic advertisement that compares its organic processes making soy milk products to conventional food-processing methods. The company is passionate about organic foods, and an infographic design gives it the chance to show the data behind its passion side by side with data about conventional food. This is a great way to convey information that consumers may not realize.

FIGURE 2-15:

Side-by-side comparison as an infographic advertisement

coolinfographics .com/Figure-2-14

Source: Making an Organic Choice, *SoNice, Earth's Own Food Company Inc.*

PR Infographics

Similar to advertisements, companies also use infographic designs for public relations (PR) with press releases. The objectives of PR are different than advertisements. Instead of directly trying to sell a product, a PR strategy may use an infographic to build awareness of products and brands, to provide information to shareholders, or to increase the value of the brand. Infographics used for PR can be published as a supplement to a text-only press release, or the entire press release can be contained in the infographic design.

Many companies consider coverage by the news media as a more affordable and credible form of advertising than traditional advertising. Many people are more likely to pay attention and believe information from a news report than an advertisement, even though the information may be coming from the same source: the company's PR department.

When Honda announced the 2013 Accord, the design was a major design change to the car, inside and out. As a part of its PR content strategy, it released the infographic design, *Accord: 30 Years of American Craftsmanship* (Figure 2-16). Honda's primary target audience were members of the press. This one design was used as content in a handful of different ways:

- The infographic was printed and displayed on 7-foot banners at press events all across the country.

- A USB drive with a PDF file of the infographic was given out in the press kits provided to attendees.

- The infographic was made available as media content on the Honda North America press website, which can be accessed only with login credentials given to members of the press.

The objective of the infographic was to get attention and coverage from news sites and blogs covering the automotive industry. Many automotive-related sites published the infographic as part of their coverage of the 2013 Accord release. Only after all the press events were complete was the infographic published publicly on the Honda News Flickr account to make it available to the general public.

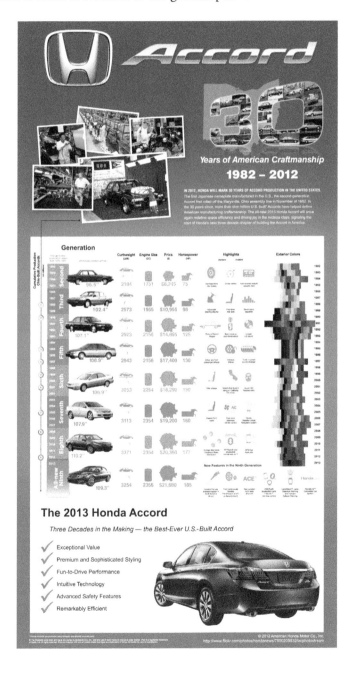

FIGURE 2-16:

Infographics can be used as part of a Public Relations campaign

coolinfographics .com/Figure-2-16

Source: Accord: 30 Years of American Crafts-manship, *Honda North America*

Hotels.com maintains a dedicated section of its press website just for infographic designs at http://press.hotels.com/en-us/infographics/. Its market position and research give it unique insights into the overall hotel industry, and it is continually providing data and information to the press. News outlets use this information in their reporting and cite Hotels.com as the source of the research data. The appeal of the data from Hotels.com is that the PR content is fun and engaging for news audiences, which encourages media outlets to utilize the information.

Twice a year, Hotels.com releases its *Hotel Price Index (HPI)*, which is a summary of the results from its own research and survey data related to changing hotel room prices and popular travel destinations all over the world. For the last few years, it has designed and released infographics visualizing the data (Figure 2-17) along with a series of text press releases highlighting the key findings from the research. All of this is then published on its dedicated press website.

Infographic Posters

Along with the explosion of online infographics, a subindustry has begun to emerge dedicated to designing and selling large, wall-hanging infographic posters to the public. These niche designers have created some amazing designs and are creating businesses selling these posters online.

Instead of designing these posters to client specifications, this business model allows the designers to choose their own topics, select the data they want to include, and design the complete infographic poster based on their own design tastes and sense of style. These face the same risks as any consumer product. The topics and data research are completely done by the designers, and they are taking a chance that their choices will be popular enough to generate sales.

FIGURE 2-17: Hotels.com uses infographics to highlight key research findings on its press website.

coolinfographics.com/Figure-2-17

Source: Bi-Annual Price Index, Early 2011, *Hotels.com*

Infojocks

Infojocks.com is a site dedicated to sports-related infographic poster designs from infographic designer Jeremy Yingling. Self-described as the art of sports statistics, Infojocks has infographic poster designs covering the NFL, NHL, NBA, college teams, and other specific team histories. Figure 2-18 is the infographic poster titled, *Hockey: History of the Stanley Cup.*

FIGURE 2-18:
Hockey: History of the Stanley Cup **poster, Infojocks.com**
coolinfographics.com/Figure-2-18

HistoryShots.com

HistoryShots.com was created by Larry Gormley and Bill Younker, and they sell designs that combine information and art. Their designs are usually focused on the historical timeline or evolution of a particular topic, and the posters are printed on museum-grade papers. Meticulously researched, they offer amazing designs based on their interests in pop culture, sports finance, and politics. Figure 2-19 shows the incredibly detailed poster, *Genealogy of Pop/Rock Music* by designer Reebee Garofalo.

Timeplots

Timeplots.com is an information graphics firm founded by Nathaniel Pearlman. Located in Washington, DC, Timeplots has released a number of highly detailed infographic posters covering the historical timelines of various political topics. It has some fantastic designs covering the history of the Presidency, the Supreme Court, the Senate, the House of Representatives, both major political parties, and more. Figure 2–20, *A Visual History of the American Presidency* is the poster that visualizes details about election results and the state of the country during each term.

Pop Chart Lab

PopChartLab.com is an infographic poster design firm located in Brooklyn, New York, founded by Patrick Mulligan and Ben Gibson. They have created some amazingly detailed posters covering the evolution of Apple products (Figure 2-21) or incredibly complex network diagrams showing the relationships between the varieties of beer, the full array of culinary tools, a taxonomy of hip-hop, and many more mappings of cultural topics.

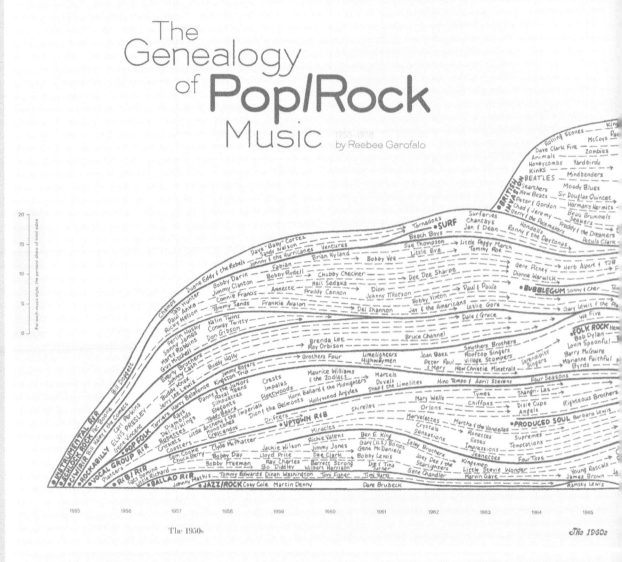

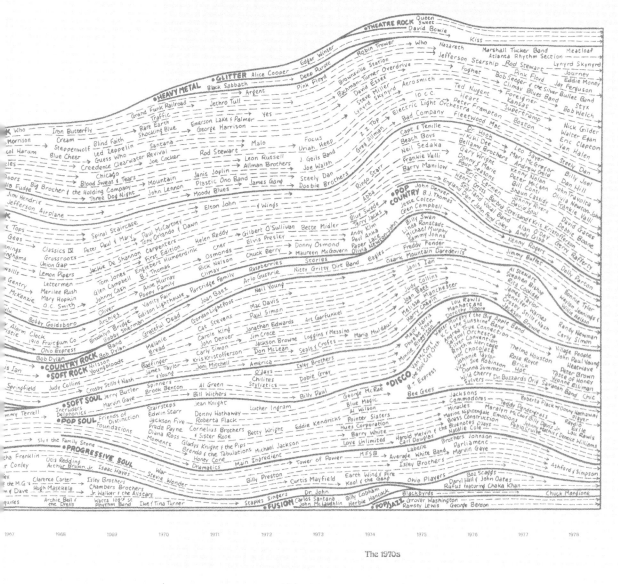

The 1970s

Concept and design: Reebee Garofalo

Revised and updated from the book Rock N' Roll is Here to Pay: The History
and Politics of the Music Industry by Steve Chapple and Reebee Garofalo

Graphics services: Darice Raley and Jean Nenaland

Special thanks to: Sam Kopper, Elger MacDougal, Beverly Mire, Rory O'Connor, Robert
Pollen and Norm Walker

Sources: Billboard, Cashbox, Gillet's The Sound of the City, Rolling Stone's Rock Encyclopedia
and Whitburn's Top Pop Records

music is clearly a subjective process and in some cases it
may be to be arbitrary. The performers shown here represent only
to a commercial bubble — the major hit makers of a
music is the most figurative; it may or may not be the most
artistically important. Such are the vagaries of the
a commodity system.

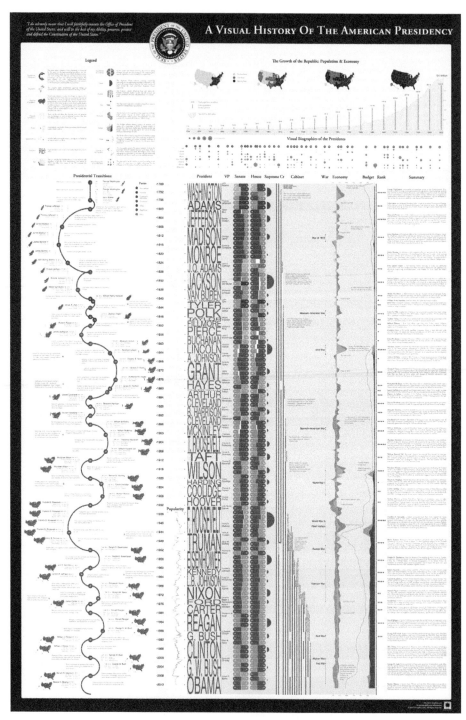

FIGURE 2-20: *A Visual History of the American Presidency* poster, Timeplots.com

coolinfographics.com/Figure-2-20

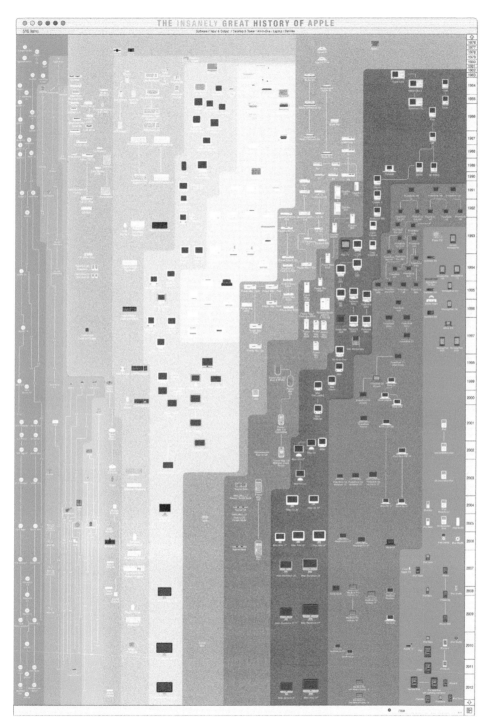

FIGURE 2-21: *The Insanely Great History of Apple* poster, PopChartLab.com

coolinfographics.com/Figure-2-21

Intellectual Property Issues

Intellectual property law is a murky quagmire of legal opinion, interpretation, and confusion. Still, there are some fundamental issues that infographic designers must consider. The following observations are drawn specifically from the author's experience with U.S. laws.

Infographic designers have the responsibility to produce work that conforms to legal requirements and doesn't put their company or their clients at risk. Clients expect designers to be the experts in these areas, and infographic designers should have a good understanding of these four areas:

- ▶ Copyright
- ▶ Creative Commons
- ▶ Trademarks and Fair Use Doctrine
- ▶ Using images and illustrations

Copyright

Copyright law exists to allow the creators of designs (the copyright holder) the ability to control how other people are allowed to use, copy, or distribute their creative works. Sharing creative work without first getting explicit permission in the form of a license is called *copyright infringement* and is generally regarded as illegal. This law is what enables creative professionals to charge for their work and also protects their work from being copied by competitors. It applies to any type of creative product, such as photographs, art, books, music, graphic designs, videos, and of course infographics.

Designers make a living selling their creative work, and any time someone else uses their creative work without first getting a license, the designer loses potential income. When creative professionals find their work being used without their permission, the ugly process of cease-and-desist letters and lawsuits begins.

In the United States there are essentially three basic levels of copyright protection.

The lowest level of copyright is given to original creative works automatically. In 1989, Congress amended the U.S. copyright law (specifically to conform with the Berne Convention Implementation Act) making the use of copyright notices optional. Most infographic designers use this level of protection because they believe this automatic protection completely covers them; however, in practice, this level of protection is the hardest to enforce in court and any awarded damages are often lower.

If a designer does not include any mention or notice of copyright protection in an infographic, the design is still protected under copyright law.

NOTE

The second level of protection is claimed when the official copyright symbol (©) is displayed on the infographic, along with the year and name of the copyright owner. Designers can add the copyright notice to their original design work without any cost or official paperwork. By adding this explicit notice of copyright, publishers have clearly communicated their claim of copyright ownership and make any argument of "innocent infringement" a difficult defense. I recommend this level of protection to all of my clients as the best way to cover an infographic design with copyright protection.

The highest level of copyright protection is an officially registered copyright. To achieve this level, the publisher must submit the final published creative work to the United States Copyright Office and pay a registration fee, which establishes a copy of the work on file and an official date of registration. This level is the easiest to defend in court and can pay the highest damages. However, this level of protection is generally overkill for infographic designs that are going to be widely shared on the Internet.

Creative Commons

In 2001, Creative Commons (CC) was founded as a licensing alternative to traditional copyright licenses. Designed to provide for more open sharing of creative works while still controlling some key rights for the publisher, Creative Commons is often seen as the ideal license for infographics.

Even though Creative Commons is an open sharing license, many mistakenly think it means giving up all of their rights and publishing their work into the public domain. This is absolutely not true. Creative Commons is a type of copyright license that allows the owner to encourage sharing of their creative work, while still retaining control of how it is used.

A Creative Commons license is free for anyone to use and has a number of options that can be adapted to the needs of each specific design. The license own-  ers have to make a few choices about what they are willing to allow others to do with their work; this will define the correct license to use.

The most common license used for infographics is identified by four two-letter codes as CC-BY-NC-ND. Designers should display the official license image shown in Figure 2-22 in the infographic image itself. That way, the license remains accessible to readers no matter where the infographic is posted.

FIGURE 2-22:
Creative Com-
mons license
CC-BY-NC-ND
creativecommons
.org/choose/

Table 2-1 shows the four aspects as they relate to an infographic design.

TABLE 2- 1:
Four aspects of a
Creative Commons
license

CODE	ASPECT	DESCRIPTION
CC	Creative Commons	Identifies that the creative work is covered by a Creative Commons license.
BY	Attribution	Any use of the infographic must include a link or credit back to the original author. The license owner can define the title, name, and URL address of the original source that must be included whenever anyone reposts the infographic design.
NC	Noncommercial	This enables anyone to copy, redistribute, transmit, and repost the infographic only for noncommercial purposes. Others may not sell or profit from your infographic without getting specific permission from the owner.
ND	No Derivative Works	Everyone may use or redistribute your infographic only as long as the design remains unchanged. They may not modify or alter the infographic design without getting specific permission from the owner.

The easiest way to generate a CC license is for the content owner to go to the Choose a License page at creativecommons.org/choose/, shown in Figure 2-23, make attribute selections, and then use the license image that the site generates. If you need a larger version of the license image to include in the infographic design, there are higher resolution versions available on the creativecommons.org/about/downloads page. If the publisher uses the HTML-embedded code generated on this page to display the license on its web page, it also contains some additional metadata for web browsers.

FIGURE 2-23:

Choosing a Creative Commons license
creativecommons
.org/choose/

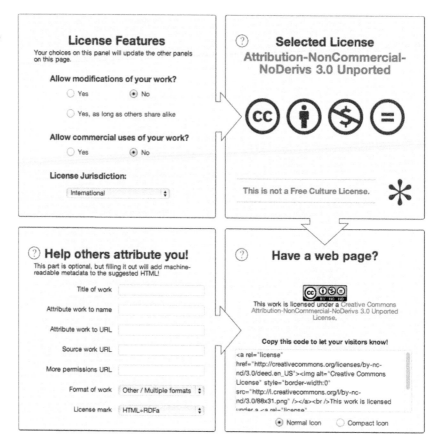

Trademarks and the Fair Use Doctrine

Trademark protection is often confused with copyright protection, but they are two different things. *Copyrights* protect complete creative works, and *trademarks* protect distinctive words or symbols associated with specific companies, products, or services. The test for trademark infringement is called "likelihood of consumer confusion."

If you are designing an infographic for your own company, of course you have the rights (and probably the responsibility) to include your company's trademarked logo in the design. This clearly identifies the company as the publisher of the infographic design and is necessary for the infographic to have any positive effect on the brand perception.

But what about including trademarked logos from other companies?

There is an exception to the trademark law called the Fair Use Doctrine that allows for limited use and publishing of a trademark in certain cases without permission of the owner. For infographics, your design needs to pass two tests:

1. Use of the logo can't make it appear that the infographic is designed or published by the company whose logo you are using.

2. Use of a company's logo can't imply that the company funds, authorizes, approves, supports, or endorses the infographic.

However, you can use another company's trademarked logo to identify or compare that company. *The Conversation Prism 4.0* from Brian Solis and JESS3 in Figure 2-24 is a popular infographic design that prominently displays hundreds of trademarked logos from other companies. In this instance, the logos are used to identify the major companies in the different types of social media businesses.

An average reader of the infographic would not be confused that any one of these companies is the original publisher or endorses the design. Using trademarked logos in this way passes the two tests for fair use, and they did not need to get permission from all of those companies.

THE CONVERSATION PRISM

Brought to you by
Brian Solis & JESS3

For more information
check out conversationprism.com

FIGURE 2-24: Fair use of trademarked company logos

coolinfographics.com/Figure-2-24

Source: Brian Solis and JESS3

Images and Illustrations

Beyond company logos, most infographic designs incorporate many images and illustrations. They might be photographs, illustrations, or vector art designs. Infographic designers need to have the appropriate rights to include any image that isn't an original design of their own.

Probably the most common way (and at the same time the worst way) to find images to include in an infographic design is to perform an image search in Google or Bing. Just because it has been published on the Internet does not make it public domain! Actually, it's just the opposite. As mentioned in the earlier section, copyright law automatically covers all original creative works, even if it doesn't have a copyright notice or include the copyright symbol.

Using images found through an Internet search, you are likely putting yourself and your client at risk of copyright infringement. An infographic designer needs to be certain the images included in a design are available through a public license. If you're designing an infographic for business reasons, you could unintentionally be putting your company at legal and financial risk.

Royalty-free stock image sites (like iStockPhoto.com or Shutterstock.com) are the best solution to ensuring that you have the required permissions to include an image in your infographic design. When you purchase a design asset (photo, illustration, vector art, video, and so on) you are actually purchasing a license to use that artwork. *Royalty-free* means that you can include that artwork in your commercial design without paying an on-going royalty to the designer. When designing infographic projects for clients, you should make sure that all of the images you include as part of the final infographic are either your own original designs or licensed royalty-free images.

In additional to icons and illustrations, hundreds of data visualization design elements have begun to become available on the royalty-free stock image sites. Figure 2-25 is a collection of vector art objects called *Infographic Elements* and is available for purchase from iStockPhoto.com. This collection is meant to help an infographic designer with predesigned visual elements that make the design process faster. Designers must still modify the visualizations to match the data included in their infographic design.

FIGURE 2-25:

Infographic Elements by Artvea

coolinfographics
.com/Figure-2-25

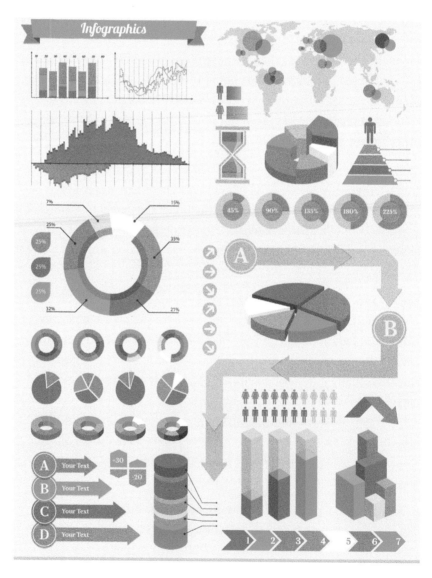

An infographic designer doesn't need to create all these visual elements from scratch. In general, infographic designs are not meant to be pieces of art; they are visual storytelling with data and information. If designers spend most of their time designing custom illustrations, the project is going to take much longer and cost much more than necessary.

AIGA, the Professional Association for Design

The legal issues are complicated, and all of them aren't covered here. You should consider an additional source of information meant to help designers understand and navigate the legal landscape.

AIGA, the professional association for design, (www.aiga.org) is an excellent resource for graphic designers about a wide variety of issues. It publishes a number of articles, case studies, videos, and webinars and a complete guide to *Design Business and Ethics* that covers copyright and trademark issues in more detail. The complete guide is available online at www.aiga.org/design-business-and-ethics/.

> *The AIGA Design Business and Ethics guide outlines the critical ethical and professional issues encountered by designers and their clients. [The guide] is mailed to all new professional- and associate-level members when they join.*
>
> AIGA WEBSITE

Should You Copyright Your Infographic?

Online infographics defy the traditional thinking behind protecting creative work online. With the exception of the infographic posters, publishers are generally not attempting to sell online infographics. Actually, it's quite the opposite. Most infographic publishers are actively trying to get their infographics shared, posted, linked, e-mailed, and even printed as frequently as possible but without any payment or licensing. It's viewed as a huge success for a company to have its info-graphic reposted on a major site that drives thousands of views.

In the case of online infographics, the purpose of a copyright needs to be thought about differently. Even though they may not be trying to sell their infographics, designers and companies should still copyright their infographic designs. A copyright prohibits others from modifying the design, claiming it as their own, or selling the infographic without the creators' consent. These are still important aspects of publishing creative work.

For example, even though all the examples included in this book have been published publicly online, available for anyone to view, they are all covered by copyrights. Because this book is a product for sale, it is considered a commercial use of those designs. To republish them in this book, I needed to get official permission from each publisher or designer for a copyright license to include their infographic designs.

So, should infographics be copyrighted? Yes. They are automatically covered by a copyright, but adding the official copyright notice to an infographic removes any ambiguity or misconceptions. Publishers should be clear and obvious about what rights they are granting to others related to their infographic designs.

Final Thoughts

Online infographics are a powerful content tool for companies to share information, build awareness, and drive traffic to their websites. They have exploded in popularity in the last few years, and their use will continue to grow going forward.

Infographic designers need to understand the objectives of an info-graphic project so they can make informed decisions about the format, orientation, and content that should be included in each design. Good infographic designers can bring together storytelling, data visualization, graphic design, online strategy, and legal understanding together to make a successful infographic.

References

1. Alan H. Monroe, *Principles and Types of Speech*, (Chicago: Scott, Foresman, 1935).

Links

Many of the images in this chapter can be viewed by using the following links or going to www.wiley.com/go/coolinfographics.

1. *Mobile Youth: Teens & Cell Phones*, PrepaidPhones.com:
   http://infonewt.com/portfolio/client-work/18409928

2. *What guests want*, Hotels.com:
   http://press.hotels.com/en-ca/more-infographics/
   hotels-com-amenities-survey/

3. *The History of Swimwear*, BackyardOcean.com:
   http://www.backyardocean.com/History-Of-Swimwear-Bikini-
   Thong-Infographic-s/758.htm

4. *Cool Infographics Gallery* on Pinterest:
   http://pinterest.com/rtkrum/cool-infographics-gallery/

5. *Our Amazing Planet: Top to Bottom*, LiveScience.com:
   http://www.livescience.com/27551-our-amazing-planet-top-to-
   bottom-mountaintop-to-ocean-trench-infographic.html

6. *Solar Savings: A Solar Innovation Story*, Extra Space Storage Inc.:
   http://www.extraspace.com/infographics/solarpower/

7. *The Common Cook's How-Many Guide to Kitchen Conversions*, S.B.Lattin Design:
   http://sblattindesign.wordpress.com/2012/01/03/measure-up/

8. *The Lifespan of Storage Media*, CrashPlan:
   http://www.crashplan.com/medialifespan/

9. *Most Polluted Cities in United States 2012*, American Lung Association (stateoftheair.org):
   http://infonewt.com/portfolio/client-work/18409910

10. *Cancer: Incidences of Cancer in the United States of America*, MesotheliomaHelp.net:
    http://www.mesotheliomahelp.net/news/
    cancer-charity-infographic

11. *Can Washroom Soap Make You Sick?*, GOJO Industries:
    http://www.gojo.com/NoMoreBulkSoap

12. *How Our Laws Are Made*, Mike Wirth and Dr. Suzanne Cooper Guasco, PhD:
    http://www.mikewirthart.com/?projects=how-our-laws-are-made

13. *How Affiliate Marketing Works*, Rae Hoffman, Sugarrae.com:
    http://www.sugarrae.com/affiliate-marketing/how-affiliate-
    marketing-works/

14. *How to Pair Wine with the Bright, Bold Flavors of Southeast Asia*, P.F. Chang's China Bistro, Inc.:
    http://www.pfchangs.com/inspired/infographic.aspx

15. *Making an Organic Choice*, SoNice, Earth's Own Food Company Inc.:
    http://www.sonice.ca/good-for-you/organic-choice

16. *Accord: 30 Years of American Craftsmanship*, Honda America:
    http://www.flickr.com/photos/hondanews/7950209832

17. *Bi-Annual Price Index, Early 2011,* Hotels.com:
    `http://press.hotels.com/en-us/more-infographics/`
    `us-hpi-first-half-2011-results/`

18. *The Genealogy of Pop/Rock Music* poster, Reebee Garofalo,
    HistoryShots.com:
    `http://www.historyshots.com/Rockmusic/index.cfm`

19. *A Visual History of the American Presidency,* Timeplots.com:
    `http://www.timeplots.com/collections/all/products/`
    `a-history-of-the-us-presidency`

20. *The Insanely Great History of Apple,* PopChartLab.com:
    `http://popchartlab.com/collections/prints/products/`
    `the-insanely-great-history-of-apple`

21. *The Conversation Prism 4.0,* Brian Solis (`http://www.briansolis.`
    `com`) and JESS3 (`http://JESS3.com`):
    `https://conversationprism.com/`

22. *Infographic Elements* Artvea:
    `http://www.istockphoto.com/stock-illustration-22855224-in-`
    `fographic-elements.php`

Relevance is a search engine's holy grail. People want results that are closely connected to their queries.

—Marc Ostrofsky, *Get Rich Click!*

3

Infographics and SEO

Normally, the objective of an online infographic design project is to increase traffic and links to the company website. The company that publishes an infographic wants to build the awareness and equity of its brand (or product) and increase its position in search engine results related to its business.

This is the realm of Search Engine Optimization (SEO) strategies, and in the last few years infographics have become a powerful content tool for companies to employ that encourages site links and increases their overall site relevance. When a company publishes an engaging, well-designed infographic on its site, many people post it on their own sites with links back to the company and share it within social media with their own networks of friends and followers.

Search engines calculate a score for a web page's credibility and authority as one way to quantify its relevance to specific keywords. They use complex, proprietary algorithms that use many different signals. Some of these classify for relevance, others for quality of content, and others for overall importance on the Internet. One of the most famous is the Google PageRank classifier, which considers both the number and quality of links pointing at a page to determine its standing. All of these combine together to determine the search engine rank score of a web page for a specific search.

The higher a specific company's website page scores for a particular search, the higher the link to that page appears in the search results for users searching with those keywords. The goal is to have the company website appear as high in the list of results as possible. The best results appear on the first page of search results for the keywords related to the business, and the best result a company can achieve is the coveted top position of the #1 ranked search result.

Google's PageRank is a logarithmic scale (not linear) from 0–10. To help people understand the concept, Elliance designed the infographic shown in Figure 3-1 in 2008, and it's still used by people everywhere to help explain PageRank. The "climbing a mountain" visual metaphor is effective, but it's important to understand that every page on a website has its own PageRank. So, the homepage of a company site may have a PageRank of 5, but an internal page may only have a PageRank of 2.

In general terms, the more links to a specific company web page from outside websites, the higher that page's rank becomes. Links from web pages that have high PageRanks of their own are more valuable links. However, it's a moving target. All the search engines frequently change their algorithms to improve their services, and the most recent links and visitors to a site are what matter most. A website could be on the front page of search results today, but tomorrow appear on page four because an algorithm was updated.

This chapter won't make you an SEO expert, but it covers the basics of effectively using infographics as a part of an SEO strategy.

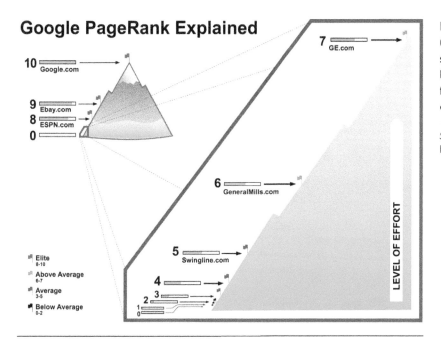

Google PageRank Explained

10 Google.com
9 Ebay.com
8 ESPN.com
0

7 GE.com

6 GeneralMills.com

5 Swingline.com

4

3
2
1
0

Elite
8-10
Above Average
6-7
Average
3-5
Below Average
0-2

LEVEL OF EFFORT

ELLIANCE

FIGURE 3-1:
Google PageRank scores pages on a logarithmic scale from 1-10.
coolinfographics .com/Figure-3-1
Source: Google Page Rank Explained, *Elliance*

The Search Engine Challenge

Search engines are in business, too, and they need to provide a valuable service to their customers to keep them coming back to use their search service. If you perform a search, and the results aren't close to what you are looking for, that reflects poorly on the search engines' brand. They want to provide the right results to their users because that's their business, and it's what convinces people to return to use their search engine again in the future.

Producing the search results that you rely on (and take for granted) is an incredibly tough technical problem, as shown in the infographic in Figure 3-2, from Stone Temple Consulting. According to Matt Cutts, head of the Webspam team at Google, the size of the Internet was measured at more than 100 trillion web pages. Each search engine company (Google,

Microsoft Bing, and so on) has its own spiders crawling all these pages on the web to parse both the text and the links from every page. They create their own massive index of the Internet and then query the index to provide the search users with a clean list of relevant results.

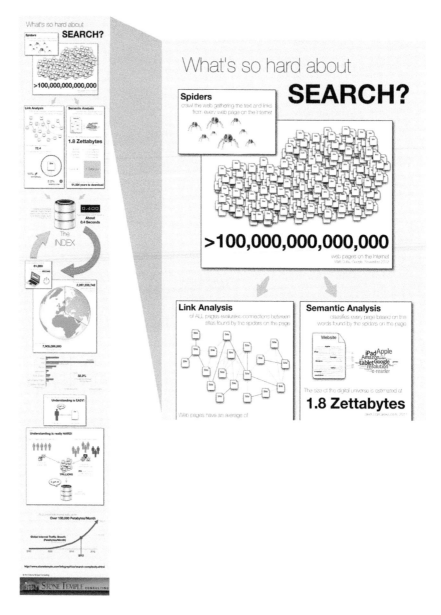

According to comScore, in August 2011, there were 61,000 Internet searches performed every second[1]—which makes it impressive that the search engines can query their own index of the Internet and return valuable results in less than a second every time.

When you, as a search engine user, consider the benefits of a good search engine, you can easily evaluate four aspects of the results to judge the success of the search:

- ▶ **Speed**—How fast did I get my results?

- ▶ **Quantity**—How many results did I get?

- ▶ **Relevance**—How relevant were the results I got?

- ▶ **Coverage**—Were all of the important pages included in the results? Any major pages missing?

When searching for the term infographics on Google today, 14,300,000 results are found in 0.15 seconds. Wow!

However, the most important of the four aspects is relevance. It's not how many results or how fast they appeared. If all 14 million of those results aren't what you are looking for, you would be extremely unsatisfied. In fact, you would probably be happier to get fewer, excellent results even if it took a little extra time.

In 2013, the Microsoft Bing search engine started an ad campaign comparing the relevance of its search results directly head-to-head with Google (Figure 3-3). The folks at Microsoft know what's important to users, and its marketing campaign competes with the market leader, Google, directly on the aspect that users care about most: relevance.

FIGURE 3-3:
The Microsoft Bing search engine is competing directly against Google on the basis of relevance.

www.bingiton.com

Source: Bing It On adver-tisement from Microsoft

The Objective of SEO

From a marketer's perspective, the objective of using an infographic as SEO content online is to improve where its company web pages appear in search results for related keywords, and ultimately increase the number of visitors to the site. Infographics have become a popular tool for this because they are so easy to read and easy to share, which creates more links and views for the company that published the infographic.

When an infographic becomes extremely popular online, it's referred to as "going viral." How popular? There's no numeric threshold value of views that content has to reach to be considered "going viral." The process of going viral online means that an ever-increasing number of people are viewing and sharing the content, usually increasing with each generation. An example of this is shown in Figure 3-4. If 10 people share the original infographic, and each of those shares is shared again by two followers, and each of those shares is shared again by two followers of the second generation, and so on, the growth could be exponential, but it's still measured in comparison to a web page's normal traffic.

In practice, when an infographic goes viral, it means that the page views and shares on social media outpace your normal content by a significant margin. It's all relative. So if a post on your company blog normally gets 500 views per day, but suddenly one post gets 5,000 views because you posted a cool infographic, it probably "went viral." You have to consider its success in comparison to other content you have published because there is no easy way to observe or measure the sharing phenomenon.

A more ambitious goal is to achieve publication on one (or many) of the major online news sites. Links from sites with high PageRank scores can be much more valuable than links from small, personal blogs. So, the goal is not only to get a high number of views, but also to get links from high value sites. The high value sites that are the most valuable depend on your industry. Which news sites post articles about your company, your industry, and your competitors?

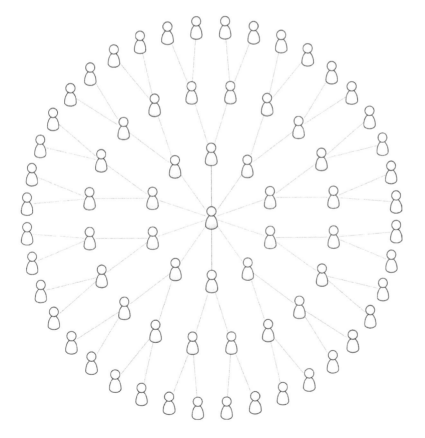

FIGURE 3-4:
The viral phe-
nomenon where
each generation
of social-sharing
causes at least two
additional posts

The Link Bait Challenge

Link bait is a phrase used to describe any content that has been specifically crafted to attract a significant number of views and links from other websites. Usually, the content used for link bait is something chosen to have broad appeal to the widest possible audience. That way, the company that publishes the content has the best chance to get as many links and views as possible.

For many, link bait has earned a bad reputation and can be perceived to be a shady form of online marketing. Even the term link bait sounds like it's related to spam, but it really isn't. Every infographic online could be considered link bait, because they are all trying to attract more traffic with visually engaging content. You'll see link bait online in different formats, things like shocking gossip, surprising news, amazing photos, funny videos, Top 10 articles, and of course, infographics. The best topics for link bait are controversial subjects or topics with strong emotional appeal. Link bait is neither good nor bad; it depends on how it is used. All of the cool infographics shown in this book are good link bait designs. In contrast, an infographic that leads readers to a malicious site that loads malware onto their computers would definitely be considered to be bad link bait.

The problem comes from content that isn't relevant to the site that publishes it. When the topic of the infographic is not related to the site that publishes it, the search engines have a hard time determining if a link should be considered as an endorsement of the company.

As an example of infographic link bait, the *James Bond: 50 Years of Movies* design in Figure 3-5 is a well-designed infographic. It contains lots of great information for fans of James Bond movies, a beautiful color palette, engaging icons, and the data is easy to understand. The infographic was popular online with tens of thousands of views, thousands of shares in social media, and hundreds of outside pages posting the infographic with links back to the H&R Block web page. By all accounts, the infographic "went viral" and you can see in Figure 3-6 that a Google image search found 284 sites that had reposted the infographic.

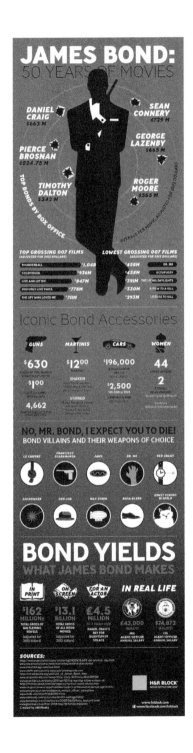

FIGURE 3-5:

An example of a cool infographic used as link bait

coolinfographics
.com/Figure-3-5

Source: James Bond: 50 Years of Movies, *H&R Block*

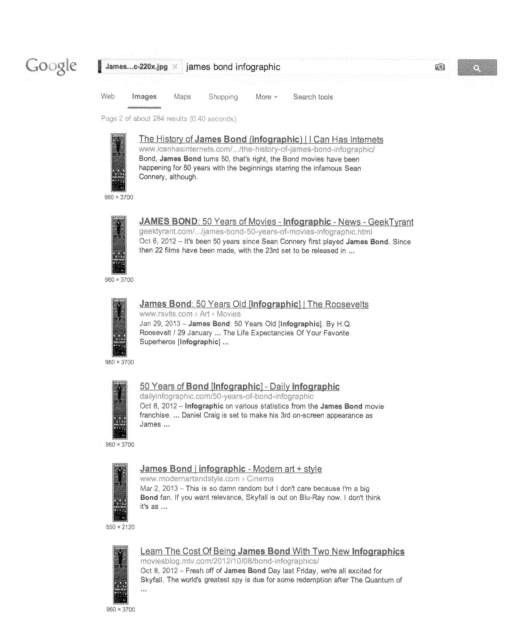

FIGURE 3-6: Google image search finds 284 sites that reposted the infographic image.

This is a good use of link bait to drive traffic to the site (there's no malicious intent). The challenge for search engines is that the topic of James Bond movies has nothing to do with H&R Block's business of preparing tax returns. Algorithmically, all those views and links back to the infographic landing page on H&R Block's site have the potential to increase the site's overall score in each of the search engines. In turn, the higher score causes H&R Block's site to appear higher in search results.

However, this is not what the search engines want to happen. This could be perceived as a method of gaming the system that uses infographic link bait as a strategy to raise the score of the H&R Block website. Is it a good infographic? Absolutely. Should links to the infographic page raise the credibility of H&R Block for tax preparation services? Probably not. The act of people linking to the infographic because they like James Bond movies should not be interpreted as an endorsement of H&R Block's services.

It's All About Relevance

At this point, the search engines don't have a good way to solve this challenge. Today, link bait infographics are effective as an SEO tactic and can successfully raise a website's overall score.

This is a problem that Google is actively trying to solve. In 2012, Matt Cutts, head of the Webspam team at Google, specifically mentioned this challenge with infographics during an interview with SEO expert Eric Enge[2]:

> In principle, there's nothing wrong with the concept of an infographic. What concerns me are the types of things that people are doing with them. They get far off topic, or the fact checking is really poor. The infographic may be neat, but if the information it's based on is simply wrong, then it's misleading people.
>
> The other thing that happens is that people don't always realize what they are linking to when they reprint these infographics. Often the link goes to a completely unrelated site, and one that they don't mean to endorse. Conceptually, what happens is they really buy into publishing the infographic, and agree to include the link, but

they don't actually care about what it links to. From our perspective this is not what a link is meant to be.

I would not be surprised if at some point in the future we did not start to discount these infographic-type links to a degree. The link is often embedded in the infographic in a way that people don't realize, vs. a true endorsement of your site.

This comment has a number of companies, SEO consultants, and infographic designers worried that Google may start discounting all infographic links across the board. Even beyond infographics, it's a challenge for all types of link bait content (text articles, photos, videos, interactive pages, and so on) but infographics in particular have been used heavily for this type of SEO tactic.

Now, a year after Matt Cutts' comment, you haven't seen this type of change yet, but Google makes major updates to its algorithms multiple times each year. They might figure out a method to differentiate unrelated link bait content and lower the impact of those links to the PageRank calculation.

To protect against any form of link bait discounting in the future, companies and designers should focus on publishing relevant infographics. This can protect links to your site that are relevant to your business and should always be considered to be a valid endorsement of your site by the search engine algorithms.

Figure 3-7, *Streamlining your digital life with the new iPad*, an infographic from NextWorth, is an example of relevance. Published shortly before the release of the iPad 3 in 2012, this design focused on many of the older electronic gadgets that the iPad's functionality had replaced. NextWorth is in the business of buying back older consumer electronics gadgets from people and recycling them. The infographic design is fun, engaging, and relevant to the NextWorth business. A link to the infographic inherently should imply an endorsement of recycling old gadgets and supporting its business.

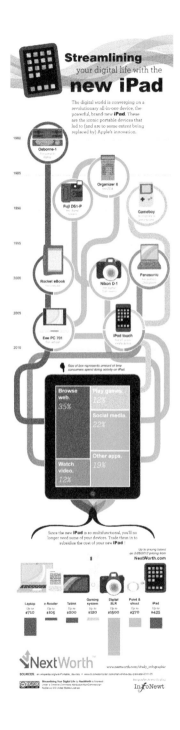

FIGURE 3-7:
The topic of replacing electronic gadgets is directly relevant to Next-Worth's business.
coolinfographics
.com/Figure-3-7

Source: Streamlining your digital life with the new iPad, *NextWorth*

To remain relevant and in the good graces of the search engine companies, you should avoid any actions or practices that could be considered "spammy." Search engines continually work to improve their algorithms, and something that helped a web page score yesterday could actually hurt the score today as the algorithms are improved and the programmers devise ways to detect any questionable promotional efforts. Some algorithm updates have even punished websites that were seen as practicing unscrupulous methods of increasing their page value, by actively lowering their page scores.

Online Lifespan

Online lifespan is the amount of time that an infographic remains relevant to audiences. Topic and data selection here are crucial. When choosing the topic of an infographic, many companies fail to understand the importance of online lifespan.

From a designer's perspective, it generally takes the same amount of time and effort to fill an infographic design with current, trending information as it does to include information that can have long-term value to the readers. In a financial sense, it costs about the same to design an infographic that will only be popular for one week as it does to design an infographic that will be useful to readers for a year or more. The infographic design will be roughly the same size, with a similar amount of illustrations, text, and data visualizations.

You need to consider the goal of the infographic project when choosing the topic and the range of data included. If the objective of the infographic project is to drive traffic and build links to the company website, you don't want an infographic that will be outdated or forgotten a week after you publish it. If the objective is to increase brand awareness in a short amount of time, a hot, trending topic could be more successful.

From an SEO perspective, the most recent views and links are often more heavily weighted. So even if you publish an infographic that goes viral, if it happened three years ago, it probably isn't providing much of a positive effect on your search engine score ranking today.

On May 1, 2011, the big news story of the day was the U.S. operation that killed Osama Bin Laden. There were a handful of infographic designs developed quickly that were published within 24 hours of the news breaking. Figure 3-8 shows one of these designs from Column Five Media that does a great job of clearly telling the story of events leading up to the operation and visually showing readers what was known about the operation in Bin Laden's compound. A lot of effort went into creating the design in a short period of time, and the end result is a well-designed infographic. However, the topic was so tied to the hot trending news of the day that when the news cycle moved on to other stories, interest in the infographic went away as well. The online lifespan of this infographic was only about one week. After that, views and links diminished rapidly.

The *Death & Taxes 2014* poster in Figure 3-9 is a popular design that visualizes the President's proposed budget and is redesigned and republished each year. It's a huge undertaking for the designers, and the final design becomes obsolete a year later when a new budget cycle begins. Its online lifespan lasts for one year.

Many designs can have significantly longer lifespans. *The History of Halloween* in Figure 3-10 from FrightCatalog.com is an unusual case. The infographic is a timeline of events that have led up to the modern day Halloween holiday, so even though its online lifespan will be many years, it's mostly only relevant during the month of October. This actually works nicely for the publisher, an online retailer of Halloween costumes, because it adds visitors and traffic to its busiest month… every year.

BRINGING DOWN BIN LADEN

After the gunfire, U.S. forces swept the fortified compound in Pakistan and left with a trove of hard drives, DVDs and other documents that officials said the CIA was already poring over. The hope: clues leading to his presumed successor, al-Qaida No. 2 Ayman al-Zawahiri.

PRE-OPERATION TIMELINE

AUGUST 2010
US President briefed on a 'possible lead' on bin Laden's location. Residence of a courier with close ties to bin Laden is found in Abbottabad, Pakistan.

SEPTEMBER 2010
CIA works with the President on a set of assessments that leading to the conclusion that bin Laden is possibly in the mansion at Abbottabad.

MARCH 14—APRIL 28
The President hold five National Securitu Council (NCS) meetings for the development of a plan to 'bring bin Laden to justice'.

APRIL
Believing the intelligence to be credible enough, the President initates military preparations.

8:20 AM ON 4/29/11
President Obama gives final order to pursue the operation before flying to Alabama.

MAY 1ST OPERATION
(Eastern Time)

OSAMA BIN LADEN COMPOU

U.S. NAVY SEALS

2:00 PM
Obama has final meeting with advisors and signs 'kill order'.

2:30 PM
US Navy Seals take off from Ghazi Airbase for Islamabad to launch operation Sunday morning.

3:10-3:15 PM
Choppers circle Abbottobad several times before engaging.

3:15 PM
With President Obama and team watching live, via Predator drone feed, Navy SEALs raid and sweep the compound.

FIGURE 3-8: Breaking news as an infographic topic: online lifespan = one week

coolinfographics.com/Figure-3-8

Source: Bringing Down Bin Laden, *Column Five Media*

AD, PAKISTAN

TWEETS IN THE NIGHT

Twitter user Sohaib Athar, a 33-year old IT consultant and resident of Abbottabad unkowingly tweeted the operation as it unfolded:

@ReallyVirtual

Helicopter hovering above Abbottabad at 1AM (is a rare event).
3:08pm EST

Go away helicopter - before I take out my giant swatter :-/
3:15pm EST

The abbottabad helicopter/UFO was shot down near the Bilal Town area, and there's report of a flash. People saying it could be a drone.
3:22pm EST

And now, a plane flying over Abbottabad...
3:44pm EST

I guess Abbottabad is going to get as crowded as the Lahore that I left behind for some peace and quiet. *sigh*
4:10pm EST

Interesting rumors in the otherwise uneventful Abbottabad air today
6:39pm EST

...

Uh oh, now I'm the guy who liveblogged the Osama raid without knowing it.
11:41pm EST

news
on.
9%)

-4:00 PM
Downed helicopter destroyed by US forces in "window-shattering explosion".

10:30 PM
Obama announces Osama bin Laden's death to the world.

1:10 AM
Burial preparations begin.

3:30 AM
Osama buried in the North Arabian Sea from the USS Carl-Vinson.

FIGURE 3-9: Online lifespan lasts as long as the data is current: budget data = one year

coolinfographics.com/Figure-3-9

Source: Death & Taxes 2014, *Timeplots*

United States 2014 Federal Budget

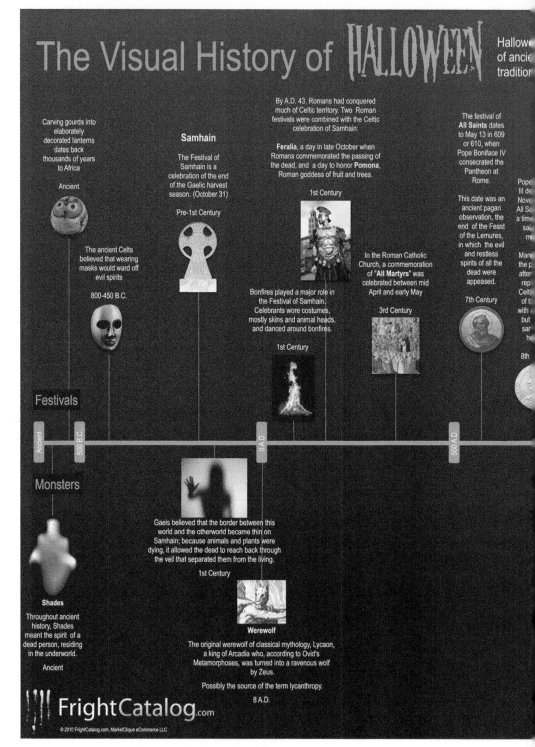

FIGURE 3-10: Online lifespan = one month, every year

coolinfographics.com/Figure-3-10

Source: The Visual History of Halloween, *FrightCatalog.com*

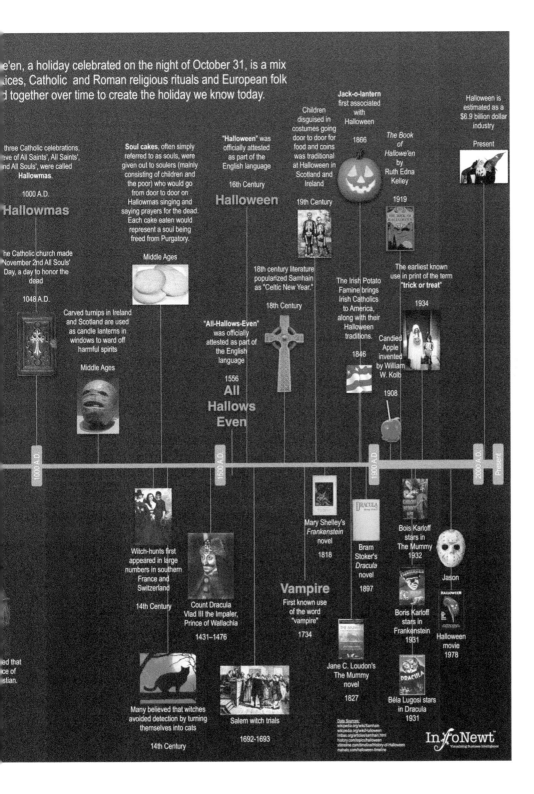

...e'en, a holiday celebrated on the night of October 31, is a mix ...ices, Catholic and Roman religious rituals and European folk ...d together over time to create the holiday we know today.

Jack-o-lantern first associated with Halloween
1866

Children disguised in costumes going door to door for food and coins was traditional at Halloween in Scotland and Ireland

The Book of Hallowe'en by Ruth Edna Kelley
1919

Halloween is estimated as a $6.9 billion dollar industry

Present

...three Catholic celebrations, ...eve of All Saints', All Saints', ...nd All Souls', were called **Hallowmas**.
1000 A.D.

Hallowmas

Soul cakes, often simply referred to as souls, were given out to soulers (mainly consisting of children and the poor) who would go from door to door on Hallowmas singing and saying prayers for the dead. Each cake eaten would represent a soul being freed from Purgatory.

Middle Ages

"Halloween" was officially attested as part of the English language
16th Century

Halloween
19th Century

...he Catholic church made ...November 2nd All Souls' Day, a day to honor the dead
1048 A.D.

Carved turnips in Ireland and Scotland are used as candle lanterns in windows to ward off harmful spirits
Middle Ages

18th century literature popularized Samhain as "Celtic New Year."
18th Century

"All-Hallows-Even" was officially attested as part of the English language
1556

All Hallows Even

The Irish Potato Famine brings Irish Catholics to America, along with their Halloween traditions.
1846

The earliest known use in print of the term **"trick or treat"**
1934

Candied Apple invented by William W. Kolb
1908

1000 A.D.   1500 A.D.   1900 A.D.   2000 A.D.   Present

Witch-hunts first appeared in large numbers in southern France and Switzerland
14th Century

Count Dracula Vlad III the Impaler, Prince of Wallachia
1431–1476

Mary Shelley's *Frankenstein* novel
1818

Vampire
First known use of the word "vampire"
1734

Jane C. Loudon's The Mummy novel
1827

Bram Stoker's *Dracula* novel
1897

Boris Karloff stars in Frankenstein
1931

Béla Lugosi stars in Dracula
1931

Bois Karloff stars in The Mummy
1932

Jason

Halloween movie
1978

...ed that ...ce of ...stian.

Many believed that witches avoided detection by turning themselves into cats
14th Century

Salem witch trials
1692-1693

Data Sources:
wikipedia.org/wiki/Samhain
wikipedia.org/wiki/Halloween
imbas.org/articles/samhain.html
history.com/topics/halloween
xtimeline.com/timeline/History-of-Halloween
mahalo.com/halloween-timeline

In**fo**Newt
Visualizing Business Intelligence

The online lifespan of the *Pairing of Wine & Food* infographic in Figure 3-11 also spans many years. Twenty years from now, the information will still be the same, and the design will still be relevant to readers. It's not like suddenly dessert wine will go well with vegetables!

Online lifespan can make a huge difference to the ongoing SEO value of any infographic and should be an integral part of the topic selection process.

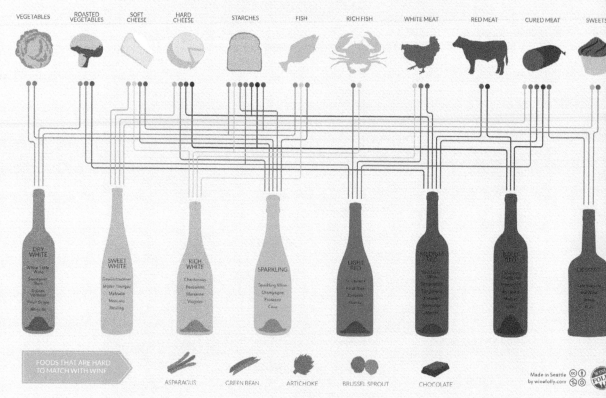

FIGURE 3-11: For general information topics, online lifespan = many years

coolinfographics.com/Figure-3-11

Source: Pairing Wine & Food, *Wine Folly*

Infographic Release Strategy

It's disappointing to see how many companies publish their new infographics online, and then just wait for people to come and find it. Many companies will spend a lot of time and resources to research data and design a good infographic but then choose not to spend any effort on marketing or promoting the infographic. Infographics are content pieces that need as much marketing support as articles, videos, advertisements, and even products.

Before a company publishes an infographic, it should carefully consider a comprehensive Infographic Release Strategy to promote the infographic. When you have a good infographic design ready to publish, you want to make sure that you maximize the benefit you get in return from the infographic.

Following are three key steps in an infographic release process:

1. Landing page

2. Self-promotion

3. Outreach

A company doesn't need to follow through with all these steps, but effort put into promotion can significantly improve the success of publishing an infographic. Most of this activity is just a commitment of effort on behalf of the company and doesn't cost a lot of extra money.

Landing Pages

The first question that needs to be addressed is, "Where should you publish the infographic?" Infographics can be published online in a hundred different ways, but many of them are not effective. Should you host the infographic on your own site, your Flickr page, as a photo in Facebook, in a guest post on another site, on an infographic gallery site, or in a blog post?

The answer depends on the company's goal for the infographic project. Normally, a company wants to attract links and visitors to its website. In that case, a company should create a dedicated infographic landing page within its own website. That way it's on a site that the company controls and is not dependent on any outside companies or services. Also, publishing and hosting the infographic on its own dedicated page gets all the benefit from the links and page views, as well as retaining complete control over the content on the page.

The landing page should have a short, simple URL, which can be used as the clear destination for links to the infographic. By pointing all the traffic and links to one dedicated landing page, it can have the best chance to achieve a high score within the search engine rankings as opposed to spreading the links across multiple locations. Also, a number of people will be typing in the web page address to find the infographic, so a short and simple URL can be important. A long, complicated URL may discourage visitors.

There are exceptions, though. If the goal is to build an audience for the company's Facebook Fan Page, developing an infographic and publishing it as new image content on Facebook would be perfectly acceptable. Links would bring new people to the company Facebook page and attract new followers.

The Image Problem

When it comes to infographics, here's the problem. Figure 3-12 shows how your infographic appears to the search engine spiders. It's just an image asset on the page with no content because the web spiders crawling sites for content can't tell what's included in an image or an infographic. They can't determine your topic, your keywords, your data sources, your key message, or any relevant information. Without text to gather and parse, the spider has nothing to send back to the search engine index.

FIGURE 3-12:
Search engines just
see a blank image
asset on the web
page.

The search engines have begun to experiment with software for face recognition, optical character recognition (OCR) and similar image searches to add context to an image, but these tools are not very effective. It's up to the infographic publisher to tell the search engines all about the infographic by adding text to the page, both visible and hidden. The dedicated HTML web page where the original, full-size infographic is hosted online is called the *infographic landing page*. You need to add text to the page describing the content and using the keywords that you want to be related to the infographic. The text is what determines the context and relevance of the infographic, and it's also the only way a search engine can truly know when to display a link to the infographic when it shows search results to its users.

There are a number of important page elements that should be included on an infographic landing page. For this purpose, imagine publishing a fictional infographic called *SEO Strategies Used by the Experts*. This doesn't exist as an infographic on the Internet today, but it may in the future. For purposes of this example, also make the assumption this is a well-designed infographic that tells a visually engaging story that people will want to share. That might be a big assumption, but if you start with a bad design, most of this effort to support the release of the infographic won't have much impact.

Keywords

The cornerstone of any SEO strategy is focusing on a short list of keywords. Keywords can be defined as the most common words entered into search queries when people search for information about a specific topic. Different keywords exist for various company sites based on the differences in industry, products, services, and information that each company offers—even different keywords for the different pages on each company's website.

Companies want to make sure that their site pages are considered by the search engines to be highly credible and relevant to the words related to their business. As a very simple example, Nike wants to be relevant for keywords like *shoes* and *footwear*, and Ford wants to be relevant for keywords like *cars* and *trucks*.

It's important to understand the keywords that people are actually using when searching. If a car dealership creates content using the words "pre-owned car," their content may not appear in the results for someone searching with the more common words "used car." Sometimes, search engines will understand that the two terms are related, but often they don't. Research should be done ahead of time to determine the most popular terms already being used to find similar content.

When publishing an infographic, it is helpful to create a short, specific list of target keywords that you would like the infographic be associated with and then use those keywords consistently on the landing page. For your fictional infographic, the list of keywords might look like this:

1. SEO
2. Search
3. Experts
4. Strategies
5. Marketing

This fictional infographic example is fairly simple with single keywords, but you can also promote multiple-word keyword phrases.

Landing Page URL

Search engines will take into account the words used in the URL of the infographic landing page on your website as a potential place to find relevant keywords. So, the best URLs use natural words that are easy for the search engines to parse and separate the words with hyphens (dashes) to clearly break them apart because spaces are not allowed in a URL address.

Google has publicly acknowledged that it considers hyphens to be word separators and underscore characters as word joiners. Don't use an underscore character unless you are purposely trying to combine words together. If you use the underscore character to separate words such as SEO_Experts, the search engines combine the words together in the index as the one-word SEOExperts. So, your landing page URL should look something like this:

```
http://coolinfographics.com/SEO-Strategies-Experts-
Infographic.html
```

It's also helpful to keep the URL as short as possible because some readers get to your infographic by typing in the address.

Title Tag

The title tag is an HTML code element that should be on every web page. The title element is included in the <head> portion of the page, and the text displays in the browser window title bar or tab.

```
<head>
<title>Expert SEO Strategies Infographic</title>
</head>
```

This is one of the first things that identifies the page content to the search engines and is especially important because the title tag is often used as the link text displayed on the search results pages. Consider using natural language with spaces and including the word "infographic" as the last word of the title tag. This helps identify the content as an infographic to both the audience and the search engines, and the last word is considered to be the least important but still relevant.

The title tag is also used by social media sharing buttons as the proposed default text for posts or tweets if no other suggested text is available. For example, unless you create some specific suggested text for Twitter, when someone uses the Twitter button on the page to share the infographic, it will propose the text from the Title Tag as the content of the tweet.

Page Title

The page title is the visible title displayed in the <body> section of the page as text. If you use the HTML code for the H1 header, the search engines knows this is some of the most important text on the page, and any included text displays on the page in a large bold font. Words in the page title are often given more importance or value than the rest of the text on the page.

```
<body>
<h1>SEO Strategies Used By The Experts</h1>
</body>
```

The actual text of the page title is often the same as the title tag, but it doesn't have to be. From a content perspective, authors usually want the page title to be as short as possible so that the text doesn't wrap on the page. Too many words here make the overall page look complicated and messy, and you can omit the word "infographic" in the page title to help shorten the text. The readers viewing the page can already see that the content is an infographic.

Description Text

The easiest thing to add to your landing page is a short paragraph of description text about the infographic. It could be text from the infographic or text that is written specifically for the landing page. This provides additional text for the search engines to index, but keep it short! The highlight of the page is the infographic; so don't scare off your visitors with too much text. When readers see too much text on the page (or within the infographic), they often tune out and leave the page without reading it because the content appears to be too dense.

Consider including a couple text links to other relevant pages within the same site in the description text. This provides two benefits. First, as the page value of the infographic landing page increases with views and links over time, these text links to other pages within the company site become more valuable. Second, people that post the infographic on their own blog or social media account often copy the entire description text as extra content to include in their post. Remember, they need text for the search engines to index on their own pages, too, and this can create additional valuable text links to the pages on your site.

However, keep any included text links relevant to the infographic topic. Some infographic landing pages have text links to unrelated pages, so they could build on the success of the infographic. Although it can be effective, readers see this as spammy.

Infographic Image Filename

The search engines even look at the name of the infographic image file to try to find words that describe the content. If the image filename is just numbers identifying the image, such as IMG1234567.jpg, the search engines just ignore it, but you don't want to miss any opportunities to link your keywords to the infographic. The easiest thing to do here is to use the main words from the title tag as the filename. So following your fictional infographic, this could be the filename of the infographic image you load onto the landing page:

SEO-Strategies-Experts-Infographic.JPG

Just like the preceding landing page URL, the filename should use hyphens as word separators. Avoid using underscore characters between words, because Google considers those to be word joiners.

Alt Text Description

An important HTML element for infographics is the alt attribute of images that enables the browser to display text describing an image when displaying images on-screen has been turned off in the browser. Due to modern Internet access speeds, the practice of viewing web pages without displaying images is rare, but the HTML element remains and is used heavily for search engine indexing.

The alt text description should be written as a brief description in natural language. The content here should ideally be a single sentence to describe the infographic and can also be used by many screen readers for people with visual impairments. Accessibility software will speak the text of the alt description out loud for people that have trouble seeing the images, which makes a natural language description that much more important.

The alt text description is included in the HTML code that identifies the actual image file displayed on the page.

```
<img src=" SEO-Strategies-Experts-Infographic.jpg" alt="Top SEO
strategies used by expert marketing consultants to improve the
PageRank of web pages">
```

The one thing you don't want to do is to stuff the alt text description with a long string of keywords. Not only is this practice spammy, but also the search engines can recognize this and will reduce any value the alt text description would have provided to the page. This is also incredibly rude and irritating to the visitors that use a screen reader.

Social Media Sharing Buttons

An infographic landing page should absolutely include sharing buttons for the major social media networks. Companies should make sharing their infographic as easy and painless as possible, and including the sharing buttons on the landing page is the most popular way to share the infographic.

One way to add buttons to the landing page is to use separate, individual, dedicated buttons from each of the social networks. A web developer can copy and paste the HTML code provided by each social network site onto the page. This method keeps the relationship simple and direct between the landing page and the social network but requires more work by the web developer.

The more popular way is to use one of the sharing button aggregator services. These services enable developers to add only one block of HTML code to the landing page which displays a number of buttons for the various networks. The major advantage of this method is the convenience of one central service for both the code and the tracking analytics. The downside may be that the aggregator also has access to your analytics, if that is a concern.

The major sharing button aggregator services are:

- ▶ AddThis: www.addthis.com

- ▶ ShareThis: www.sharethis.com

- ▶ AddToAny: www.addtoany.com

In practice, sharing buttons should always be displayed "above the fold" on the landing page—meaning, they should be visible at the top of the page without any scrolling. Many readers will only view the top portion of the infographic and make the choice to share it in their social networks. Only a small portion of the readers make it all the way to the bottom of the page, so it's less effective to place the sharing buttons there.

In some cases, especially for very tall infographics, sharing buttons can also be repeated at the bottom of the page as an added convenience for the reader.

Embed Code

Embed code is a section of HTML code that displays on the web page as text. The code is similar to the HTML image display code used on the landing page, but this code is intended for other blog authors to copy and paste as an easy way to display the infographic on their own sites. This code is included in the <body> section the page.

The advantage of making the embed code available on the landing page is huge for the publisher. The code can be written to display the correct infographic image and provide a link back using the correct URL for the infographic landing page. In addition, using the embed code can make the process of posting an infographic incredibly convenient for bloggers.

There are two parts to adding a block of embed code to your infographic landing page. First is writing the HTML code you want bloggers to copy, and second is adding the <textarea> code to your own page so the code appears on your page as text instead of actually displaying the infographic. This is important because when people view your infographic landing page, you want their browser to display the code instead of trying to interpret it and display the infographic image a second time.

The embed code for your fictitious infographic might look like this:

```
<body>
Please share this infographic on your site by copying and pasting
the code below
<p>
<textarea style="width:540px;height:100px">
<a href= "http://coolinfographics.com/SEO-Strategies-Experts-
Infographic.html">
<img src=" SEO-Strategies-Experts-Infographic-small-500px.jpg"
alt="Top SEO strategies used by expert marketing consultant to
improve the PageRank of websites">
</a>
<p> SEO Strategies Used By The Experts - An infographic by the
team at <a href="http://coolinfographics.com" >Cool Infographics</
a>
</textarea>
<body>
```

On your infographic landing page this will display the embed code text in a small text box as shown in Figure 3-13. This is an easy way to make the image display code available to anyone to copy and paste into their own site or blog. Instead of uploading the image file onto their own server, this code will display the infographic image from your server when someone views their page. It's a nice way to help bloggers save space on their servers because they don't need to host the image file.

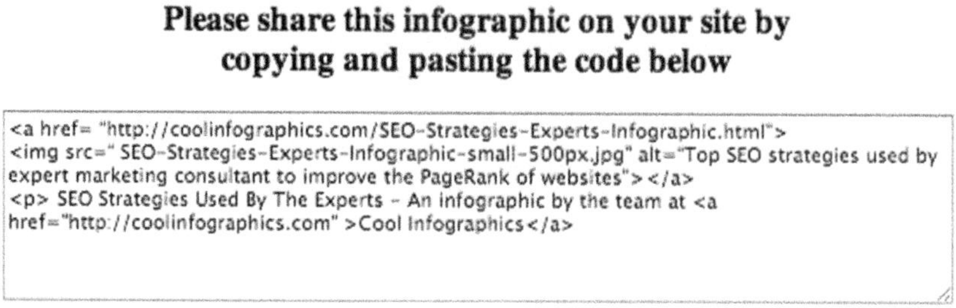

FIGURE 3-13:
The <textarea> element will display the HTML code in a small text box.

Please share this infographic on your site by copying and pasting the code below

```
<a href= "http://coolinfographics.com/SEO-Strategies-Experts-Infographic.html">
<img src=" SEO-Strategies-Experts-Infographic-small-500px.jpg" alt="Top SEO strategies used by
expert marketing consultant to improve the PageRank of websites"></a>
<p> SEO Strategies Used By The Experts - An infographic by the team at <a
href="http://coolinfographics.com" >Cool Infographics</a>
```

Following are six key aspects to understand about what is included in this example embed code:

1. A simple request above the code asking bloggers to use the embed code.

2. All of the HTML code is visible in the box. Too much code text would run past the bottom of the box, which would hide a portion of the code from view. The box will display a scroll bar, but it can feel like you are hiding some of the HTML code on purpose.

3. When displayed on the blogger's site, the infographic has a clickable link back to the original infographic landing page at the URL defined by the publisher. This lets you choose where you want the link to go.

4. A smaller, 500 pixel-wide JPG image file of the infographic is used as the source for the image that is displayed on the blogger's site. This is more likely to fit into the smaller space of blog formats (see Chapter 2, "Online Marketing Infographics"), and will load faster than using the size parameters to display a larger image.

5. An alt text description is written by the publisher to maximize its SEO value.

6. An additional line of text can be displayed under the infographic as a caption with a text link to the front page of the company website.

With the help of a good web developer, much more could be done within the embed code, including some spammy SEO practices you should avoid like adding a long string of keywords or linking to unrelated pages. Filling the embed code with keywords and text links is obviously unnatural, and the search engines are smart enough to ignore that type of content. Publishers should be transparent about the code they offer to bloggers by making all the text visible on the page so that bloggers can see what code they would be adding to their own sites.

The code should also be short and simple like the example embed code above. Even if all the code is written with good intentions, a long, complicated block of code has a greater chance of including spammy code hidden within it. Most bloggers are not web developers proficient with HTML and may not understand what all the embed code means. A long block of code has a high probability of scaring off bloggers because putting unknown HTML code they don't understand on their site is potentially risky.

The embed code is also just a suggestion to bloggers to use. They can paste the code as-is into their sites, or modify the code any way they see fit. If they want to change the alt description, they are free to do so. As the publisher, you are providing the code as a convenience.

In practice, only a small portion of bloggers actually take advantage of using the embed code to display an infographic on their blog. Usually, they download the JPG image file itself or display the image by linking directly to the hosting server. That leaves the flexibility to choose their own link, write their own alt text description, or choose not to include them at all.

However, it is definitely worth the effort to make the embed code available on the infographic landing page because it can maximize the value of the links from those bloggers that do use it. The reality is that the infographic has a life of its own on the Internet, and the publisher has little control over how it is shared.

Self-promotion

The second part of the release strategy is self-promotion. Many companies already have existing communication channels established with customers, investors, suppliers, and the media. After an infographic has been published publicly with a dedicated landing page, a company should broadcast that URL as widely as possible through their own channels. You never know whose network of followers will reach the right audience.

This is where you should blow your own horn. This is marketing, and you are pitching the infographic to your audience as valuable content. If they like the infographic, they will share it with their own networks…and if those followers like it, they will share it with their own networks…and if those followers like it they will share with their own networks…and so on. That's one way a worthy design can "go viral."

The opportunity is that promoting your infographic through the existing company communication channels is essentially free. It just takes some effort by the employees, and companies can control how much time they ask employees to spend on promotional activities. This is also an opportunity for a company to take advantage of the different forms of presence they have established on the Internet.

Company Communication Channels

How can visitors find the infographic on the company website? If you establish a dedicated infographic landing page as previously mentioned, it's now a custom page within the website that's accessible only to people that know the URL or click a link from another site. What about people who visit your website on their own? How can they get to the infographic or even know it exists?

Depending on the company policies surrounding control of website development, the ability to make changes to the website varies dramatically. A large, global corporation may need months of review and even legal approval to add a single link to the website homepage. A small, nimble startup might be willing to add a link to the homepage within minutes.

Table 3-1 shows the most effective places companies can add links to an infographic they have published.

WEBSITE AREA	DESCRIPTION
Navigation	Most sites have a consistent form of navigation throughout the site. A navigation bar across the top or navigation links down the sidebar are common. Where you add the link to the infographic depends of the topic of the design.
Front page link	A small thumbnail image on the front page is the best way to draw viewers in to see the full-size infographic, but even a text link on the front page can drive a lot of your website's organic traffic to view the infographic.
Product page link	If the infographic topic is specifically related to one of the company's products or services, a thumbnail or text link to the infographic on the product page can also help reach the target audience.

TABLE 3-1:
Effective link locations

WEBSITE AREA	DESCRIPTION
Blog	The company blog is an ideal place to promote the infographic. Use the smaller 500-pixel version of the image in the blog post and link to the dedicated landing page, so that readers can find the full-size version.
Press Releases	If press releases are a part of the website, write a press release about the key message of the infographic that includes the image and a link to the landing page to reach an entirely different audience than the blog.
Media Library	Upload a copy of the infographic file to the media library on your website to allow media contacts access to download the design and include it in any articles.

Often companies also have some more traditional, legacy forms of communication. You might include the infographic in regularly scheduled emails or printed newsletters physically mailed to customers. Use these communication channels as an additional way to share the infographic with a broader audience and include the link to the infographic landing page.

Company Social Accounts

These days, it's highly likely that your company maintains its own social network accounts on Facebook, Twitter, Google+, Flickr, Pinterest, and so on. Companies should absolutely post links to their own infographic on every social media account they have and should post it multiple times. If you post only once, most of your audience will miss it. Your social media followers aren't watching all the time, and if they aren't paying attention, your post will scroll off the bottom of the page before they have a chance to see it as other new content is posted into their news feeds. When you log in to Facebook, you probably don't scroll back to where you left off yesterday and read everything. You probably read only the top few pages and then move on to other things. Anything further down in your feed is never seen.

There's some good data supporting this behavior. Bitly.com is a popular link-shortening service. Because it is so popular across many services, it has some amazing quantitative data about social media links. As you might imagine, when new content is posted online, there is an initial surge of activity by readers clicking the links to view the new content, but then the traffic decreases over a long period of time. Nothing truly dies on the Internet, so the content may continue to get a small number of views even years later.

In 2011, bitly.com published an analysis of what it calls the mean half-life of the links posted to various social networks using its service. By its definition, the *half-life* of a link posted to social media is the amount of time at which this link will receive one-half of the total number of clicks it will ever receive.

What bitly.com found was quite surprising. You can see the chart it created from the data in Figure 3-14, and the initial surge of clicks is obvious. From the bitly.com blog post:[3]

> We looked at the half-life of 1,000 popular bitly.com links and the results were surprisingly similar. The mean half-life of a link on Twitter is 2.8 hours, on Facebook it's 3.2 hours, and via "direct" sources (like email or IM clients) it's 3.4 hours.

On average, this means that after about 3 hours, your link has dropped low in the news feeds of your followers and they aren't seeing your post anymore. Not surprisingly, if they don't see the link, they don't click the link. This is data from 2011, and since then more people have joined social networks, and more content is posted every day. If this analysis were repeated today, the half-life would probably be even shorter because of the increasing velocity of tweets and posts as they scroll down the page faster and faster every day.

FIGURE 3-14:

A posted link will get half of the clicks it will ever get in the first 3 hours.

Source: Half-life of social media links, *bitly.com*

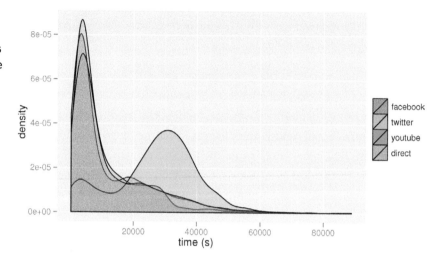

You can also see on the chart that videos on YouTube had a much longer half-life of 7.4 hours, but that information is not applicable to the majority of infographics posted online. Most infographics are not videos and don't get posted to YouTube. However, this strategy wouldn't be much different for infographic videos, based on the much longer scale of an online lifespan that covers months or years.

So how can you use this information to your benefit? There are two parts to a company's social media strategy based on this data:

First, a company should post links to an infographic multiple times over a period of time. How long? Post once a day for a week and no more than twice in one day. Posts should be at least 5 hours apart to catch a different portion of your audience that pays attention to its social networks at different times of the day. Some people check Facebook on lunch breaks and other people don't check until they get home in the evening. Spread the posts out to different parts of the day.

Second, there is a high likelihood that a small portion of your audience will see a few of your posts linking to the same infographic. You don't want these people seeing you repeat that exact same text from earlier. Each post should be written differently. Highlight a different piece of information from the infographic and include both an image (if the social network allows images) and the link to the landing page. Some social networks can automatically find and display the image when you add the URL link.

Each post should be treated like a headline. You want to catch the attention of your audience and entice them to want to read more. If your company has them, involve the copywriting and PR staff to help write the text of the different posts. They are experts at writing these ready-for-press releases and advertisements.

Kickoff Sharing

The last thing you should leverage from within a company is the existing pool of employees. Share the infographic internally and invite all your employees to share it publicly within their own social networks. This has the potential to kickoff the sharing counters on the infographic landing page and may reach some networks of people that don't follow any of the company's communication channels.

The social networks rely on the momentum of frequently shared content to promote the most popular posts. A popular post is shown to more users, which, in turn, can make it even more popular. Asking your employees to help kick-start this cycle of sharing can trigger the promotion of posts linked to your infographic. Many people also look specifically for the current trending posts or most popular topics.

The challenge is that many companies have a big hurdle to overcome here with their employees. Most employees don't work for the marketing or PR departments and they may fear that posting anything related to their company could impact their continued employment. That is, they don't want to get fired. They may want to keep their work life separate from their personal life. It may be fear that they could be misunderstood as speaking on behalf of the company. The company may have specifically asked them not to post any information about the company to protect confidential information.

However, online infographics are a different type of public company information. The objective is to share the infographic with as many people on as many different sites as possible. Hopefully, the infographic is sharing some type of new, surprising, insightful data about the company's industry, market, research data, or products. The company should be proud of this message and want everyone to share it.

To overcome this hurdle, companies need to proactively give employees permission to share the infographic...in writing. Usually an internal e-mail is all it takes. Normally, this message mentions something about the topic of the infographic, how excited the company is to share this information with the public, and, of course, the link to the infographic landing page. Politely request that employees become involved to help kickoff the launch of the infographic and use the sharing buttons on the landing page to share the infographic with their own social networks. Some employees won't participate, but many will.

The one thing you should never do is demand or require employees to share any of your content. This quickly becomes a lose-lose scenario. A company can quickly create a lot of animosity from employees and put the company at risk of a lot of bad publicity. Seriously, if people don't already want to share the infographic on their own, and you feel like you need to compel people to share the infographic, you're doing it wrong.

Promotion, Publicity, and Outreach

The third part of the release strategy is Outreach. This is the activity of marketing the infographic to other authors and sites outside of the company. The hope is that they will appreciate your infographic and post a link. This can be a murky practice that gets into some questionable, spammy practices, but you should remain strong and stay focused on the best practices to build organic links to your infographic.

Again, the search engine companies are constantly trying to improve their algorithms to filter out spam and artificial links so their users get good search results. You want your outreach activity to focus on contacting actual authors and bloggers that may have an interest in the infographic. If someone posts your infographic because they like it, and they think their audience will like it, you don't need to worry about future algorithm updates.

Remember that links from sites with high scores are the most valuable. There are a number of tools that can help you determine the rank of a particular web page. A simple one to use is PRChecker.info (www.prchecker.info) that enables you to enter the URL of any web page to determine its current Google PageRank.

Topic-Specific Blogs

Unless it's someone's personal blog, most blogs have some focus on a topic they specialize in. The Cool Infographics blog obviously focuses on infographics, but you can consistently find blogs related to any niche topic you want. If your infographic design is about chocolate cupcakes, you can find hundreds of cupcake-themed blogs to consider for your outreach plan.

Research online to find the blogs related to your infographic topic. You can easily use Google Blog Search (www.google.com/blogsearch) to search for blogs related to keywords from your infographic. Click the

Search Tools button at the top of the results page and you can choose between Posts to find specific authors that have posted articles related to your topic or homepages to find entire sites.

An effective method is to look at the list of sites that already link to your existing website content. You have to dig into your company's web analytics or use one of the site explorer tools listed next. These sites are aware of your company and liked some of your prior content enough to post it on their site. They are likely to be receptive to any additional quality content from your company.

After you make a list of potential sites, a little extra digging can help narrow it down by determining which blogs are most valuable to include in your outreach plan. No one has time to contact 500 blogs, so focusing your effort is important.

The following list covers five different aspects of blogs that you should research and use to help evaluate the value of any links to your infographic:

- ▶ **Active?**—Blogs are created easily and abandoned just as easily. Check the dates on the most recent posts to make sure they still actively post content. If the last post was a year ago, cross it off your list. Don't waste your time on abandoned blogs.

- ▶ **Rank?**—The easiest statistic to check is the Google PageRank of each blog you find. There are a number of different tools online that can reveal SEO data about websites, some free and some paid. Try using the PageRank Status extension for the Google Chrome browser (pagerank.chromefans.org) to display the PageRank of any page you visit. There are other SEO tools that score websites using their own metrics that are also useful to help determine how valuable a link to your infographic could potentially be. Open-SiteExplorer from SEOmoz (www.opensiteexplorer.org) scores sites with a measure called Domain Authority, and the MajesticSEO

Site Explorer (www.majesticseo.com) evaluates sites based on measurements called Trust Flow and Citation Flow.

- ▶ **Traffic?**—It's harder to determine how much traffic a site receives, but it's certainly helpful information to determine the potential reach of a posted link to your infographic. Because site traffic is not public information, a few sites have tools that can estimate site traffic, such as Quantcast (www.quantcast.com) and Compete (www.compete.com). The numbers are an estimate, but a ballpark number is probably good enough to evaluate an outreach target site.

- ▶ **Followers?**—It's fairly easy to determine a rough estimate of the social audience of blogs. In addition to the traffic estimate, check out their social media presence. How many Facebook followers do they have? How many people follow them on Twitter? If available, how many people subscribe to their RSS feed? How many people have them in circles on Google+? How many followers do they have on Pinterest? These can all help paint a picture of how many people might be exposed to your infographic when posted to their social networks.

- ▶ **Infographics?**—Browse or search the site to see if they have posted infographics from outside web pages before. Some sites post only their own content, so it's good to know if a blog is open to publishing good infographics from outside sources.

After you narrow down your list of blogs to include in your outreach plan to something more manageable, the next challenge is determining how to reach them. Of course, you can always use the Contact page of the blog (if there is one) to reach the blog author, but a cold contact like that can get lost among all the other contact messages.

A more effective way to persuade an author or site to share your infographic is to establish some form of direct communication. Email is best, but many people hide their email addresses to reduce the amount of spam they receive. Find and connect with them through their social media accounts. For example, you could follow them on Twitter. If they follow you back, that would enable you to send them a private Direct Message (DM) to make contact. If they accept a connection from you on LinkedIn, you can send them a message or view their email address on their portfolio page.

When writing a message to a blog author, make it personal. I receive approximately 400 submissions every week to the Cool Infographics blog, and if the message is obviously a template or a form letter, I ignore it. I've seen the exact same message submitted 10 times on the same day with only the link changed. Humans are pattern recognition machines (Chapter 1, "The Science of Infographics") and it's easy to spot the scripted messages that have been copied and pasted into the e-mail. These go straight into the trash.

A good message should be written directly to the blog author and should contain relevant information. Why would their blog audience be interested in the infographic? What prior posts have they published on similar topics? What content have they posted from your company before? What prior posts from the bloggers have you helped share in your own social networks?

Make sure you include the URL link directly to the infographic landing page. Don't try to send them the infographic JPG image file as an attachment. You don't want them to host the infographic image on their site because then they don't need to link to your page. Just send the URL link, and let them use the embed code or sharing buttons from the landing page. They can also get the JPG from the landing page if that's how they would like to post it on their own site. It's often helpful to include a short text description of the infographic in the e-mail so that they can paste that into their blog post as additional text, even if it's the same text description from the landing page.

After you release your infographic into the wild, it takes on a life of its own. Ultimately, you don't have control over what happens to it. You will undoubtedly see both positive and negative comments about it, and from an SEO perspective, it's all good. If people post links and talk about your infographic, your web page rank can benefit.

News Media Sites

News related sites are always looking for good content to publish, but they are also constantly bombarded with hundreds or thousands of story ideas, editorials, press releases, and infographics. If you work for a medium- or large-size company, you may already have an internal PR department or contract with an external PR firm that has an existing list of media contacts. You know these media contacts already post articles relevant to your industry, so take advantage of them. That's a huge benefit of working for a larger company.

In addition, many popular, high-ranking media sites often post infographics submitted from the outside, but the challenge is getting your infographic onto their radar. Some have a system for submissions on the website, but some obscure that process so that they don't get thousands of submissions every day.

Many news sites are focused on a specific topic area, like politics, the environment, health issues, or technology. The selection of news sites to include in your outreach plan depends on your specific infographic topic; however, many news sites cover a wide variety of topics that could be applicable to many different infographic topics.

- ▶ **GOOD Magazine**—www.good.is

  Good Magazine loves infographics. It has made data visualization and infographics an integral part of its culture both online and in print. Create a free account on its website and upload your own infographic as content that the community can learn from.

- ▶ **Mashable**—www.mashable.com

  Mashable is a popular online news site that generally focuses on technology, business, and innovation content. It has a dedicated page for story submissions open to the public and includes links to its editorial staff on Facebook and Twitter.

- ▶ **Smashing Magazine**—www.smashingmagazine.com

  Smashing Magazine posts content generally related to technology, online lifestyle, web development, graphics, and design. The Contact page has a form to submit suggestions that are reviewed by its editorial staff.

- ▶ **The Next Web**—www.thenextweb.com

  The Next Web covers content related to the latest news about Internet technology, business, and culture. On its Contact page, it lists tips to pitch a story (your infographic) and has a contact form to use at the bottom of the page.

You can also submit press releases about your infographics to a number of PR distribution services. These services can make your infographic, along with text and links, available online to news services and websites, and accessible to the search engine spiders. Your company may already have an account with one of these services, but if not, they offer affordable pricing options for individual press releases.

- ▶ **PRWeb**—www.prweb.com

  PRWeb offers a variety of paid options to upload a press release that gets submitted to major news sites and search engines.

- ▶ **PRLog**—www.prlog.org

  PRLog offers both free and paid options to submit a press release for distribution.

- ▶ **PR Newswire**—www.prnewswire.com

  PR Newswire offers a handful of plans at different price points to distribute and track your press release. There are separate plan options for small businesses and nonprofit organizations.

A different strategy would be to approach specific authors instead of news outlets because they may post content across multiple sites. This is more likely to succeed as a long-term strategy. Find authors that post about your company's industry and start interacting with them. Add comments on their published content, post links to their articles, share links in your company social media accounts, and follow them on the social networks they use. Cultivate an on-going relationship with authors related to your industry, and they will be more receptive when you have quality content to share. They may even follow you back and pick up on your infographic from your own self-promotion efforts without any prompting.

Infographics Sharing Sites

When I started the Cool Infographics blog (coolinfographics.com) in 2007, it was one of a handful of websites on the Internet that focused on information design, data visualization, or infographics. I could count on my fingers the number of sites online that published similar content. As a fan myself, I had to visit only a small number of sites to keep up with infographic design news online.

However, in 2013, there are now hundreds of blogs, Tumblr pages, Flickr photo groups, Pinterest boards, Facebook fan pages, and sites that exist for the sole purpose of posting infographics. Over the last few years, a large group of people have become fans of good infographic designs, regardless of the topic of the design. There's an audience that loves to see good infographics that have made infographics a part of their daily information consumption.

These curated gallery and review sites are the easiest group of sites to approach as a part of an outreach plan. They are actively looking for infographics to post as content for their readers, and many of them allow you to self-publish by creating a user account and uploading your infographic to the site. These sites can help generate a large number of views and links to your infographic landing page.

Different sites approach the process of accepting infographics for publication differently. Some sites post every infographic they can get their hands on to build a huge showcase of infographics and some sites filter the infographics and choose the ones they post based on review criteria such as topic or design.

For example, I'm selective about which infographics I post on the Cool Infographics blog. I mentioned earlier that I get approximately 400 submissions every week to the Cool Infographics blog, but I post only a handful on the blog every week. With that many submissions through the site contact page, it's a serious challenge to keep up. A good infographic submission might be unread in my inbox for months before I find it, and then it might be much longer before I get around to writing a blog post about it.

An additional advantage of these sites is that you may reach an audience you had never considered before. Readers of infographic sites may not have any reason to visit sites related to your company's product or service, but when they see your infographic, it may attract their attention and build awareness.

Here's a short list of infographics sites for your reference. This list is constantly changing as smaller sites collapse and new sites are launched every day, so I attempted to include the more long-lasting sites. I do maintain an ongoing list of current infographics sites on the Cool Infographics blog. You can check for the most current list at coolinfographics.com/links/.

Infographic Self-publishing Sites

These sites enable people to create a free account and upload their own design work. When people view the infographic you uploaded on these sites, they also have easy sharing buttons and embed code automatically generated so viewers can share them easily. This might not be as powerful as using the embed code from your own infographic landing page, but it's convenient and easy to use.

▶ **Flickr**—www.flickr.com

Use your own account (free or paid) to upload the infographic image into your own photostream. After the infographic is in your account on Flickr, you can add it to groups focused on sharing infographics by joining them. If your infographic topic is relevant to other photo groups, you can also join them and add the infographic as well.

▶ **Visual.ly**—visual.ly

Visually has built a tremendous showcase of infographics. After you create a free account, you can upload your infographic to be included in the gallery. The site enables you to include a short text description and links to the source site and designer. When you view infographics on Visually, there are tools for easy sharing and it also allows viewers to like or comment on the infographics. Popular infographic designs are featured on Visually's homepage.

▶ **Visualizing.org**—www.visualizing.org

Visualizing.org is a free community site to share data visualizations and infographics designs. Upload your own infographics; they are made available to anyone for viewing and commenting. They also maintain a large library of public data sets and host visualization design challenges.

▶ **Graphs.net**—www.graphs.net

Graphs.net is a free gallery site that enables you to upload your own infographics. The site also provides space to include a text description and a link to the original source URL.

▶ **Love Infographics**—www.loveinfographics.com

Love Infographics is a free gallery that enables people to create an account and upload their own infographics. The infographics can include a text description and links to the original and enables other designers to add comments.

▶ **VisualizeUs**—vi.sualize.us

VisualizeUs is an image-sharing site that includes a large collection of infographics intended as inspiration for designers. Create an account and install its browser widget to upload your infographics to the site.

Free Infographic Submission Sites

Free infographic submission sites can be run by anyone, and new sites appear (and disappear) every day. Just like researching the topic related blogs, you should also research the web analytics of any infographics gallery sites to help determine which sites can be most valuable in your outreach plan.

These sites have free reign to control the content they post and are under no obligation to post any infographic you submit. Just like the blogs, try to connect with the author to break through the clutter. On free sites, there's no barrier of entry. So, every infographic gets submitted to these sites, often multiple times, which is annoying. That's a lot of noise that your infographic design has to break through to get noticed.

▶ **Cool Infographics**—coolinfographics.com

On Cool Infographics, I strive to post the best examples of infographic designs I can find. I post only a handful of infographics each week out of the hundreds of submissions and infographics I find on my own. This careful selection has built the site into one of the strongest links you can get from an infographics gallery site. Submit your link and message through the Contact page.

▶ **Visual Loop**—www.visualoop.tumblr.com

Tiago Veloso has built Visual Loop into one of the largest and most popular infographics galleries. You can find infographics, portfolios, interviews, Pinterest boards, and much more. This site makes the commitment that every infographic submitted will be posted to its Tumblr page, which then has the chance to be posted on its other channels. Submit your infographic through the Contact link on the page.

- **Chart Porn**—www.chartporn.org

  Chart Porn is a great collection of the most visually appealing data visualizations, maps, charts, and infographics designs. The site is curated by Dustin Smith, and you can submit your infographic to the e-mail address on the About page.

- **News I Like**—www.newsilike.in

  Bharat Prajapati posts infographics along with his own reviews of the designs on a frequent basis. Use the Submit page to send the URL link to your infographic landing page.

- **Submit Infographics**—www.submitinfographics.com

  Submit Infographics posts selected infographics along with descriptive text, links, and a review by a designer. It requires a minimum of 100 words in your description to be considered.

- **NerdGraph**—www.nerdgraph.com

  NerdGraph posts multiple infographics each day and enables anyone to submit infographics for review through its Submit page. Although it doesn't post them all, it includes a text description, keywords, a link back to the original, and a promise to send an e-mail notification when the infographic is posted.

Paid Infographic Submission Sites

A number of infographic gallery sites charge for submissions to be considered. Usually it's a small fee to cover the author's time to review the infographic and compose a blog post. The pay wall also helps reduce the amount of submissions the site receives to only those publishers serious enough to pay the fee. Some sites even offer a range of services with different prices, from free up to expensive premium listings.

Unlike the totally free sites, there's an implied agreement that your infographic will definitely get posted if you pay the fee and probably not if you don't pay. If you pay the money, you should expect to get coverage and links. This addresses the uncertainty of submitting to the free sites that have the freedom to ignore your submission. Fees listed next were current as of 2013 and will change over time.

It's unclear whether the search engine companies will consider these to be spammy paid links in the future, but currently these small fees seem to fall below their radar. In the SEO industry, paid links are considered to be a questionable practice of link building, and the search engine companies are constantly developing ways to eliminate the impact of paid links in their algorithms. Your company must choose its own level of risk tolerance and if the value of links from these paid sites are worth the fees. On the other hand, for a small marketing expense (approximately $1,000 total) you can be guaranteed to get your infographic onto all these sites.

- **Infographics Showcase** ($100)—www.infographicsshowcase.com

  Infographics Showcase will post a review of your infographic design with grades for both design and information. Pay the fee, and within 7 days it will post the infographic, along with a thorough written review. Use the PayPal button on the Submit page to start the process. As it states on the page: "*We will take the good and the bad, but we prefer the good. Bad infographics, get bad reviews.*"

- **Infographic Journal** (Free-$25)—www.infographicjournal.com

  Infographic Journal accepts both free and paid submissions. The staff filters free submissions to choose which ones get posted, but it guarantees that paid submissions will be posted. Use the form on the Submit page to send it the URL link, description, and embed code of your infographic.

- ▶ **Infographic Love** ($60)—www.infographiclove.com

  Infographic Love requires that a text description of at least 200 words be submitted along with the infographic, and it features only well-designed infographics with good research. Use the PayPal button on the Submit page to start the process.

- ▶ **Daily Infographic** (Up to $350)—www.dailyinfographic.com

  Daily Infographic consistently posts one good infographic every day and has built a large following. If you submit your e-mail address, it will send you details about the fees to submit and feature your infographic on the site.

- ▶ **Infographics Archive** (Free-$399.95)—www.infographics archive.com

  Infographics Archive offers a range of prices from free submissions with no guarantee to be listed, up to $399.95 for a 10-day spotlight package. Use the PayPal button on the Submit page to start the process.

- ▶ **Amazing Infographics** ($100)—www.amazinginfographics.com

  Amazing infographics will post your infographic along with a text description and two supporting links that you can use to link back to your landing page or company website. Use the PayPal button on the Submit page to start the process, and your infographic should be posted within 7 days.

- ▶ **Infographic Gallery** (Free-$30)—www.infographicgallery.co.uk

  Infographic Gallery enables both free and paid infographic submissions. Only paid submissions are guaranteed to be posted. Use the forms on the Submit page to start the process.

▶ **Info-Graphic** (£20)—www.info-graphic.co.uk

Info-Graphic posts only paid infographics submissions. On the Info-Graphic Submit page, you can send your infographic along with a preferred title, text description, URL link, keywords, and embed code. Use the PayPal button to submit payment.

Hundreds more free and paid infographics sites exist online, so this list will naturally change over time. Do your own research and leverage this community of infographic fans to help build an audience for your own infographic designs.

Final Thoughts

The goals of most online infographics are to build awareness, reach customers, drive website traffic and improve placement in search engine results. A cool infographic design alone is generally not enough. Don't publish an infographic and just hope that people show up to see it. It takes some extra effort to maximize the return on investment a company makes into the data research and infographic design efforts.

Leverage these insights and tactics to give your infographic the best possible chance for success. Your infographic needs to be visible to the search engines and easy to find for readers. Build a good infographic landing page, share the infographic through all of the company's communication channels, and reach out to authors and sites that will consider your design to be valuable content for their readers.

Combine all of these efforts together with a cool infographic design and you have the formula for an extremely successful project.

References

1. comScore Releases March 2013 U.S. Search Engine Rankings,
   http://www.comscore.com/Insights/Press_Releases/2013/4/
   comScore_Releases_March_2013_U.S._Search_Engine_Rankings

2. Matt Cutts and Eric Enge Talk About What Makes a Quality Site,
   July 2012, http://www.stonetemple.com/matt-cutts-and-eric-
   talk-about-what-makes-a-quality-site/

3. bitly.com, How long will people pay attention? September 2011,
   http://blog.bitly.com/post/9887686919/you-just-shared-
   a-link-how-long-will-people-pay

Links

Many of the images in this chapter can be viewed by using the following links or going to www.wiley.com/go/coolinfographics.

1. *Google PageRank Explained*, Elliance:
   http://www.elliance.com/aha/infographics/google-pagerank-
   explained.aspx.

2. *What's so hard about search?* Eric Enge, Stone Temple Consulting:
   http://www.stonetemple.com/infographics/search-complexity
   .shtml

3. *James Bond: 50 Years of Movies*, H&R Block:
   blogs.hrblock.com/2012/09/25/50-years-of-bond-james-bond-
   infographic/

4. *Streamlining your digital life with the new iPad*, NextWorth:
   http://www.nextworth.com/ipad3_infographic

5. *Bringing Down Bin Laden*, Column Five Media and Namesake:
   http://columnfivemedia.com/work-items/namesake-
   infographic-breakdown-of-the-takedown-%E2%80%94-osamas-
   last-hour/

6. *Death & Taxes 2014*, Timeplots: http://www.timeplots.com/collections/catalog/products/death-and-taxes-poster-2014

7. *The Visual History of Halloween*, FrightCatalog.com: http://www.frightcatalog.com/halloween-history/

8. *Pairing Wine & Food*, Wine Folly: http://winefolly.com/review/5-tips-to-perfect-food-and-wine-pairing/

The more strikingly visual your presentation is, the more people will remember it. And more importantly, they will remember you.

—Paul Arden, *Whatever You Think, Think The Opposite*

Infographic Resumes

The principles behind good infographic design have recently made their way into the resumes of individuals. Job candidates are looking for new ways to make their resumes stand out from the crowd, quickly communicate their top attributes, and be more memorable to the prospective employer who may review hundreds of resumes for an open position. Infographics are a fantastic way to tell your story to a potential hiring manager—and they're cool too!

This rising trend of infographic resumes is a hotly debated topic. Recruiters, candidates, resume writers, hiring managers, and human resources managers can have widely opposing, strong opinions. Some believe that adding any graphics to a resume is unprofessional and may lead to a candidate not being considered for a position. Many others are huge supporters of graphic resumes because they break the monotony of all-text resumes and stand out from the pile of resumes reviewed.

As discussed in Chapter 1, "The Science of Infographics," the research behind visual communication of information shows that visualizations can often be more effective than text alone. Although traditional illustrations and images are mainly appropriate for graphic designer-type roles, the advent of infographic design brings credible data visualizations to candidates seeking any type of role. Whether it's a complete infographic design or just including small data visualizations in a text resume, visualizing a candidate's key information on a resume is quickly becoming popular.

Michael Anderson's infographic resume shown in Figure 4-1 was one of the first infographics resume designs to be published online and go viral in social media. This caused me to originally take notice of the concept of infographic resumes. Posted online in 2008, the design was colorful, eye-catching, and broke the traditional resume mold. A link to Michael's resume was posted on the Cool Infographics blog in 2010, but it was also featured on hundreds of sites and blogs including some mainstream sites such as Mashable, Business Insider, Fast Company, and FlowingData.

The infographic resume visualizes his work history as an area chart timeline, with work experience above the date line and his educational accomplishments below. His resume states that "Area represents relative energy expenditure over time," which is a subjective value that Michael created to design the chart. The overlapping nature of the design is appealing because it also shows concurrent activities clearly. The Daily Intake and Output is a fun, lighthearted chart of the amount of each activity plotted over his waking hours from 8 a.m.–2 a.m.

Michael Anderson
RÉSUMÉ / INFOGRAPHICS

theportfolio.ofmichaelanderson.com
lunyboy@yahoo.com | 304-382-5145
HC 63 BOX 2340 | ROMNEY, WV 26757

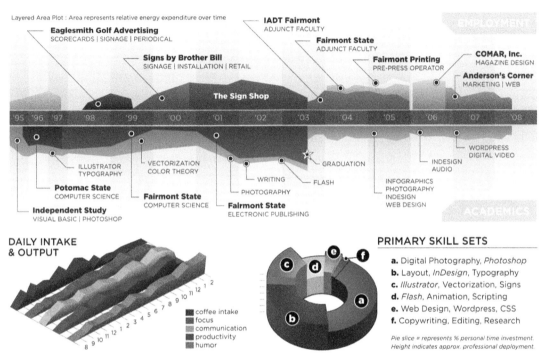

FIGURE 4-1:
Infographic resume—Michael Anderson
Coolinfographics.com/Figure-4-1

The Primary Skill Sets visualization is a doughnut chart with two dimensions. The angles of the pie slices represent his personal time spent developing each skill and the height of each slice shows the amount of time each skill has been used in a professional capacity. For example, it shows that Michael has spent a lot of personal time in photography, but that skill has not been utilized much in his professional career. Again, the values are estimated by Michael, so they are subjective and just meant to be indicative of his skills. Also, notice that no values are shown on any of the visualizations. Actual values had to be created to design the charts, but they aren't shown because they aren't needed. This removes unnecessary information and keeps the design simple.

This design stands on its own as a preview to his full text resume. Because this design doesn't replace his traditional resume, it gave Michael the opportunity to cut out most of the lengthy text descriptions and let the visualizations stand by themselves. It's a great tool to attract the attention of both prospective employers and freelance clients, and anyone interested has the contact information required to learn more about Michael.

The definition of an infographic resume is:

> *A visual account of an individual's history and abilities that uses data visualization design to communicate key portions of a job candidate's skills, history, education, or other relevant information.*

The key distinction that makes infographic resumes unique is that the graphic elements visualize important information and help tell a better story about the job candidate. It's not just about adding graphic elements but communicating data or information more effectively.

Graphic designers have been designing creative, colorful, artistic resumes with illustrations, fonts, images, and photographs for decades; however, the idea of using data visualizations to create a new style of resume has taken hold only in the last few years. A handful of designs began appearing online in 2008, as the awareness and popularity of online infographics was beginning to build momentum. The trend has continued to grow at an accelerated pace, and by January 2013, thousands of infographic resumes incorporating data visualization could be found online.

In Figures 4-2 and 4-3, Faz Besharatian's infographic resume appears next to his traditional text resume. His work history has been visualized in a timeline that highlights the length of time Faz spent in each role and the skills that were required.

In this instance, there is more complete information contained in the text resume. The infographic resume serves three purposes: to attract attention, to highlight the roles and companies in his history, and to demonstrate his graphic design ability. If interested parties want to learn any of the details, such as accomplishments, responsibilities, or specific achievements within each role, they can learn more from the full-text resume. Faz makes both versions available for anyone to download from his website.

It's still the early days for infographic resumes, but they will probably become mainstream in the next few years. In the future, an all-text resume will be seen as boring and dated, reflecting poorly on the job seeker. Recruiters and hiring managers will appreciate the speed and ease of reading from infographic designs and will begin to experience frustration with the extra time and effort required to search for key information hidden within an all-text resume.

The quality of these infographic resume designs covers the full spectrum. There are some fantastic, inspiring designs online, but there are also some "cringe-worthy" designs as well. As designers continue to experiment with different design styles, they are beginning to learn what works in the field of resumes. Most people design their own infographic resume. The market for professionally designed infographic resumes is a new type of service now offered by many designers and design firms.

FAZ*reSume*

faz@fazfolio.com
www.fazfolio.com
240.481.0335 (UTC -05)
1211 13th Street NW, #102
Washington, DC 20005

Faz Besharatian *Creative Leader – Design Evangelist – Team Player*
Living in Washington DC, wandering everywhere.

Objective:
To pursue a challenging career in design, with the opportunity to be a part of a team creating compelling concepts and solving interesting problems.

Professional Experience:
Faz LLC [CEO – 2011-Present]
Consultant + Entrepreneur + UX Designer

Welocalize [Sr Product Manager – 2011]
Developed business requirements, and prototype solutions, for a translation service company's next-generation of products. Drove strategy and provided user experience oversight.

Responsibilities included:
- Creating business requirements and UI specifications
- Recommending best practices in developing multiple versions at once
- Establishing time lines and drafting design documents
- Identify and prioritize existing usability issues and define solutions to address them
- Converting requirements into actionable items that can be implemented in a user interface
- Develop, oversee, and polish all UX project deliverables

AARP [Design Director – 2007-2011]
Established the tone for AARP.org's creative direction. Guided the digital strategy and user experience for the 40 million member organization. Managed the user experience team – Web Designers and Information Architects – and collaborated with product, development and editorial teams towards enhancing the AARP's online engagement with its members.

Responsibilities within product design business unit included:
- Helping shape the business unit road-map and thereby AARP's digital strategy
- Translating strategy to feature development during the agile sprint cycle
- Collaborating with business development and sales groups to stay on track with revenue goals
- Selecting platforms and working with partners during initial content integration
- Working closely with product managers, developers & quality assurance professionals
- Reporting to top management on progress and performance

AOL [Principal Designer – 2005-2007]
Implemented user interaction in support of AOL services. Designed prototypes and high-fidelity models that explored potential design directions well before production. Worked with program managers and business stake-holders to drive future product direction and business strategy. Teamed with Information Architects and User Interface professionals on numerous concepts, mood boards, screen mocks, visual specs, and design requirement documentations. Collaborated with – and gave direction to – design agencies and internal product teams.

Corcoran College of Art + Design [Adjunct Faculty – 2004-2008]
Instructed semester-long college courses, covering web fundamentals and theories of interface design.

US Airways [Design Manager – 2004-2005]
Established creative direction for a transportation/travel web site. Drove corporate design and brand standards and worked closely with outside agency on redesign effort. Designed and conducted usability tests and other research with representative users. Provided user interface and usability consultation to product management and development teams with specific increased sales revenue goals.

Terrapin Systems [Art Director/Web Designer – 2003-2004]
Developed and managed projects ranging from identity systems and collateral materials to multimedia. Conceptualized, planned, designed, and produced for a wide range of web-based channels; including web sites, micro sites, emails, online applications and rich media.

Independent Designer
[Art Director/Designer – 2002]
Worked under both direct contract and freelance arrangements.

USWeb/CKS (became marchFIRST) [Art Director – 1999-2001]
Art directed the design and implementation of high profile client projects, including: on-line banking site for PNC Bank; kiosk design for US Airways; identity development for Capital.com; promotional CD-ROM for US Airways; web site design for Shop@AOL commerce channel.

Low + Associates
[Senior Designer – 1997-1999]

Snyder Communication
[Graphic Designer – 1995-1996]

Maryland Media
[Graphic Artist – 1993-1995, part-time]

For extended description of all positions, please visit http://www.linkedin.com/in/fazthepersian.

Educational Experience:
Yale School of Management,
New Heaven, CT [2010]
Certificate, Business Perspectives for Creative Leaders

University of Maryland,
College Park, MD [1995]
Bachelor of Arts in Graphic/Advertising Design

Key Skills:
Identifies, addresses and solves complex user interface and information design problems by providing multiple viable solutions.

Possesses expert diagramming and screen layout skills and creates high-level concept maps, navigation maps and wire frames.

Collaborates with other disciplines to define the vision and requirements for a product or programming area.

Possesses thorough understanding of industry standard applications/technologies, such as HTML, CSS, AJAX, Flash and Publishing Systems.

Reviews competing products and recommends design solutions that differentiate the company's products from those of competitors.

Works with business owners, producers, technology personnel, designers and researchers on specific projects to create final interface features.

Develops user profiles, with emphasis on human error control, display issues, visual interaction and task/objective analyses.

Proficient in industry standard authoring, graphic, layout and sequencing tools.

FIGURE 4-2: Text resume—Faz Besharatian

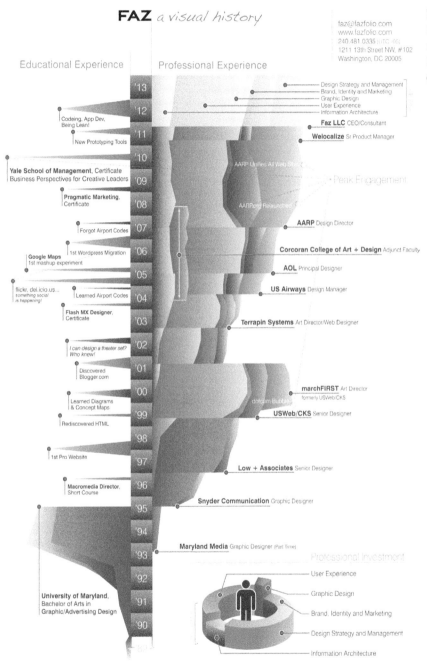

FAZ *a visual history*

faz@fazfolio.com
www.fazfolio.com
240.481.0335 (UTC -9)
1211 13th Street NW, #102
Washington, DC 20005

Educational Experience   Professional Experience

'13 — Design Strategy and Management
Brand, Identity and Marketing
Graphic Design
'12 — User Experience
Information Architecture

Codeing, App Dev,
Being Lean!

Faz LLC CEO/Consultant

'11

Welocalize Sr Product Manager

New Prototyping Tools

'10

AARP Unifies All Web Sites

Peak Engagement

Yale School of Management, Certificate
Business Perspectives for Creative Leaders

'09

Pragmatic Marketing,
Certificate

'08

AARP.org Relaunched

Forgot Airport Codes

'07

AARP Design Director

1st Wordpress Migration

'06

Corcoran College of Art + Design Adjunct Faculty

Google Maps
1st mashup experiment

'05

AOL Principal Designer

flickr, del.icio.us...
*something social
is happening!*   Learned Airport Codes

'04

US Airways Design Manager

Flash MX Designer,
Certificate

'03

Terrapin Systems Art Director/Web Designer

*I can design a theater set?
Who knew!*

'02

Discovered
Blogger.com

'01

Learned Diagrams
& Concept Maps

'00

marchFIRST Art Director
formerly USWeb/CKS

dotcom Bubble

'99

USWeb/CKS Senior Designer

Rediscovered HTML

'98

1st Pro Website

'97

Low + Associates Senior Designer

Macromedia Director,
Short Course

'96

Snyder Communication Graphic Designer

'95

'94

Maryland Media Graphic Designer (Part Time)

'93

Professional Investment

'92

User Experience

'91

Graphic Design

University of Maryland,
Bachelor of Arts in
Graphic/Advertising Design

Brand, Identity and Marketing

'90

Design Strategy and Management

Information Architecture

FIGURE 4-3:
Infographic
resume—Faz
Besharatian
Coolinfographics
.com/Figure-4-3

Key Benefits

The three key benefits of infographics designs discussed in Chapter 1 are what also make infographic resumes game changers to the job market.

First, visual designs stand out from the pile of text-only resumes and attract attention. Hiring managers and human resources departments are skimming hundreds, if not thousands, of resumes for open positions. An infographic resume breaks the pattern and draws the reader's attention. The first step to landing a new job is to get the hiring manager interested enough to learn more and an infographic resume can get a candidate that extra attention.

Second, data visualization can make the understanding of a candidate's unique information faster for the reader. Recent research has concluded that a recruiter or hiring manager looks at an individual resume for only an average of six seconds[1]. By visualizing a candidate's key information using data visualization design techniques, the reader can learn more about the candidate in that same short timeframe. Six seconds reading an infographic resume is more effective than six seconds reading a text resume. This means that hiring managers may understand more about job candidates that have infographic resumes.

Third, because of the *Picture Superiority Effect*, anyone reading an infographic resume is much more likely to remember the visualized information three days later. The visualized data triggers the reader's visual memory and the recruiter or hiring manager is more likely to remember that candidate after reviewing many resumes. This significantly improves the chances of a candidate to advance to the next step in the hiring process.

What's the Risk?

The risk of using a poorly designed infographic resume is that they can quickly and effectively demonstrate that a job candidate would not be a good hire for the company.

A poor design could:

- Be visually unappealing

- Visualize data incorrectly

- Fail to visualize the relevant information

- Confuse the reader with too many visualizations

- Highlight the wrong attributes for the desired position

- Use an inappropriate design tone (such as, a fun, lighthearted design style when applying for a serious role)

- Not print correctly if not designed to fit standard paper sizes

A poor design can stand out from the pile of job candidate resumes and create a negative impression with the recruiter just as fast and effectively as a good design can create a positive impression.

Many of the best practices behind designing a good text resume apply to designing an infographic resume as well. Being concise and focused is critical. Candidates need to identify clearly their key strengths related to the type of position they would like to attain. An infographic resume should focus on communicating those key strengths quickly and clearly to the recruiter. If the design visualizes everything possible from a candidate's history, the key strengths are likely to get lost in the visual noise, and the recruiter could become frustrated trying to read the resume.

Just like every other resume, if the reader becomes confused, annoyed, or frustrated, the candidate's resume can quickly end up in the trash.

Designing an Infographic Resume

Remember that infographics tell stories. Infographic resume designs should be used to tell the story about job candidates. The story can include their background, history, education, skills, experience, achievements, accomplishments, roles, successes, aspirations, goals, and more.

The key to an effective infographic resume is to use data visualization design to highlight only the most important aspects for a specific individual. The visualizations draw the readers' attention to the key information, and with the Picture Superiority Effect, that is the information from the resume most likely to be remembered. So, a younger, less experienced candidate might highlight education and software skill proficiencies, but an older, mature candidate could highlight major accomplishments and employment over many years with respected employers.

The design challenge is to tell a simple story that is quick and easy to understand. The mistake many people make when designing an infographic resume is to attempt to visualize everything they can. Too many data visualizations can create excess visual noise and confuse the readers. The hiring managers may not understand the key attributes of the job candidate within those short few seconds they have to review the resume. As a general rule, the best designs include three or fewer data visualizations in the design. As an additional benefit, focusing on only the key attributes demonstrates to the hiring manager the candidate's ability for clear and concise communication—a desirable skill for any position.

The first step in the design process is to identify which aspects of an individual's history are the most beneficial while also considering what is most relevant and important to the prospective employer. After the key aspects have been identified, the designer can begin to focus on which types of visualization design are appropriate to include.

Most infographic resume designs focus on a combination of these three key types of information:

1. Timeline of education and work experience

2. Relative experience and proficiencies among key job skills

3. Geographic locations

Timeline Designs

Designers have the same variety of design options for visualizing an individual's history as seen in other infographic designs.

Randall Knapp included a timeline of his programming experience as part of an overall infographic design (Figure 4-4). He used an area chart with overlapping colors to highlight the different types of activities over a 7-year period. Even though the timeline is the main focal point, it's part of a larger design that includes additional information and a separate visualization of skill proficiencies.

The overlapping areas on the timeline also do a great job showing concurrent activities. We lead parallel lives, not sequential ones. Many people have roles that overlap each other, as well as with educational and other activities. A visual timeline is the best way to show that type of information that gets lost in a text-only resume. Going to school at night or working two jobs shows significant dedication and motivation in an individual's history. With a text-only resume, the reader must take time to put together the timing of different activities to understand overlap or gaps in a candidate's history. With a visual design, overlapping activities and gaps between roles are understood within seconds.

Timelines usually highlight an individual's history related to one or more of the following activities:

- ▶ Time spent at learning institutions or earning degrees

- ▶ Time spent working for different companies

- ▶ Time spent holding different roles or positions

- ▶ Time spent as a member or volunteer for organizations

- ▶ Time spent using different software applications

- ▶ Time spent in different locations

- ▶ Major events or milestones in a person's career

FIGURE 4-4:
Timeline focused infographic resume—Randall Knapp
Coolinfographics.com/Figure-4-4

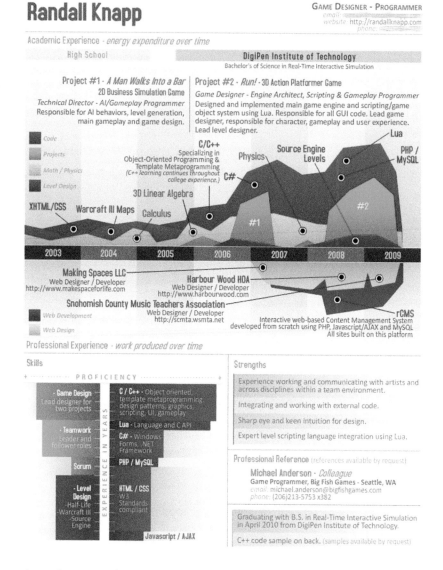

Area charts are the most common data visualization design for timelines, but designs using line charts, number lines, and overlapping shapes are also common.

Although many designs incorporate timelines as one element of an overall layout, designer Mike Wirth effectively used a large timeline visualization as his entire infographic resume design (Figure 4-5).

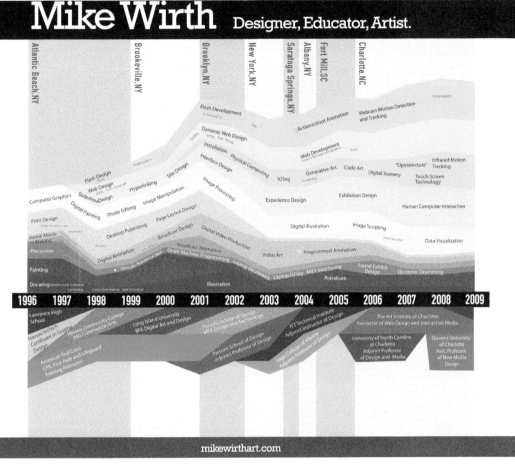

FIGURE 4-5: Infographic timeline resume—Design by Mike Wirth

Coolinfographics.com/Figure-4-5

In Mike's resume, the years along the x-axis become the backbone of the entire design. It's a central design element around which all the other information is placed on the page. The locations he has lived are shown as gray-colored columns in the background, and instead of overlapping colored sections, he uses a stacked area design to show the overall increase in total experience over time.

Although a completely different design style, Duncan McKean's infographic resume (Figure 4-6) takes a similar approach by making the entire infographic resume design into a timeline visualization.

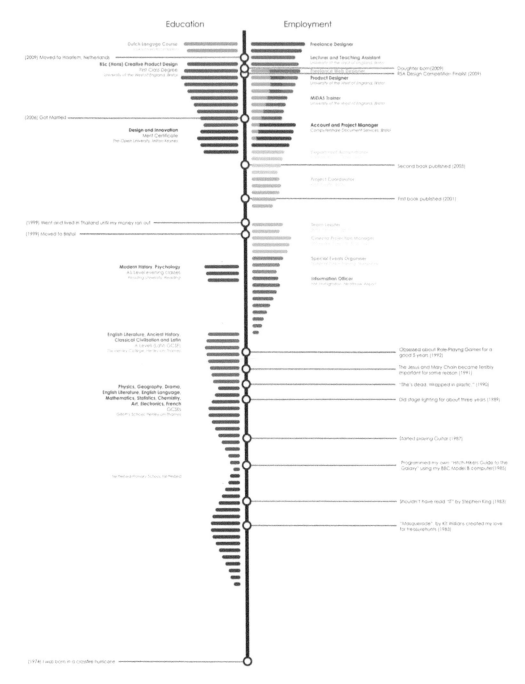

cv.duncan**mckean**.com

FIGURE 4-6: Infographic timeline resume—Duncan McKean
Coolinfographics.com/Figure-4-6

A job candidate's work and education history over time is one of the most important pieces of information to a recruiter or hiring manager. An infographic timeline can visually demonstrate a candidate's history in an engaging way that's faster and easier to understand.

Relative Experience Designs

Levels of experience in different job skills are normally qualitative and subjective. The candidate may consider himself to be highly skilled at project management, but not have any firm numeric data to back up that claim. That's where relative experience comparisons come into play.

Hana Tesar's infographic resume (Figure 4-7) is based on showing her skills in relation to each other. There are no numbers shown as value labels on the bar charts, but visually she is telling the reader how her skill levels compare. The implication is that the highest bars are not only her strongest attributes, but also implies that they are areas in which she is exceptionally skilled when compared to other candidates within the job market. She has some experience in all the skills shown, but the highest bars are the ones she wants to highlight most to a potential employer or client.

This is where visually comparing multiple attributes with a data visualization becomes effective. In Figure 4-8, Navdeep Raj uses a different skills comparison in his resume design. The different job skills are shown with bars of varying size. This communicates to the reader that the candidate's skills are strongest in User Experience and Information Architecture compared to the other skills that he thought were also appropriate to include. The candidate does have some skill in 3-D animation, but it's weaker than the other skills.

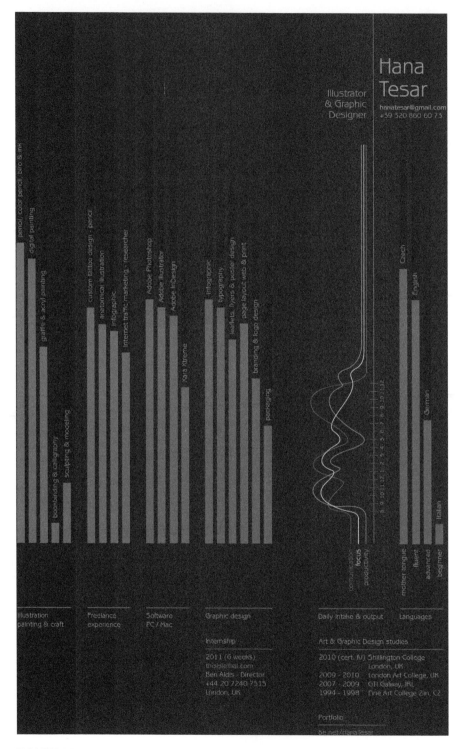

FIGURE 4-7: Relative experience resume—Hana Tesar

Coolinfographics.com/Figure-4-7

FIGURE 4-8:
Skills visualization resume—Navdeep Raj

Coolinfographics.com/Figure-4-8

Visualizing the skills in relation to each other allows the candidates to communicate their subjective strengths in key areas without needing to assign specific numeric values to each skill.

Bar charts are the most common visualization to show skills, but there are many other design styles that could also be used. Circle sizes, sliders, bubble charts, Sankey diagrams rose diagrams and more can also be effective visualizations to display proficiency among multiple skills.

Geographic Designs

Where a candidate has lived and worked can also be relevant information on a resume. Maps are a common design element to show not only employment locations, but also to visualize length of stay, the sequence of the locations, or the many different countries visited in the course of a career.

A map visualization dominates the space on Ana Foureaux Frazao's 2-page infographic resume (Figure 4-9). Her prior roles in International Public Relations are clearly shown to the reader and strongly reinforce her international experience. The locations of her positions are color-coded by the type of work she did and the map design is simplified by removing all the country borders.

Maps have a unique challenge when used as data visualizations in a resume. The design needs to illustrate enough spatial information to make the identified locations easily recognizable to the audience, but too much detail (such as terrain, borders, cities, and roads) may also create unwanted visual noise. The focus of the design should be the key information the candidate wants to communicate, not a pretty map.

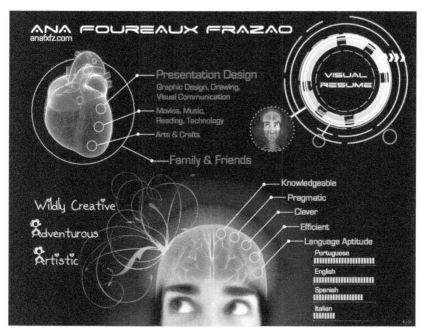

FIGURE 4-9:
Geographic info-
graphic resume—
Ana Foureaux
Frazao
Coolinfographics
.com/Figure-4-9

The design should also limit the amount of geographic information displayed to only the required area. If a candidate has worked in three different cities in the state of California, a map of the entire United States is not needed. If a candidate has worked in five cities across Canada, the entire world map would take up valuable space. The real estate on the resume page is too valuable to waste. The infographic should show only as much map space as needed to include all the highlighted locations in a recognizable space.

Chris Robertson's resume (Figure 4-10) shows diverse locations including multiple states in the United States and also locations in foreign locations, such as Dubai and Lebanon. Instead of showing an entire world map, Chris shows only the relevant states and countries and pinpoints the city locations where he has worked. This saves space and allows Chris to place the locations along a timeline. This design also gave Chris space to include additional information such as his title, the companies he worked for, and a few major client projects.

Company Logos and Icons

One of the easiest and most effective ways to add visual design elements to a resume is by including company logos. Companies have spent a lot of effort, time, and money to build their brand equity and recognition of their logos. Prior employment with a recognized company is a positive attribute in employment history and reflects well on the candidate for a new position. When people include the name of a prior company on their resume, one of the primary desired benefits is that respect for a recognized company will transfer some of that good will to the job candidate.

In traditional text resumes, people use many different text adaptations to emphasize the different companies they have worked for in the past. Bold, italics, different font type, or larger font size are all used to make the names of companies stand out from a page full of text as key information.

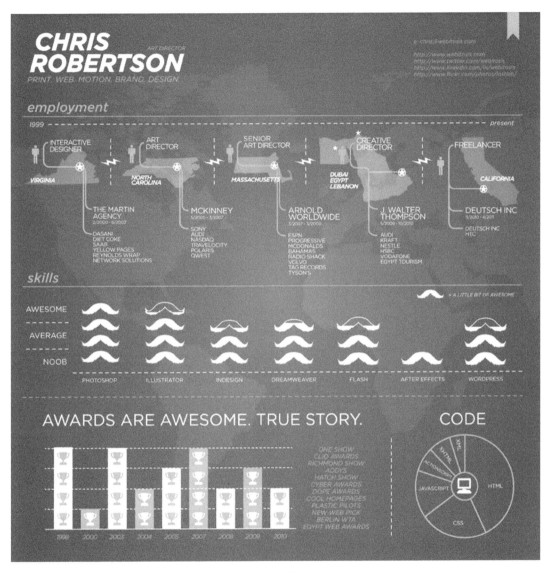

FIGURE 4-10: Infographic resume with map data—Chris Robertson
Coolinfographics.com/Figure-4-10

After reading the study from The Ladders (mentioned earlier) that concluded most recruiters look at each resume for only six seconds, Adrian Saker created this logo-only resume, using logos from both the companies he worked for, the client projects he was involved with, and additional logos for skills, education, and interests (Figure 4-11).

ADRIAN SAKER
CREATIVE DIRECTOR

adriansaker@gmail.com

FREELANCE

 McCANN WORLDGROUP

 Ogilvy

 GREY

 ■R/GA

 J W T

 M&CSAATCHI

 EURO RSCG

 Coca-Cola BURGER KING MasterCard Glenfiddich at&t

 IBM AMERICAN EXPRESS

 Twix  TOSHIBA Tanqueray USbank

 verion

 Microsoft Schick Merrill Lynch

 ON THE BORDER

 LG  Depo-Provera VOLVO

FIGURE 4-11: Logo resume—Adrian Saker
Coolinfographics.com/Figure-4-11

STAFF

EDUCATION

MEMBERSHIPS

INTERESTS

SKILLS

The addition of graphic logos from the different companies included in prior work experience can draw the reader's attention. If the companies are known and recognized by the reader, the logos can quickly make a candidate's work history easy to understand. If those companies have a positive reputation, the job candidate may instantly leave a positive impression on the hiring managers, even before they read a single word of the resume.

Based on this principle, LinkedIn, the site dedicated to professional connections, has begun displaying company logos on everyone's profile pages if it has one available from an official Company Page, as you can see from the author's profile (Figure 4-12). When people add a company position to their personal work history in their LinkedIn account, if they choose a company that LinkedIn already recognizes, the official company logo displays on the individual's profile page.

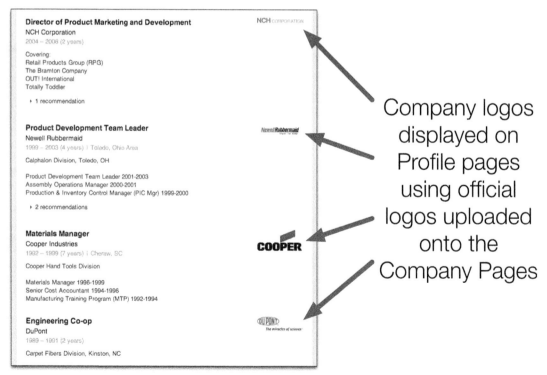

FIGURE 4-12: Company logos shown on LinkedIn profiles

There are many posts and articles online about understanding the legal issues surrounding the use of trademarked company logos. Many people do not understand trademark law and especially the Fair Use doctrine. In a reference to a company, especially in a list of multiple companies, the Fair Use doctrine enables the use of a company's trademark when referring to that company. More information about the Fair Use Doctrine is covered in Chapter 2, "Online Infographics," but it's worth repeating that trademark law is different across countries, so it's worth understanding local laws.

Sascha Kuntze used many company and brand logos in his infographic resume (Figure 4-13). In this design, the logos are used to represent past clients and also his social media presence. The reader is likely to recognize some of the mainstream logos included in this design, and the value of Sascha's work is elevated based on his association with these respected companies.

David P. Ingram's use of logos in his resume (Figure 4-14) is also effective. The logos draw the eye and attention instantly and creates the first impression the resume leaves on the reader. For example, Sony is generally regarded as a company with a tremendously positive reputation, especially related to its training of high-quality employees. The first impression on a hiring manager reading his resume might be that David comes from a reputable company, so David's resume is probably worth the extra time to read thoroughly.

As a hiring manager sorts through a pile of a hundred resumes, getting through that initial filter determining which resumes are worth serious consideration is a huge advantage for any job candidate.

SASCHA KUNTZE

Associate Creative Director
Conceptualizer, Writer, Director

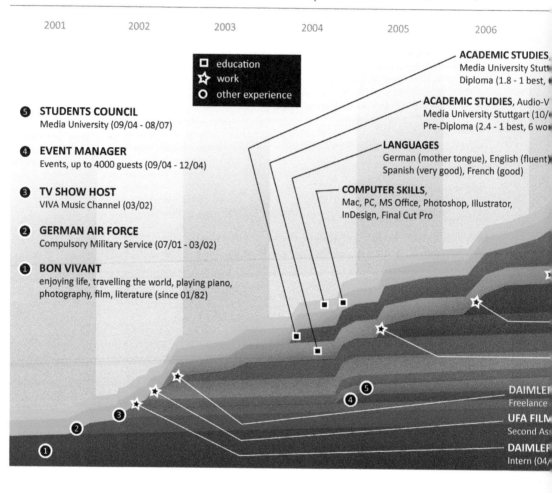

2001   2002   2003   2004   2005   2006

☐ education
☆ work
○ other experience

⑤ STUDENTS COUNCIL
Media University (09/04 - 08/07)

④ EVENT MANAGER
Events, up to 4000 guests (09/04 - 12/04)

③ TV SHOW HOST
VIVA Music Channel (03/02)

② GERMAN AIR FORCE
Compulsory Military Service (07/01 - 03/02)

① BON VIVANT
enjoying life, travelling the world, playing piano,
photography, film, literature (since 01/82)

ACADEMIC STUDIES,
Media University Stutt...
Diploma (1.8 - 1 best,...

ACADEMIC STUDIES, Audio-V...
Media University Stuttgart (10/...
Pre-Diploma (2.4 - 1 best, 6 wor...

LANGUAGES
German (mother tongue), English (fluent)...
Spanish (very good), French (good)

COMPUTER SKILLS,
Mac, PC, MS Office, Photoshop, Illustrator,
InDesign, Final Cut Pro

DAIMLE...
Freelance

UFA FILM...
Second As...

DAIMLE...
Intern (04...

clients

You Tube
twit...
Go...
ca...

rec...

portfolio: www.thisguyprobablycostsalot.com
email: kuntze@gmx.de
mail: PO Box 74170, Dubai, UAE

FIGURE 4-13:
Infographic resume using logos—
Sascha Kuntze
Coolinfographics
.com/Figure-4-13

2008   2009   2010

Marketing
/07)
ent of MBA

achelor

NEW
Associate
Creative Director
since 2011

— **OGILVY & MATHER**, Dubai
Copywriter (since 10/07)

— **MARS**, Viersen
Marketing Snickers, consulting graduand (03/07 - 09/07)

— **JUNG VON MATT/FLEET**, Hamburg
Copywriter (03/06 - 09/06)

— **SPRINGER & JACOBY**, Hamburg
Copywriter (03/05 - 09/05)

V.MEDIA, Stuttgart
2 - 09/03)

M, Munich/Berlin
Unit manager (07/02 - 09/02)

V.MEDIA, Stuttgart

I AM THE SUM OF WHAT I'VE DONE.

Hi,
my name
is Sascha.
I'm 30 years
old. And as
you can see
from all
these
facts:
I'm German.

This CV
shows
you how
everything
I've done in
my life
accumulates
to what
I am
today.

I'd love to
hear
from you.
And if
you want
to hear
from me,
follow
me
on twitter:
@dailyinspired.

iews

2 followers

7110 hits

18 features

3 lost

14 won

1 GOLD CLIO
2 MERIT ONE SHOW
1 SILVER CANNES LION
3 BRONZE NEW YORK FESTIVALS
3 BRONZE CANNES LIONS
4 FINALIST LIAA 14 FINALIST CANNES LIONS
1 GRAND PRIX EFFIE 12 GOLD DUBAI LYNX
1 GOLD EFFIE
1 BRONZE LIAA
4 BRONZE CLIO
4 D&AD IN BOOK
3 GOLD MENA CRISTALS
2 BRONZE EPICA 3 FINALIST MENA CRISTAL
13 BRONZE DUBAI LYNX
3. EXHIBITION STAND OF THE YEAR
1 FINALIST CLIO
6 SILVER DUBAI LYNX
1 SILVER EPICA

zoom to view

David P. Ingram
Product Management Specialist

I MAKE THE DESIGN AND DELIVERY OF GREAT SOFTWARE HAPPEN

MAKE NOTES HERE

(415) 691-0187
dpingram@gmail.com
San Francisco Bay Area

Career

UBL — JANUARY 2011 - NOW
Name Dynamics, Inc.
SVP Product (ubl.org)
Define product strategy and roadmap •
Manage specification, delivery & deployment

Bb — MAY 2008 - DECEMBER 2010
Brownbook.net
Founder and CEO
Conceived of & developed the business •
Manage product development • Achieved
750,000+ visitors/mo & 20,000+ listings/mo

MAY 2006 - APRIL 2008
ShareNow.com
Product Director
Managed prod. strategy, design & delivery •
Grew from 3 to 30 people in Oxford & LA

MAY 2003 - SEPTEMBER 2005
British Telecom & Sony
Product Consultant
Defined and developed the business plan for
monetization on BT.com • Redesigned sales
prop. & processes • Implemented new
prospecting processes & CRM tools

Key Skills

Business Cases, Use Cases,
SORs, PRDs, Process Flows,
Wireframes, Prioritization,
Resources Management,
Scheduling, Delivery
Management, SCRUM,
UAT & QA, On Time,
In Budget, To Specification

Understand, Clarify, Prioritize,
Focus, Define, Commit, Do,
Deliver, Iterate

What's David Like?

I can summarize my opinion of David in **3**
words: **capacity, passion, commitment.**
— John Ball, Principal, Verto Group, LLC

David's **drive** and **focus** is amazing.
— Stewart Townsend, Sun Microsystems

A rare exec with a good grasp of both
technological and **strategic** issues, and
the ability to **execute**.
— Andrew Shorland, LocalSEOGuide.com

David has great strategic insights, **laser
focused** delivery every time, easily
understands key issues and opportunities,
then always delivers **exceptional results.**
— Marc Lyne, CTO, BT Directories

Top qualities: **Great Results, High
Integrity, Creative.**
— Graeme Horsfall, Microsoft Corporation

1
Number of products
killed before launch

7
End-to-end new
product developments
successfully deployed
in the last 3 years

88%
Annual revenue growth
at Izodia while Group
Product Manager

93
Number of independent
press articles about my
projects

300%
Amount I increased partner contract
values in my first 3 months at UBL

$1,600,000
Funds I raised to launch brownbook.net

$2,000,000
Value of first-year sales of the product
I designed at Scoot

$8,000,000
Funds raised while at sharenow.com

MY WHEELS
Why? Less fuel
+ more fun

For more:
linkedin.com
/in/davidingram

FIGURE 4-14: Company logos on infographic resume—David Ingram
Coolinfographics.com/Figure-4-14

Software Application Logos

Infographic resumes initially grew in popularity with a younger generation of graphic designers and social media managers. These roles require an expertise in multiple software applications and web services key to the job, and using the application icons is similar to using company logos. Many of the primary applications are instantly recognizable by their icons.

Unlike company logos though, the software icons generally serve as a visual acknowledgment of the requirements for the job. The icons instantly show the hiring manager that the candidate has the software skills required for the open position, but doesn't position him above any other candidates that also possess the required skills unless more information is added.

Tina Chen's resume (Figure 4-15) displays the four different software application icons that she primarily uses for her design work to demonstrate proficiency in each of them. Her other information, like years of experience, foreign language fluency, and the overall design itself are what set Tina apart from other candidates.

Additional visuals, such as the relative experience designs mentioned earlier can be used in combination with the software icons to add information. In Figure 4-16, Aníbal Maíz Cáceres' infographic resume shows the software icons integrated into a relative experience bar chart that shows his varying proficiency level in each application. Aníbal also makes the resume available online in multiple languages (English, Spanish, and French), and the use of icons reduces the amount of text that needs to be translated for each version.

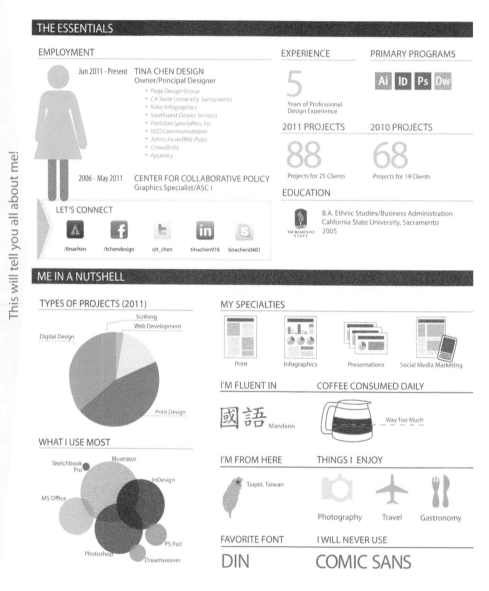

FIGURE 4-15: Resume with Software Icons—Tina Chen
Coolinfographics.com/Figure-4-15

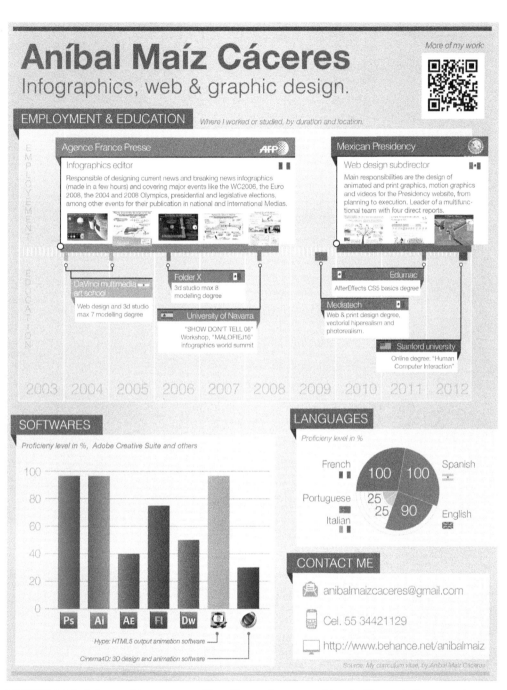

FIGURE 4-16: Infographic resume with software icons combined with a relative experience visualization—Aníbal Maíz Cáceres

Coolinfographics.com/Figure-4-16

Using an Infographic Resume

Because infographic resumes are still relatively uncommon in the job marketplace, the next challenge is how candidates can use them effectively in a market in which most resumes are still text-only. Initially, infographic resumes were embraced by candidates looking for graphic designer, web designer, social media, and web development roles. After the first couple of years, the trend quickly spread into other fields, and many infographic resumes have been used for more traditional roles such as CEOs, vice presidents, managers, accountants, actors, and IT professionals.

Job Application Systems

The biggest hurdle facing the use of infographic resumes are the automated job application systems (also called application tracking systems) used by many companies. These online systems prompt the job applicant to input or upload their resume file into a database, usually as text-only or Microsoft Word format. The application system then parses the text into key words that are automatically organized into predefined categories. The key words are loaded into a central database so that hiring managers and human resources departments can easily query the database to match open positions with job candidates.

Any visual design and even traditional text formatting from the resume becomes irrelevant because the hiring company never sees the original document, just the collected text. This means that even if job applicants have an infographic resume, its usefulness will be effective only when their resume is sent through e-mail, displayed as part of the candidate's online profile (personal website, LinkedIn, Facebook profile, and so on) and when physically shown to a potential employer in face-to-face interviews.

There are only two formats that I have seen to be effective when using an infographic resume as part of a job search: a separate, standalone infographic resume design and a combined design that integrates the data visualizations into the full-text resume.

Standalone Infographic Resume

So far, the most common format for an infographic resume is a separate infographic design used as a summary to supplement a traditional text resume. This format means the candidate still needs to maintain a separate, traditional, all-text resume that can be used in job application systems and interviews so that potential employers have the resume format they require. The infographic resume is used to initially generate interest and awareness in a job candidate, and then the text resume is used to provide full details.

Mino Parisi's resume shown in Figure 4-17 is a great example of this. His infographic resume includes a timeline of his work and education history and a series of doughnut charts that show the relative amount of experience using different software applications (color-coded) in different types of design work. This standalone design is a snapshot look at many of Mino's key attributes but is mostly graphics with minimal text. His full text resume (in Italian) is available separately and includes the full details of his history (Figure 4-18).

Using an infographic resume in this manner essentially uses the infographic design as an advertisement to get attention or build awareness of the candidate. The infographic design would attract the attention of the employer or client, who can then look to the traditional resume for full details.

In this format, the infographic resume is a supplement to the traditional resume. It's not a replacement.

FIGURE 4-17:
Standalone info-
graphic resume—
Mino Parisi
Coolinfographics
.com/Figure-4-17

Mino Parisi
Guidonia Montecelio, 00012 Roma
📞 +39 3294922879 • skype: mino_parisi
✉ minoparisi@gmail.com
Be www.behance.net/minoparisi
in it.linkedin.com/in/minoparisi

MINO PARISI
graphic, web & UX designer

SKILLS

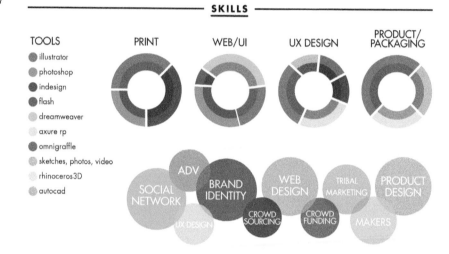

TOOLS
- illustrator
- photoshop
- indesign
- flash
- dreamweaver
- axure rp
- omnigraffle
- sketches, photos, video
- rhinoceros3D
- autocad

PRINT   WEB/UI   UX DESIGN   PRODUCT/PACKAGING

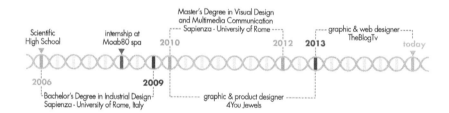

SOCIAL NETWORK   ADV   BRAND IDENTITY   WEB DESIGN   TRIBAL MARKETING   PRODUCT DESIGN
UX DESIGN   CROWD SOURCING   CROWD FUNDING   MAKERS

EDUCATION & EXPERIENCE

Scientific High School

internship at Moab80 spa

Master's Degree in Visual Design and Multimedia Communication
Sapienza - University of Rome

graphic & web designer
TheBlogTv

2010   2012   **2013**   today

2006   **2009**

Bachelor's Degree in Industrial Design
Sapienza - University of Rome, Italy

graphic & product designer
4You Jewels

ADDITIONAL INFORMATION

videogames geek culture   electronic music circuit bending   glitch art new media   lomography DIY cameras   do it yourself 2.0 maker/open culture

Mino Parisi
graphic, web & UX designer

born in Rome (Italy), 7 March 1987
living in Guidonia Montecelio, 00012 Rome (Italy)

📞 +39 3294922879 / skype: mino_parisi

✉ minoparisi@gmail.com

🔵 www.minoparisi.com

🔵 www.behance.net/minoparisi

🔵 www.flickr.com/minoparisi

🔵 it.linkedin.com/in/minoparisi

FIGURE 4-18:
Separate text
resume—Mino
Parisi

WORK
EXPERIENCE

graphic & web designer, TheBlogTv spa, Rome (IT)
social media marketing and media design agency
22 July 2013 - today

product & graphic designer, 4You Jewels, Rome (IT)
jewelry brand
01 March 2010 - 19 July 2013

graphic & product designer, Moab80 spa, Rome (IT)
furniture design company
01 April 2009 – 22 July 2009

EDUCATION

**Master's Degree in Visual Design and Multimedia
Communication**, "Sapienza" University of Rome -
grade:110/110 cum laude.

Bachelor's Degree in Industrial Design,
"Sapienza" University of Rome - grade: 102/110

High School Diploma (Scientific Studies),
Liceo Scientifico "L. Spallanzani", Tivoli - grade: 76/100

COMPUTER
SKILLS

Software: Photoshop, Illustrator, Dreamweaver, Indesign,
Flash, Axure RP, Rhinocheros 3D, Cinema4D, AutoCAD.

Programming language: html/css, Processing.

Hardware: Arduino.

LANGUAGES

Italian (mother tongue);
English (B2).

WORKSHOP

Agile Processes for Innovation Collaborative, 2012
Global Service Design Jam Rome 2013
Global Game Jam Rome 2013
Pretotype @ Opencamp 2013
MolyJam Rome 2013

AWARDS

1° Prize graphic design contest: Segni d'Incontro 2011
Merit Award at international LotusPrize Awards 2012

ADDITIONAL
INFORMATION

Organizer and tutor at: PopUp Makers Roma, Circuit
Bending workshop and MolyJam Rome 2013.
I like: video games, cyberpunk, comic books, electronic
music, circuit bending, makers and DIY photography.
I am a member of: UX Book Club Roma, Arduino User
Group Roma, Fablab Roma and Roma Makers.
European driving licence: B

As a variation to this format, the infographic resume design can be inserted as a separate page in a Microsoft Word document or PDF file that also includes the full-text resume pages. This allows the applicant to submit only one file in e-mail or online. When the potential employers view or print the resume, they have both the infographic resume and the full-text resume available as separate pages. Mino's resume above is available online as a single PDF file for download that includes both the infographic and text resumes as separate pages.

Combined Infographic Resume Design

An effective alternative infographic resume format is for the designer to embed individual data visualizations directly into the text resume. The advantage of this design format is that the candidate has only one document that includes both the visual design and the full text. The visuals are adjacent to the full-text details in the design, so there's little eye movement for a reader to find the detailed information about the candidate.

Vanessa Wilson's infographic resume (Figure 4-19) demonstrates this beautifully. The full-text descriptions of each role are connected to the visual timeline running down the left side of the page. The overlap between education, work experience, and volunteer work is easily seen, and the complete text description of each is also readily accessible to the reader.

This combined design format can be accomplished by inserting the data visualizations as images into a standard Microsoft Word document and wrapping the resume text around the visualizations. A more advanced method would be to use a desktop publishing application such as Adobe InDesign to integrate the visualizations with the text.

Taking this idea one step further, if the data visualizations are charts designed in Excel, the charts can be linked to the data source so that any updates to the data automatically propagate into the resume design.

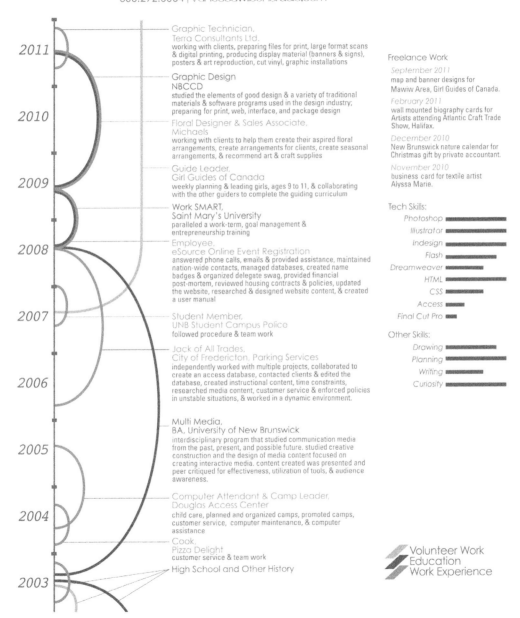

vanessawilson
506.292.0064 | vanessawilsonstudio.com

2011

Graphic Technician,
Terra Consultants Ltd.
working with clients, preparing files for print, large format scans
& digital printing, producing display material (banners & signs),
posters & art reproduction, cut vinyl, graphic installations

Graphic Design
NBCCD
studied the elements of good design & a variety of traditional
materials & software programs used in the design industry;
preparing for print, web, interface, and package design

2010

Floral Designer & Sales Associate,
Michaels
working with clients to help them create their aspired floral
arrangements, create arrangements for clients, create seasonal
arrangements, & recommend art & craft supplies

2009

Guide Leader,
Girl Guides of Canada
weekly planning & leading girls, ages 9 to 11, & collaborating
with the other guiders to complete the guiding curriculum

Work SMART,
Saint Mary's University
paralleled a work-term, goal management &
entrepreneurship training

2008

Employee,
eSource Online Event Registration
answered phone calls, emails & provided assistance, maintained
nation-wide contacts, managed databases, created name
badges & organized delegate swag, provided financial
post-mortem, reviewed housing contracts & policies, updated
the website, researched & designed website content, & created
a user manual

2007

Student Member,
UNB Student Campus Police
followed procedure & team work

Jack of All Trades,
City of Fredericton, Parking Services
independently worked with multiple projects, collaborated to
create an access database, contacted clients & edited the
database, created instructional content, time constraints,
researched media content, customer service & enforced policies
in unstable situations, & worked in a dynamic environment.

2006

Multi Media,
BA, University of New Brunswick
interdisciplinary program that studied communication media
from the past, present, and possible future. studied creative
construction and the design of media content focused on
creating interactive media. content created was presented and
peer critiqued for effectiveness, utilization of tools, & audience
awareness.

2005

Computer Attendant & Camp Leader,
Douglas Access Center
child care, planned and organized camps, promoted camps,
customer service, computer maintenance, & computer
assistance

2004

Cook,
Pizza Delight
customer service & team work

High School and Other History

2003

Freelance Work

September 2011
map and banner designs for
Mawiw Area, Girl Guides of Canada.

February 2011
wall mounted biography cards for
Artists attending Atlantic Craft Trade
Show, Halifax.

December 2010
New Brunswick nature calendar for
Christmas gift by private accountant.

November 2010
business card for textile artist
Alyssa Marie.

Tech Skills:

Photoshop
Illustrator
Indesign
Flash
Dreamweaver
HTML
CSS
Access
Final Cut Pro

Other Skills:

Drawing
Planning
Writing
Curiosity

Volunteer Work
Education
Work Experience

FIGURE 4-19: Combined infographic resume—Vanessa Wilson
Coolinfographics.com/Figure-4-19

With this design style, it's important that all the information still exists in the text. We don't want to replace information with the graphics. When submitted to job application systems, the automated text-parsing ignores the images but still has access to the full text. If a text-only file format is required, exporting the document to a .txt file from Microsoft Word can remove all the images automatically.

The primary challenge of this format is keeping the resume short. If the goal is to maintain a one-page or two-page resume, the candidate needs to reduce the amount of text included to make room for the visualizations.

Publishing Infographic Resumes Online

The strategy for releasing an infographic resume online is similar to releasing an online marketing infographic. Candidates should establish the main landing page location for the resume and then link to that landing page whenever they share the infographic resume. In the case of the infographic resume, the landing page would normally be hosted on the candidate's personal website, but the resume landing page could also be hosted on an image site such as Flickr.com, Behance.com, Visual.ly, or Pinterest.com.

Wherever the infographic resume is hosted online, it is important to make viewing and sharing the file simple and easy. Different file format versions should be readily available to download for any potential employer or client. At least a PDF version should be available for download, but a Microsoft Word version is also recommended.

The ability to share the infographic resume in social media easily can also be effective to get your resume in front of the right people. Sharing buttons from the major social media services should definitely be included on the landing page. Many people that are not potential employers may appreciate the design and want to share within their networks (like in this book). This would be a fantastic outcome for any infographic resume design because it gets more people looking at the resume and more chances that it will catch the attention of a potential employer or client. That's how I came across all of the examples included in this book!

Recently, LinkedIn added an easy way to share an infographic resume on an individual's profile. Users can now add images and links as a part of their background summary that displays at the top of the profile page. By adding the URL of the resume landing page, LinkedIn can display a thumbnail of the infographic resume that links to the landing page URL when clicked.

Designing Infographic Resumes for Print

One area definitely worth mentioning is that hiring managers, recruiters, and HR managers are likely to print out your infographic resume on an office printer. It may be printed, photocopied, and faxed without your knowledge, so you need to design one with that in mind.

First, assume it will be printed on standard-size paper. The tall format infographic style is not a good design choice for infographic resumes. In the United States, that means 8.5" $\times$ 11" letter-size paper. In other parts of the world, it may mean 297 $\times$ 210 mm A4-size paper. Because the position may be in another country, the applicant should understand the standard local paper sizes in the locations where you may be applying for a job. The design of an infographic resume should be sized to fit the proportions of the page and use a font size big enough to be legible when printed.

Second, the designer won't have any idea what kind of printer might be used to print out the resume. Laser or inkjet? Color or black and white? High or low resolution? A good designer will test printing the design on the lowest features to make sure it's still legible and understandable. At home, the applicant can force his printer to print out the design at a lower quality level and only in black and white. Even though this may not be the primary design, it will still work when its use is out of our control.

To demonstrate, Figure 4-20 and Figure 4-21 show Kevin Burton's infographic resume as it was originally designed and desaturated to show what it would be like when printed in only black and white. All the company logos had already been converted to black and white in the original version, so those translate perfectly. The parts of the design that do have the blue colors convert to grayscale nicely and remain easy to read and understand when the color is removed.

By using a lot of grayscale elements in the original design, this infographic resume works nicely when printed without the color. Kevin doesn't need to worry about how his resume will appear when printed on a variety of different printers. It will always come out well.

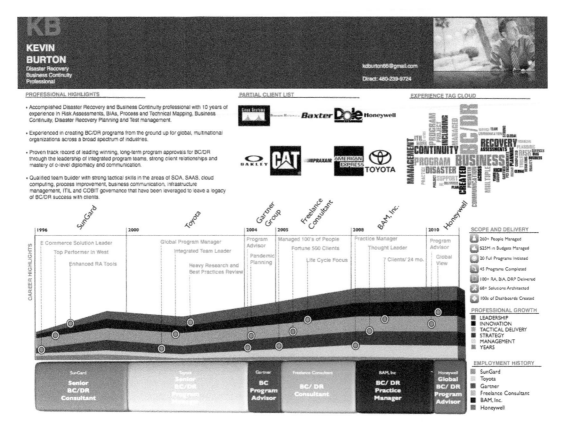

FIGURE 4-20: Original infographic resume—Kevin Burton

Coolinfographics.com/Figure-4-20

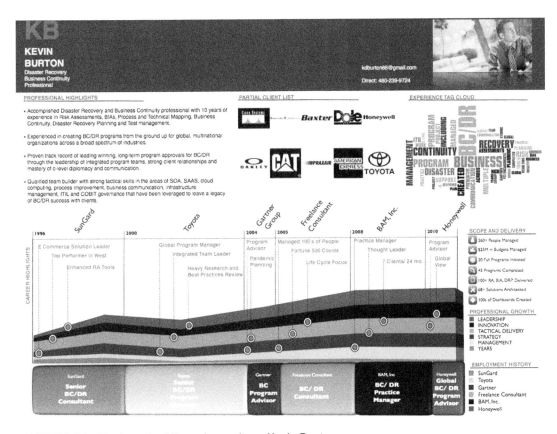

FIGURE 4-21: Black-and-white-only version—Kevin Burton

Jack Hagley took this idea one step further with his simplified, black-and-white resume design. He designed his infographic resume (Figure 4-22) with five objectives in mind:

▶ To be completely black and white, so that it always looked the same when printed

▶ To minimize the file size to make it easy to e-mail and download

▶ To use as little ink as possible when printed out by clients

▶ To be visually distinctive

▶ To contain a large amount of information

FIGURE 4-22:
Infographic
resume—
Jack Hagley
Coolinfographics
.com/Figure-4-22

Jack Hagley

Infographic Designer
www.jackhagley.com

E-MAIL
Jack@jackhagley.com

PHONE
075 19 29 36 44

TWITTER
@jackhagley

What can I do that is useful to you?

Infographics · Branding & Logos · Code · Data Journalism · Processing · Iconography · Photoshop · Data Visualisation · Graphic Design · Illustration · Illustrator · Problem Solving · Artworking · Concepts

Good · Better

Who have I worked with recently?

- Tesco Compare (Infographics, Content)
- Arena Media (Infographics, Content Creation, Graphic Design)
- Three Mobile (Infographics Online Content)
- Information is Beautiful (Infographics, Iconography, Artworking)
- Fly Thomas Cook (Infographics)
- Petrobras (Infographics, Illustration)
- Nell's Recruitment (Infographics)
- Love the Garden (Infographics)
- Joseph Rowntree Foundation (Infographics)

- Musse.com.br (Branding, Web Design)
- HSBC at SapientNitro (Iconography)
- Virgin Media at Avanade (Iconography & UI Design)
- Russian Standard Vodka (Design, Concept Art, Visualisation)
- Kruŝovice (Print Ads)
- The Centrifuge (Posters & Flyer)
- Herv (Album Covers)
- R. Mussak (Logo Design)
- MMMovies (Business Card)

How do I look at the world?

INTP
(Myers–Briggs)

Analytical Thinker / Wizard

Extroverted —— Introverted
Sensing —— Intuition
Thinking —— Feeling
Judging —— Perceiving

What do I do with my time?

Supper · Design · Design · Lunch · Rest · Design · PM · AM · Breakfast · Sleep

What else do I do?

Learning · Music · Reading · Films · Cooking

What's more?

Age **30** · Lucky Number **φ** · Moustaches **1**

What's my story?

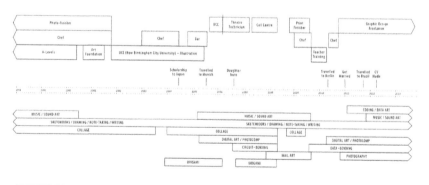

www.jackhagley.com

PAGE ONE OF ONE

BEST PRINTED A3

An infographic resume needs to be easily printed by a recruiter or hiring manager. Although many infographic designs look great online with dark background colors, that style makes an infographic resume hard to print. Even if they have a color printer available, many recruiters will avoid printing out a resume with a black background for fear of how much printer ink or toner it would use.

Infographic Resumes on the iPad (or Tablet)

Another fantastic use of an infographic resume is Dave Rodgerson's infographic resume designed to be shown and shared on an iPad (Figure 4-23). The proportions of the iPad's screen (7.75″ × 5.82″) are smaller than a standard letter-size page of paper, so the design had to be simplified even further to make sure the text was legible on the small screen. Think of this as a mini-resume or an Infographic Elevator Pitch.

In this design, most of the text has been removed. Icons and logos tell most of the story about Dave—his employers, his major clients, his education, and his professional associations. The network map of his connections on LinkedIn show Dave's connections within the color-coded industries without needing to show the names of all his connections. The word cloud is created from his social media account on mirror.me (`mirror.me`) and shows what topics Dave is most often interested in and posting about online. Visually, the potential employer or client can learn a lot about Dave in just a few seconds.

The design is best formatted as a PDF file to be cross-platform and cross-device compatible. That means it can be viewed on the iPad using the Apple iBooks app, or even from within an e-mail message if it has been sent to someone. No requirement to install an extra app from a third-party is necessary. Using the built-in functions of the iPad, the two-finger pinch gesture can zoom in and zoom out of the design while showing it to someone.

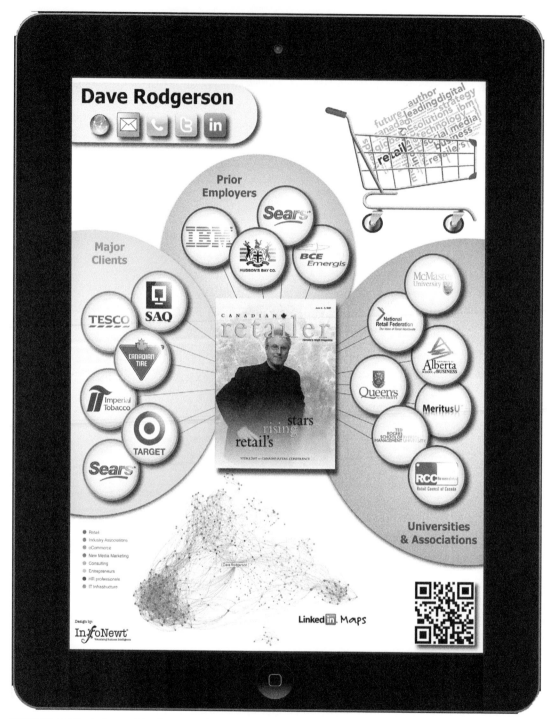

FIGURE 4-23: Infographic elevator pitch—Dave Rodgerson

Coolinfographics.com/Figure-4-23

The secondary benefit of the PDF format is that all the HTML links included in the PDF file are functional. Each of the company logos and icons are tappable (or clickable) links. Dave didn't need to include the text of his e-mail address because anyone can tap the e-mail icon and it automatically opens up a new message in the default e-mail application properly addressed to him. The LinkedIn icon, if tapped, opens up his LinkedIn profile in the default web browser.

While Dave is showing his resume to someone in person, he can also e-mail it instantly to them by tapping the Share icon in the app. It automatically attaches the PDF file to a new e-mail message. The universal nature of the PDF file enables anyone to view the file on a tablet, smartphone, or computer.

Infographic Resume Design Tools

So, you want to try your hand at designing your own infographic resume?

You don't have to be a graphic designer (but it couldn't hurt). So far, most of the infographic resume designs are created manually using common graphic design software, such as Adobe Illustrator or Photoshop. Microsoft Office is also widely used to create both the individual data visualizations and the overall design.

However, with the increase in popularity of infographics, and infographic resumes in particular, a number of online services have begun to appear that offer to generate an infographic resume for the user automatically. These are not general infographic design sites. They are sites dedicated specifically to creating infographic resumes.

They all import an individual's profile information from LinkedIn.com and then enable you to edit or add custom information manually. To begin, you can choose between a handful of templates, make adjustments to the design style, choose which sections to include, and rearrange the sections as needed. Some of them enable the user to upload their text resume as the source data and additional images.

Because these sites are so new, they can definitely help a candidate stand out visually, but they start with predesigned templates. If the user just accepts the design defaults without making any changes, their resume may end up looking exactly like other resume designs the hiring manager has seen. The risk these sites will face in the future is that they could become perceived as only premade resume templates when infographic resumes become more popular and recognized.

The job candidate should always start with one of the design templates, and then customize the design using the available options to make their own resume visually unique and distinctive.

re.vu

re.vu enables users to upload example files or portfolio images of their work to be included in the resume design. Figure 4-24 shows re.vu CEO, Stephen Years' infographic resume from the website.

Recognizing that many recruiters and hiring managers will still want to see your text resume, re.vu also enables you to upload your traditional resume to make it available for download from your custom infographic resume page.

Kinzaa.com

kinzaa
Infographic resumés

Kinzaa.com adds sections where the candidate can input data to include their desired company personality, work environment, preferred neighborhoods, and expected benefits to help match the candidate with the right company. Blogger Erica Swallow's resume (Figure 4-25) is used on the site to demonstrate an example resume.

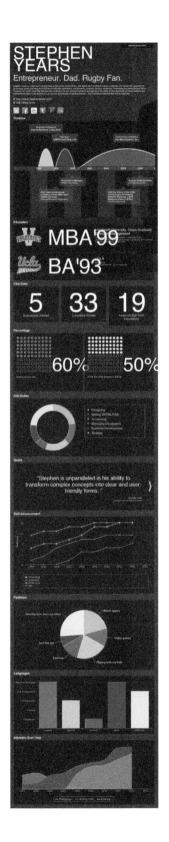

FIGURE 4-24:
re.vu designed info-
graphic resume—
CEO Stephen Years
Coolinfographics
.com/Figure-4-24

FIGURE 4-25:

Kinzaa.com info-
graphic resume—
Erica Swallow

Coolinfographics
.com/Figure-4-25

Vizualize.me

vizualize.me *beta*

Connect with a LinkedIn account and visualize.me will create an initial resume based on the information it can pull from the profile. Once the initial infographic resume has been created, the user can edit the profile information, choose from a selection of themes, and edit the design options such as colors, backgrounds, fonts, layouts, and more. Cofounder Kenneth Lee's resume is shown as an example in Figure 4-26.

The final infographic resume design is viewable using the custom URL defined by the user. The URL or visualize.me buttons can be shared in social networks. The final resume can also be downloaded as a PDF file for printing and e-mail. One unique feature of visualize .me is the stats page that will show traffic numbers of visitors to the resume page.

ResumUP.com

RESUM UP

ResumUP has one design template that is applied to all users, which you can see in Figure 4-27. Login with a LinkedIn account and ResumUP will import the data to create the initial resume. The user has control to edit the information displayed and add information about the type of position and company they are looking for. The final resume is viewable online with a custom URL or can be downloaded as a PDF file.

FIGURE 4-26:
Vizualize.me info-
graphic resume—
Kenneth Lee

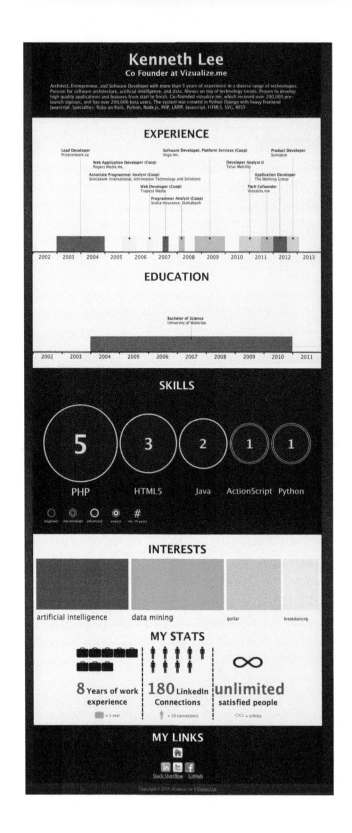

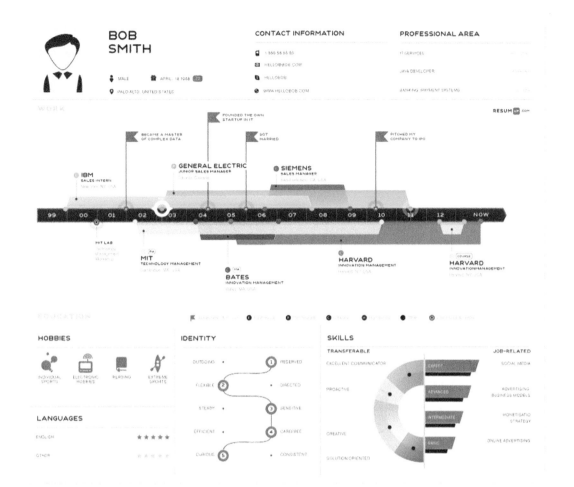

FIGURE 4-27: ResumUP.com infographic resume—Bob Smith sample
Coolinfographics.com/Figure-4-27

Cvgram.me

Anyone can login to cvgram.me with either a LinkedIn or a Facebook account. Depending on which type of account is used to login, cvgram will create an infographic resume based on the available information in the user's profile. As shown in Figure 4-28, once the initial resume has been created the user can edit their information and many of the design options (themes, colors, fonts, and more). A custom URL is created for each user to share his or her resume publicly with others directly from the site. The service is for online sharing only, so no options for downloading the infographic resume are available.

FIGURE 4-28:
cvgram.me info-
graphic resume
builder
Coolinfographics
.com/Figure-4-28

Shine

A new iPad app was recently launched in the iTunes store that will walk the user through the process of generating a personal infographic resume. Developed by Boluga, the Shine app (Figure 4-29) is free to download and includes one complete resume design template. Additional design templates and features are available through in-app purchases. Once a resume is created, the user can e-mail, share, and print copies directly from the iPad and the PDF files that Shine creates are fully text-searchable.

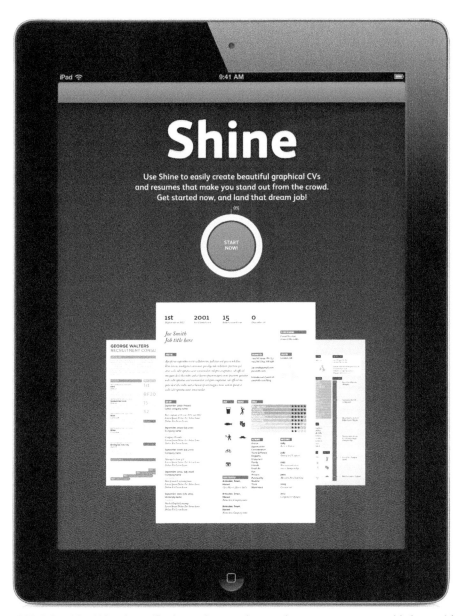

FIGURE 4-29: Shine is an iPad app that can be used to create a personal infographic resume

Coolinfographics.com/Figure-4-29

In addition, you can use any of the infographic design resources listed in Chapter 7, "Design Resources," to create the different types of data visualizations used in infographic resumes. The visuals created by these tools can be inserted into your infographic resume as one component of the overall design.

You can see my own network map (Figure 4-30) from LinkedIn InMaps (inmaps.linkedinlabs.com). InMaps is one online design tool worth specific mention in this chapter because it's a data visualization that is primarily aimed at being used as a visualization of you as an individual, which is perfect for use on an infographic resume. With user permission, the tool accesses the user's profile on LinkedIn and creates a network map of all the connections associated with that user and any interconnections between people in the user's network. It also creates color clusters of people related to the same company or industry, and creates a custom URL link that can be shared with others to view the resulting network map online. The image generated can also be easily inserted into an infographic resume design.

These network maps of connections are intended to show the reader how connected the candidate is with other professionals within a particular industry without showing the actual names of those connections. It is definitely a more qualitative design element that is indicative of how involved and engaged the candidate is with creating and maintaining connections online.

FIGURE 4-30: LinkedIn network map

Coolinfographics.com/Figure-4-30

All About You

Resumes are all about telling your story. Infographic resumes allow you to leverage the benefits of visual communication to tell your story in a more effective way. Making a resume stand out in a positive way, attracting the attention of a potential employer, making the personal information easier to understand, and making a candidate more memorable to the recruiter or hiring manager are all reasons why infographic resumes will continue to develop and become more popular.

I've accumulated hundreds of real infographic resumes in a Pinterest Board at pinterest.com/rtkrum/infographic-visual-resumes/. If you create one for yourself, send me a link. I'd love to add it to the collection!

References

1. "Keeping an Eye on Recruiter Behavior," The Ladders, 2012, http://cdn.theladders.net/static/images/basicSite/pdfs/TheLadders-EyeTracking-StudyC2.pdf

Links

1. Michael Anderson's infographic resume: http://theportfolio.ofmichaelanderson.com/resume.pdf

2. Faz Besharatian's infographic resume: http://visualresume.fazfolio.com

3. Randall Knapp's infographic resume: http://randallknapp.com

4. Mike Wirth's infographic resume:
   http://www.mikewirthart.com/?projects=infographic-resume

5. Duncan McKean's infographic resume:
   http://duncanmckean.com/projects/infographic-cv/

6. Hana Tesar's infographic resume (http://be.net/HanaTesar):
   http://www.behance.net/gallery/Creative-Resume/1855167

7. Navdeep Raj's infographic resume (http://be.net/navdeep):
   http://www.behance.net/gallery/My-Resume/6217587

8. Ana Foureaux Frazao's infographic resume:
   http://anafxfz.com/portfolio/my-visual-resume

9. Chris Robertson's infographic resume:
   http://visual.ly/infographic-resume-chris-robertson

10. Adrian Saker's logo resume (http://www.adriansaker.com):
    http://householdname.typepad.com/my_weblog/2012/04/the-
    6-seconds-recruiters-spend-on-your-resume.html

11. Sascha Kuntze's infographic resume:
    http://www.thisguyprobablycostsalot.com

12. David Ingram's infographic resume:
    http://docs.google.com/open?id=0B2u9YPf3KC_
    FYmYxYWY3ZDItMmNlOS00MjFmLTkwYTEtNGMzOGJhOGI2YzEw

13. Tina Chen's infographic resume (http://www.tinachendesign.com):
    http://www.tinachendesign.com/49207/443286/projects/
    personal-infographic-resume

14. Aníbal Maíz Cáceres' infographic resume
    (http://be.net/anibalmaiz):
    http://www.behance.net/gallery/My-visual-resume/5831227

15. Mino Parisi's infographic resume (http://minoparisi.com):
    http://www.minoparisi.com/image/CV_Mino_Parisi.pdf

16. Vanessa Wilson's infographic resume
    (http://be.net/vanessawilson):
    http://www.behance.net/gallery/Resume-Infograph/2499627

17. Kevin Burton's infographic resume
    (www.linkedin.com/in/kevindburton):
    http://visual.ly/kevin-burton-resume

18. Jack Hagley's infographic resume:
    http://www.jackhagley.com/

19. Dave Rodgerson's infographic elevator pitch on iPad:
    http://daverodgerson.com

20. re.vu CEO, Stephen Years' infographic resume:
    http://re.vu/stephen

21. Kinzaa.com infographic resume—Erica Swallow:
    http://kinzaa.com/ericaswallow/

22. Vizualize.me infographic resume—Kenneth Lee:
    http://vizualize.me/kenneth

23. ResumUP.com infographic resume samples:
    http://resumup.com/pages/pressroom#art

24. cvgram.me infographic resume tool:
    http://cvgram.me/

25. Shine, iPad infographic resume creation app:
    http://itunes.apple.com/us/app/shine-graphical-cvs-
    resumes/id630664282

26. LinkedIn Labs InMap, Randy Krum:
    `http://inmaps.linkedinlabs.com/share/Randy_Krum/3198792385`
    `5400069723005892604839494 2850`

27. Infographic Visual Resumes Pinterest Board:
    `http://pinterest.com/rtkrum/infographic-visual-resumes/`

Good design is good business.

—Thomas J. Watson

5

Internal Confidential Infographics

Online infographics are the public face of what everyone sees as *infographics*. They are shared extensively in social media and have been the driving force behind the explosive growth in using infographics and data visualizations to communicate visually over the past few years. Infographic designers can include only designs that have been shared publicly by their clients as a part of their design portfolios.

However, there is a secret, mostly unknown world of corporate infographics used to communicate more effectively inside of companies all over the world. Companies have a ton of internal data that they don't share with the public, but at the same time, they have an essential need to communicate clearly and effectively that information internally. They want their employees to all share the same understanding, so that they are all working toward the same corporate goals. They want to give their investors a clear picture of the state of the business. They want to present compelling stories about their products to their customers.

Infographics and data visualizations are powerful tools to help simplify the understanding of complex corporate data and improve the memory retention of that information by the audience.

For example, a company would want all its sales employees communicating the same message about its products to customers. The information might be product benefits, price points, shipping schedules, or competitive advantages. A clear visualization of that information can make it easier for all of them to understand and remember, but can also be used as an aid to help them communicate clearly and confidently to customers.

By definition, corporate confidential data should not be shared outside the company, and for that reason I can't share real-world examples in this book. However, I can show examples of the visual styles and types of data being visualized by companies all over the world. Here I include public, online infographic designs or example designs I created to demonstrate what can be visualized within a company.

Improving Internal Communications

Charts and graphs from Microsoft Office products (mainly Excel and PowerPoint) have become the standard way to share corporate data internally, but they are used so often that they are no longer unique and memorable to the audience.

An employee might sit through multiple PowerPoint presentations in the same day that all use the same design template. In fact, a given company might provide the same custom branded PowerPoint template to all its employees to use for presentations. In a sense, the company is dictating that all of its presentations look the same, which has the counterproductive effect of making them harder to remember.

A research report can have more than 100 charts of the gathered data, all of them using the same chart design style and the same colors. How is an employee expected to remember any of the specific details when all the charts look the same?

The problem continues to get worse each day as the amount of information a company possesses continues to grow and accumulate. Effectively sharing that information internally and making it useful to employees is becoming both more important and more difficult at the same time.

Companies can leverage the power of infographics and data visualization design as a more effective form of internal communication to disseminate clear, memorable information. However, it does take a bit of extra work to design a unique visualization or an infographic for each set of data. Sometimes it involves an infographic designer, but most of the time employees that have no training in design create these charts and graphs on their own. With reduced workforces and budget cuts, employees are usually expected to design their own presentations and reports.

The formats for publishing infographics within a company are also different. The tall format (Chapter 2, "Online Infographics") you see most often with infographics published online doesn't work well within the internal communication channels of a company. Usually, internal infographics are printed posters, presentation slides, printed handouts, PDF files, e-mail, or intranet sites.

The Fear of Confidential Information

Two goals within companies are often perceived to be in conflict: clear communication and confidentiality. Many companies fear that if they make their confidential information too easy to understand and share within the company, it may also become easy to share outside of the company (purposely or accidentally). As a result, the information often isn't designed to be understood and shared with employees who would benefit from the knowledge. However, there are effective ways to meet both objectives.

On the one hand, managers want their direct reports to be as effective as possible. In general, employees with access to information and a clear understanding of the business data are more effective than employees kept in the dark. A manager's performance is often a measurement based on the effectiveness of the employees that report directly to him, and as a result he wants to provide his employees with every tool possible to help them perform their jobs well.

On the other hand, companies should protect their confidential information because that information is often a competitive advantage. Companies may even be legally bound to protect the data they possess, such as medical information or customer credit card numbers. Along with their security obligations, they are often afraid to make any of their confidential information too easy to share outside of the company, even accidentally. For example, if a company's entire new product development roadmap for the next five years is clearly outlined in a one-page visual summary handed out during a presentation, it could be highly damaging if that one document were accidentally shared with a competing company.

In response to this fear, access to many documents of valuable, internal company information is often restricted. Many employees that would benefit from knowing this information in their day-to-day jobs are not allowed access due to paranoia within the company against that information being leaked outside.

Overcoming these two opposed objectives can be achieved by approaching them separately.

First, a company should make its internal data as easy to understand by its employees as possible. For a company to thrive: employee mistakes, misunderstandings, and misjudgments need to be minimized by any means possible, and clear communication can often eliminate the confusion that leads to these types of errors. Using good data visualization design methods can effectively disseminate information to its employees across an organization and increase the company's chance of survival.

Second, companies should definitely use corporate policies to help control the need for confidentiality. Document shredding policies, file encryption, e-mail tracking, password protection, and even physical building access control can help safeguard a company's valuable data. These policies should define the behavior of the employees but allow access to information to those who would benefit from it.

Ideally, access to valuable information internally should be easily accessible, but sharing that information outside of the company should be difficult. This helps prevent any accidental sharing of information and makes any purposeful sharing of confidential company information much more difficult.

As a case study, the work computer I use for client design projects has user accounts with requirements for strong passwords and has XTS-AES 128-bit whole-disk encryption on the hard drive. I then create a separate 256-bit AES encrypted disk image for each separate project so that my files are also completely encrypted when they are backed up to an external disk or online storage. For clients that request it, I also use encrypted e-mail to protect messages containing any data or information exchanged while in transit between the client and myself.

Don't let fear of data exposure hold back your employees from doing the best work they can. Your company has valuable information, and you must leverage that information to the company's advantage in every way possible.

Ideas for Visualizing Internal Data

One of the best parts of my job is that when I work with a client, I get a sneak peek at their internal data. I get to see some of the research and statistics that drive the decisions these companies make. I've seen hundreds of different data sets, and I enjoy helping companies find insights from their data and clearly communicate them.

This section will share a number of different types of data and visualizations that I have seen in use internally by companies. Your company may have similar data, or the data available to you may be completely different. These ideas are intended to help inspire you to visualize the data you have and make having the data more useful to the company.

Most of these examples are fairly simple and don't need powerful graphics software. By spending a little extra time, you can create most of these using standard office productivity suite applications. More specialized software would make these easier, but it's not required.

Budgets

The most common data available within companies are the numbers from budgets. This data might include the entire corporation or just an individual department. Even a small company can quickly lose grasp of where the money goes, and visualizing the budget information at some regular frequency can be extremely valuable. Some companies want to visualize the approved budget for the upcoming year, or alternatively they might visualize the actual spending from the prior year to better understand expenses.

Figure 5-1 shows an example of a budget poster. This design uses the publicly available budget numbers from the city of Bedford, Texas from the 2009-2010 financial year. This design uses proportionally sized circles to visually compare the dollar amounts, similar to the *Death & Taxes Poster* in Figure 3-9; however, this design is split into two halves to include additional data. The left half visualizes all the sources of income and the right half visualizes all the different expenses.

Visualizing with circles is an easy way to show multiple levels of hierarchical data, so departments can be broken down into additional levels of detail. The viewer can easily understand how one expense category compares to others or as a portion of the budget as a whole. Figure 5-2 shows a close-up of only the police department total split up into its smaller categories of expenses. In this design, the connecting arrows and circle outlines are color-coded to show how each expense category has changed from the prior year. Reduced budgets are shown in red, categories that didn't change are shown in yellow, and increased budgets are shown in green.

Another popular way to visualize budgets is with the treemap visualization method. David McCandless used a treemap design to visualize the 2010 budget of the BBC in, *The BBC-o-Gram* shown in Figure 5-3. In a treemap, proportionally sized rectangles are used for each department and fit together, and the entire area covered by the diagram represents the total of all budget expenses.

In this example, the rectangles are only showing select highlights from the budget, and the expenses are color-coded by category. This also allows space for a visual hierarchy that allows some of the major expenses within certain departments to be shown as smaller rectangles within the larger rectangles of their parent departments.

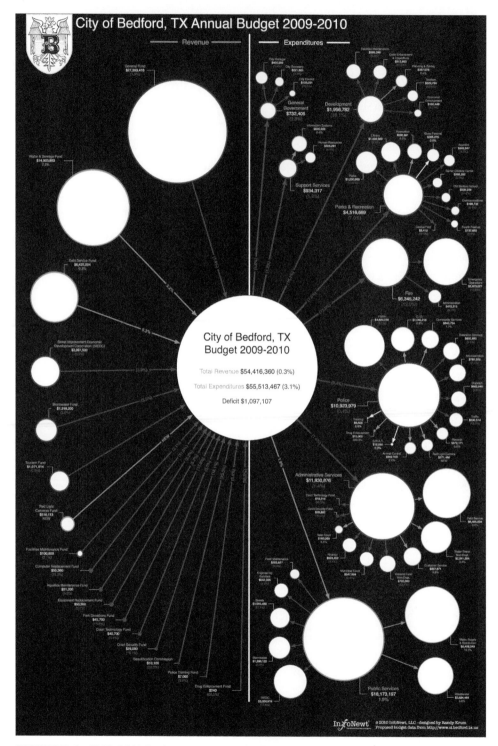

FIGURE 5-1: 2009-2010 Budget poster, City of Bedford, Texas

Coolinfographics.com/Figure-5-1

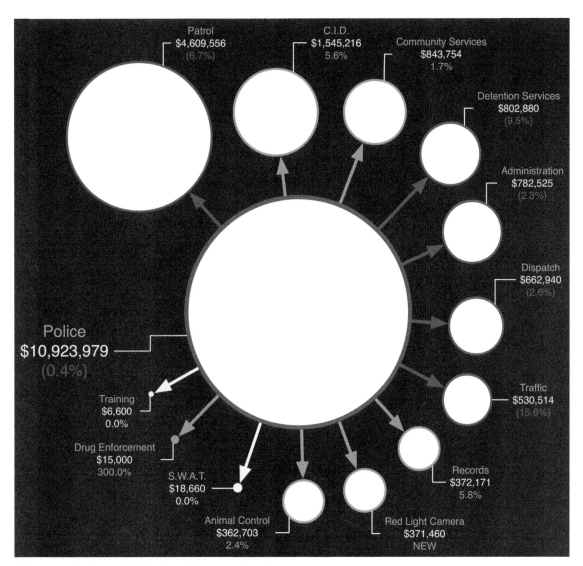

Patrol
$4,609,556
(6.7%)

C.I.D.
$1,545,216
5.6%

Community Services
$843,754
1.7%

Detention Services
$802,880
(9.5%)

Administration
$782,525
(2.3%)

Dispatch
$662,940
(2.6%)

Traffic
$530,514
(15.6%)

Records
$372,171
5.8%

Red Light Camera
$371,460
NEW

Animal Control
$362,703
2.4%

S.W.A.T.
$18,660
0.0%

Drug Enforcement
$15,000
300.0%

Training
$6,600
0.0%

Police
$10,923,979
(0.4%)

FIGURE 5-2: 2009-2010 Bedford, Texas police department expenses

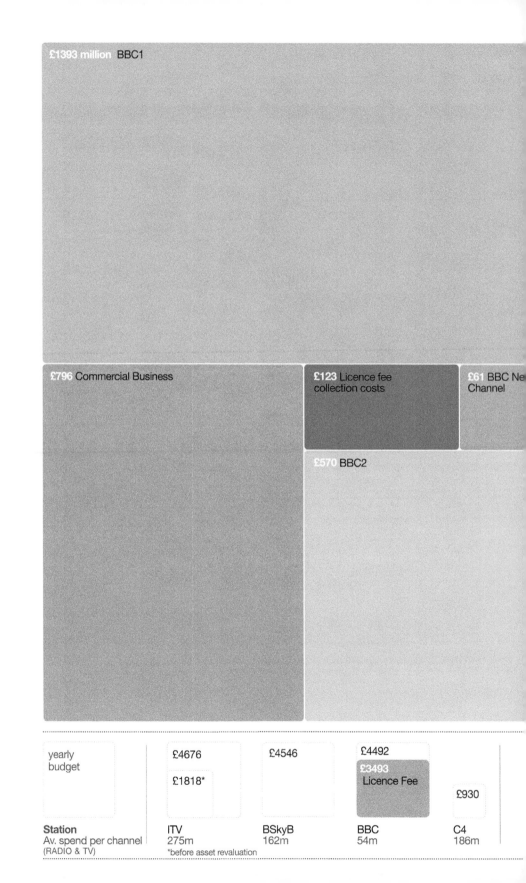

£1393 million BBC1

£796 Commercial Business

£123 Licence fee collection costs

£61 BBC Ne
Channel

£570 BBC2

yearly budget	£4676	£4546	£4492	
	£1818*		£3493 Licence Fee	£930
Station Av. spend per channel (RADIO & TV)	ITV 275m *before asset revaluation	BSkyB 162m	BBC 54m	C4 186m

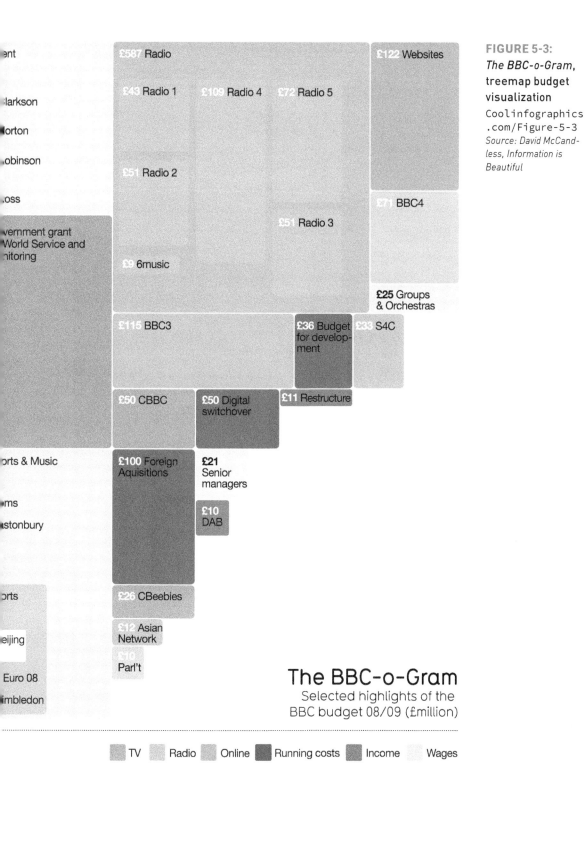

FIGURE 5-3:

The BBC-o-Gram, treemap budget visualization

Coolinfographics
.com/Figure-5-3
Source: David McCandless, Information is Beautiful

£587 Radio

£43 Radio 1   £109 Radio 4   £72 Radio 5

£51 Radio 2

£51 Radio 3

£9 6music

£122 Websites

£71 BBC4

£25 Groups & Orchestras

£115 BBC3   £36 Budget for development   £33 S4C

£50 CBBC   £50 Digital switchover   £11 Restructure

£100 Foreign Aquisitions   £21 Senior managers

£10 DAB

£26 CBeebies

£12 Asian Network

£10 Parl't

ent

larkson

lorton

.obinson

.oss

vernment grant
World Service and
nitoring

orts & Music

.ms

astonbury

orts

eijing

Euro 08

imbledon

The BBC-o-Gram
Selected highlights of the
BBC budget 08/09 (£million)

TV   Radio   Online   Running costs   Income   Wages

Sales and Profit Data

Companies often have some internal confusion differentiating between sales dollars and profit dollars. Often, the products and services with the highest sales revenue are not what earn the most profit for the company. This type of analysis can be organized by product, product line, customers, brand, geographic location, sales manager, and so on.

Figure 5-4 shows a simple visualization using opposing bar charts of annual sales and annual profit for a list of 10 products. Because the profit rate percentages are different across the available products, you can see that in this case the best-selling product is not the most profitable product for the company. This type of chart with bars going in opposite directions isn't available as a standard chart type in Excel and would have to be created manually using rectangle shapes.

FIGURE 5-4:
Sales and profit
visualization

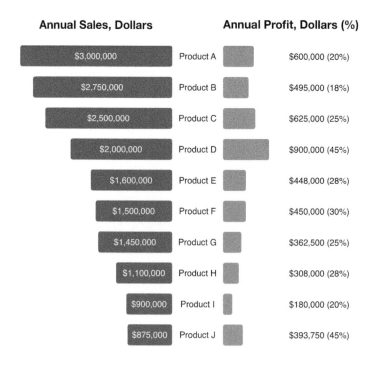

Top 10 Sales Products

Visualizing the scale of business with key customers can help everyone within a company understand how much of the company's sales come through different sales channels. Data visualizations like Figure 5-5 can be used in an annual report, a board meeting presentation, or printed out as a poster and hung in the hallway of the company office. Using the customer logos to make the information visual makes the information understandable at a glance.

Many companies like to share information internally in this manner without showing the actual values. This can inform all the employees that walk by the poster with a consistent message, but also obscure the specific detailed financial information from any visitors that happen to be visiting the office (vendors or customers).

FIGURE 5-5:
Sales by retail channel visualization

Business Processes

Clearly defined business processes are becoming essential within companies. As companies grow and hire more employees, they use formal business processes to help train and standardize their workflows across departments and locations. It could be the process to close the financial books at the end of each month, the process to inspect incoming products for quality, the process to hire a new employee, the process to handle each customer service call, or the process to make a change to the company's website. The company needs to ensure that the functions are performed the same way every time, no matter which employees are involved in the work.

Processes are generally shown as flowcharts. This is a formal, structured way to visualize a process with different symbols to represent different functions within the chart. For example, rectangles represent process steps, rectangles with tear-off bottoms represent documents, and diamonds represent decision-points.

Although they may be highly detailed and technically correct, one company could have hundreds of business processes to document. Just like a report that includes 100 similar bar charts, these flowcharts begin to all look the same to employees and are not memorable. Illustration and infographic design can help make these processes unique, engaging, and memorable to employees.

For example, Figure 5-7 shows an infographic timeline of the process to design a website designed by John Furness, the owner of Simple Square. The events are arranged along a straight timeline, but a number of additional elements of information have been added. The events are shown as circles sized to represent the estimated amount of involvement; the color coding shows the progression through the phases; individual milestones are shown connected to each phase; and the label font sizes are adjusted to show the level of importance (similar to a word cloud). This type of infographic design can be applied to many internal business processes.

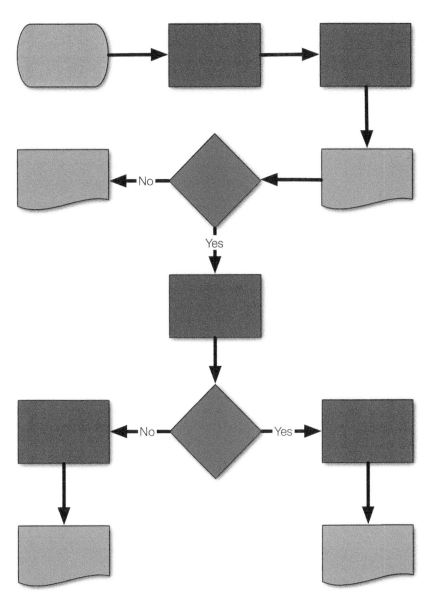

FIGURE 5-6:
Drawing a standard
flowchart

A Website Designed
MILESTONES, INVOLVEMENT, IMPORTANCE & TIMELINE

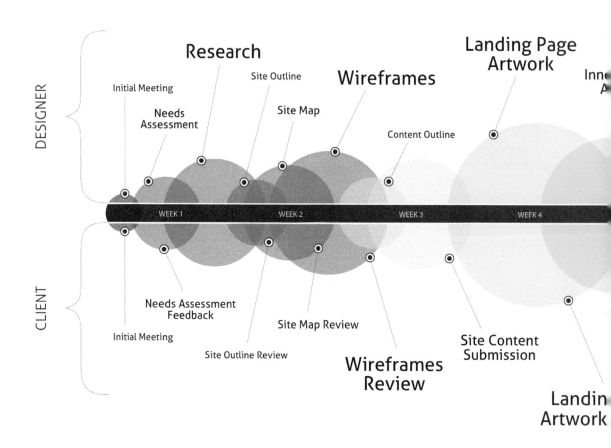

DESIGNER

Research

Initial Meeting

Needs
Assessment

Site Outline

Site Map

Wireframes

Content Outline

Landing Page
Artwork

Inn…
A…

WEEK 1 WEEK 2 WEEK 3 WEEK 4

CLIENT

Needs Assessment
Feedback

Initial Meeting

Site Outline Review

Site Map Review

Wireframes
Review

Site Content
Submission

Landin
Artwork

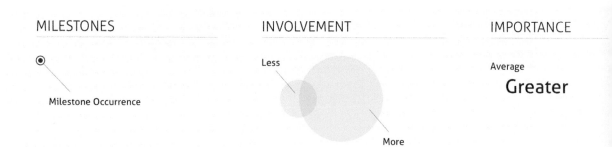

MILESTONES

Milestone Occurrence

INVOLVEMENT

Less

More

IMPORTANCE

Average

Greater

FIGURE 5-7:
A Website Designed,
John Furness,
Simple Square
Coolinfographics
.com/Figure-5-7

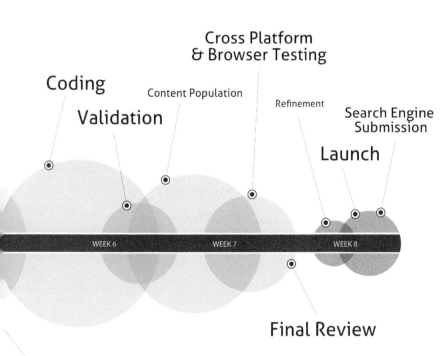

Coding

Validation

Content Population

Cross Platform
& Browser Testing

Refinement

Search Engine
Submission

Launch

WEEK 6

WEEK 7

WEEK 8

Final Review

Inner Page(s)
Artwork Review

PHASE

Initial
Contact

Planning

Development

Launch

How Affiliate Marketing Works in Figure 5-8 demonstrates a different way to visualize processes. The design visualizes a 10-step process as a path, and each event along the process is shown as a character performing an activity. The advantage of using characters in the design of a company process is that the employee audience can visualize themselves performing these functions and can more closely relate to the process.

FIGURE 5-8: Process visualized as a path with characters

Coolinfographics.com/Figure-5-8

Source: How Affiliate Marketing Works, *Sugarrae.com*

Strategies

Similar to processes, strategies usually involve a number of connected events or activities, but they may not be organized in a chronological sequence. Visual strategies are good for showing the flow of information among many connected activities so that employees or customers can easily understand how the individual activities tie together into the overall strategy.

Figure 5-9 is an example of a social media content strategy from Chris Heiler, President and Founder of Landscape Leadership. This diagram shows how different forms of online content uploaded to various social sites integrates together into the company blog, and that the primary interaction with customers and fans will take place on a company Facebook page. Of course, there would be a lot more detail about each activity in the plan, but a central diagram keeps everyone informed about the overall vision.

Quantitative Research Data

Companies often have a lot of research data. This might include market research, customer research, product performance data, consumer profiles, brand equity assessments, customer segmentation studies, conjoint research and many, many more. The complete reports from this research can easily be hundreds of pages long with detailed data tables and hundreds of charts.

This quantitative data is fairly easy to load into the three standard charts (bar chart, line chart, and pie chart) but is not always easy to understand when forced into only these three types of charts. Many times, it's worth the time and effort to experiment with different methods to visualize the same data set to find a visualization that is easier for readers to understand.

Social Media Strategic Plan

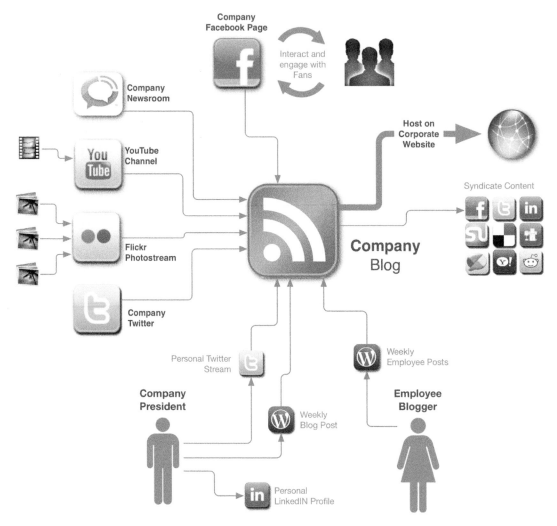

FIGURE 5-9: Example Social Media Strategic Plan

Coolinfographics.com/Figure-5-9

Source: Landscape Leadership

For demonstration purposes, I made up some quantitative research data to visualize. Seven aspects of three competing brands create 21 different statistical values from the responses. Figure 5-10 shows the default clustered bar chart from PowerPoint. In this case, this familiar format is not easy for the audience to read or understand quickly. Readers probably understand bar charts fairly well (they see them often enough), and after spending some time figuring out the color coding, they might start to make some observations by comparing the bars.

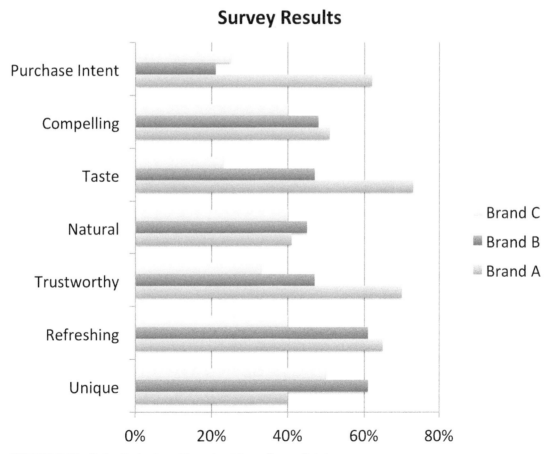

FIGURE 5-10: Default clustered bar chart from PowerPoint

However, there are many ways to visualize the same data set.

In Figure 5-11, the same research data is redesigned into a different data visualization that's much easier to understand. This one is not one of the chart styles built into PowerPoint but can be easily created manually by using the square shape tool. This example uses 10 × 10 grids of 100 squares to visualize percentages, with the values color-coded to match the brand colors.

Because the entire decimal number system is Base-10, it's easy for readers to understand instantly. Using rows that are 10 objects across is intuitive for readers, and anything different is difficult to follow. Some ineffective data visualizations in infographics have used rows of 12, 17, 20, and even 24 objects across, and it is difficult for readers to understand the values being shown. For any rows of icons or shapes, try to always stick with 10.

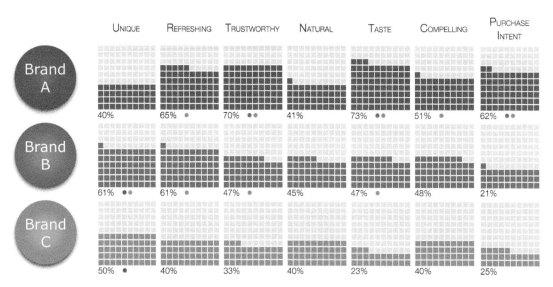

FIGURE 5-11: 10 × 10 grid redesign of quantitative research data

In research data, it is also common to note differences that are calculated to be statistically significant between the scores of the different brands. This is visualized by using matching colored dots beneath each grid to represent the other brands that are significantly lower. Brand A's trustworthiness is significantly higher than both Brand B and Brand C, so both blue and green dots are shown under that grid.

By lining them up, the viewer can quickly see that generally the overall trend is that Brand A scored better than Brand B and Brand C. It's visually easy to compare values within a brand's results and between the brands. All 21 data points are clearly visualized on one page. It's the same data, just easier to understand.

Qualitative Research Data

Qualitative research works very differently with a small number of responses or participants, and the data is often verbal or written opinions. This research data is usually gathered from focus groups, interviews, in-home research, or consumer journals. This data is important for companies to understand consumers and behaviors but should not be confused with large, statistical surveys. Any data that is not considered to be statistically significant with a low margin of error should be considered to be qualitative data.

An infographic designer needs to be careful that visualizing qualitative data doesn't mistakenly imply that the results are quantitative. Even a simple pie chart, as shown in Figure 5-12, can be the wrong visual method to use. In this example, only six people were interviewed, and four of them claimed they would buy the product from the research. Even though four out of six is mathematically 66 percent, it doesn't statistically imply that 66 percent of all consumers would be interested in buying the product. Six people certainly aren't a large enough sample size to reach that type of conclusion.

However, many readers in the audience will not be experts with math and statistics. When they see this pie chart, they will jump to the conclusion that research shows that 66 percent of all consumers would be interested in buying the product. The pie chart style hides the low number of respondents and visualizes a general percentage, which is misleading to the audience.

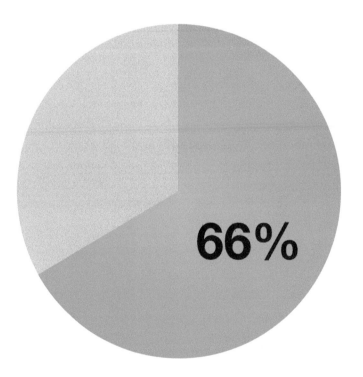

Consumer Interviews

66%

4 out of 6 people interviewed would buy the product

A better way to visualize this data would be to use character icons to represent the actual number of consumers interviewed. Figure 5-13 shows a line of six people icons with four of them colored green to literally show that four out of six people responded that they would buy the product. The audience can relate the icons to individual people from the survey, which reinforces the small sample size.

Another type of data from qualitative research is verbatim comments from people. Things people say in a focus group or write on a survey form can be single words or paragraphs of text. Word clouds are used to show the frequency particular words are used. The font size of each word or phrase is based on the frequency of mentions in the complete text from the research.

Consumer Interviews

4 out of 6 people interviewed would buy the product

FIGURE 5-13: Visualize the qualitative data literally.

To demonstrate, I gathered the text from 15,000 customer review comments about related products from Amazon.com, and used Wordle.net (www.wordle.net) to create two word clouds. Figure 5-14 includes the words from positive review comments shown in a green word cloud, and Figure 5-15 includes the negative comments shown in a red word cloud.

FIGURE 5-14: Word cloud of positive customer product reviews on Amazon.com

FIGURE 5-15: Word cloud of negative customer product reviews on Amazon.com

The nice thing about word clouds is that they are visually indicative of general sentiment, especially when seen in relation to the rest of the words. The reader can get a good understanding of the common themes between the comments, but no numbers are shown to indicate specific levels of frequency. Even with thousands of customer reviews as the data set, this is still considered to be qualitative data because there is little information about the people involved. It's not a controlled survey of a specific type of consumer. Instead, it's a random assortment of customers that happened to be motivated enough to post a review online.

Better Presentations Using Infographics

Most people are comfortable using data visualizations and infographics at work in presentations. This is where they most often see charts, tables, and diagrams used to communicate with employees in the company. However, a presentation with a bunch of slides that all look the same because the presentation designer just accepted all the design template defaults isn't going to impress anyone. In fact, the presenter can lose credibility, and the information is unlikely to be remembered by the audience.

Presentation software can be a powerful design tool but not if the user just accepts all the design template defaults. Templates are supposed to be a good place to start but not the final slide designs. If you want your presentation to stand out and be memorable, you need to design and customize your own visualizations to be relevant and engaging for your audience.

Figure 5-16 is the default chart created by one of the standard templates in PowerPoint. How many charts have you seen that look exactly like this one with only the values and the text changed? In templates, the default colors match the overall presentation theme but don't have any connection to the data.

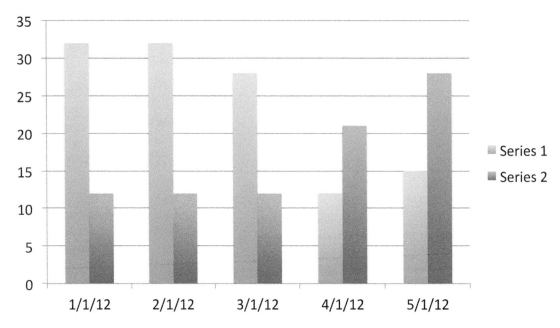

FIGURE 5-16:
Original chart
created with a
PowerPoint
template

You don't want your audience to remember that you used PowerPoint; you want them to remember your specific information. For the Picture Superiority Effect to be effective, the visual elements have to be related to the information. So you need to make the visual elements of your charts relevant to your data.

Even a handful of simple design changes can make each chart specific to its own data and easier for the audience to understand. In Figure 5-17, the same chart has been redesigned mostly using the design options available in PowerPoint. The major changes can be accomplished by following these steps:

1. Color the bars to match the branding of the data.

2. Display the data in the bars.

3. Simplify the axis labels as much as possible, down to just the month abbreviations by adding the year to the title.

4. Color the text of the month abbreviations along the x-axis to a lighter gray to help the colors of the chart become the focus.

5. Remove the axis lines, tick marks, and gridlines. For a chart this simple, they're unnecessary and add unwanted visual noise.

6. Add the specific company logo images found on those company websites on top of the bars. This establishes the meaning behind the color-coding and eliminates the need for a chart legend.

These changes obviously won't apply to every chart because your data will be different, but the idea is to make every data visualization relevant and meaningful to the audience. In this case, I purposely stayed with the bar chart visualization instead of trying different data visualization methods to demonstrate how some simple changes can make your charts much more meaningful to your audience. This is what it takes to make your data easier to understand and remember.

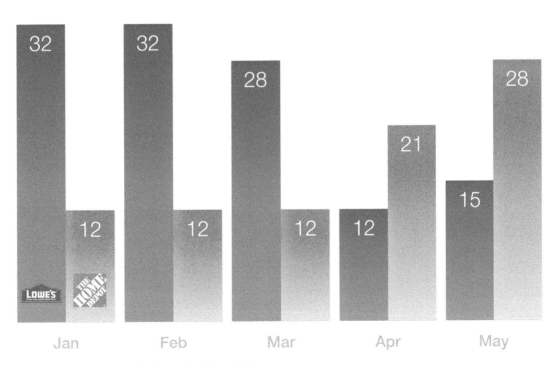

FIGURE 5-17: Chart redesigned in PowerPoint

The One-Page Infographic Handout

One of the best uses of infographics within a company is for the handouts passed out during presentations. A printed, one-page infographic handout can be much more effective when used as an executive summary of a presentation. Instead of giving everyone in the audience a thick packet with every slide from your presentation, give them just a one-page summary.

The same design principles from online infographics apply, so only the most important information should be visualized on the handout. With all the key information on one page, none of the information gets lost. The members of the audience can lay the handout on their desk or hang it up on the wall of their office, and all the key information is viewable. This keeps the message and information fresh in their minds and reinforces memory because they see it often.

If you distribute a large packet of printed pages from a presentation, the information will probably get lost when the employees return to their desks. If they leave the printed stack on their desk, they only see the top page, and the rest of the information is buried in the stack unless they make the effort to look through the pages. More likely they don't have room on their desk, so the stack of slides is either filed away in a drawer or thrown away–out of sight, out of mind.

The one-page handouts can be printed on standard letter-size paper, but many handouts are printed on the larger legal-size (8.5″ × 14″) or tabloid-size paper (11″ × 17″) available for many business-grade printers and photocopiers.

Figure 5-18 is the *2011 Wisconsin Crash Calendar* designed by Joni Graves as part of the University of Wisconsin's Transportation Information Center's ROaDS (Resources, Outreach, and Data Support) initiative using statewide data. Printed on a single 11″ × 17″ page, the Wisconsin Bureau of Transportation Safety (BOTS) uses the design as a handout for several staff meetings and multi-disciplinary meetings across the state, and it is also used at quarterly Traffic Safety Commission (TSC) meetings.

The handout displays an immense amount of data on one page. By visualizing the data in the color-coded calendar format, it presents the data in a way that is much easier for the audience to understand than just the numbers. By providing it on a one-page handout, the design allows audiences to see patterns and easily compare the frequency data between different crash causes.

Prezi Presentations

 Prezi

If you take the idea of the one-page handout to the next level, you can convert a one-page infographic into your entire presentation. Using a zooming user interface (ZUI. pronounced "zoo-ee"), a presentation tool like Prezi (prezi.com) enables you to display the entire infographic as the presentation instead of breaking the information apart into separate, individual slides.

Prezi is a presentation application alternative to the more common PowerPoint or Keynote presentations. Instead of a sequence of individual, separate slides, Prezi uses one large canvas where the user can add images, charts, text, and even videos. The software enables the presenter to define a sequential path of zooming, rotating, and moving across the canvas to focus on different parts and create the flow of a presentation. When the presentation is displayed or projected, the software animates the movement across the canvas between each step defined in the path.

For example, Figure 5-19 is a large infographic from McGraw-Hill Higher Education that was used in its sales training conferences. The complete design can be printed as a one-page handout and distributed to the audience, or printed as a poster to be displayed. Prezi can then be used as the presentation application to move the focus of the projected display to each area of discussion during the presentation (Figure 5-20).

FIGURE 5-18:

A one-page info-graphic handout allows the audience to easily see all of the data from your presentation

Coolinfographics.com/Figure-5-18

Source: 2011 Wisconsin Crash Calendar, *Joni Graves*

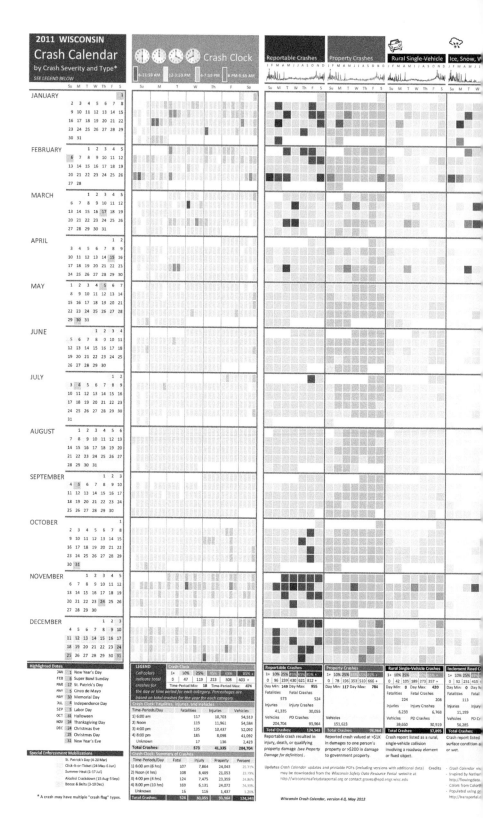

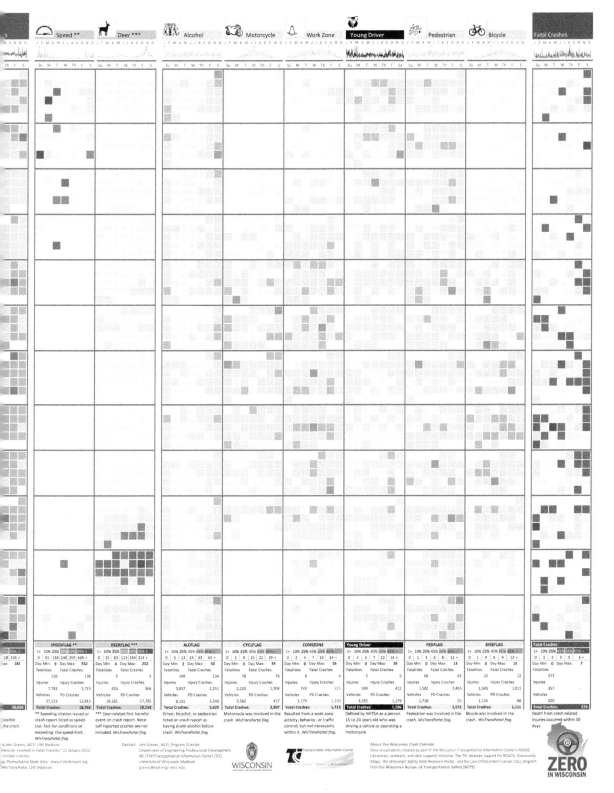

The audience can easily follow along throughout the entire presentation using the handout as a reference. Everyone in the audience has all the data on the one-page handout as a convenient takeaway document, so they have access to the information after the presentation.

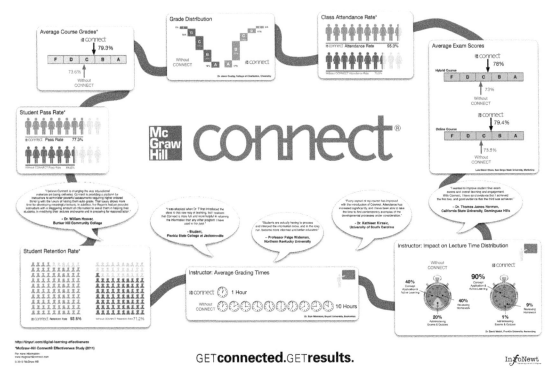

FIGURE 5-19: Large one-page infographic handout
Coolinfographics.com/Figure-5-19
Source: McGraw-Hill CONNECT

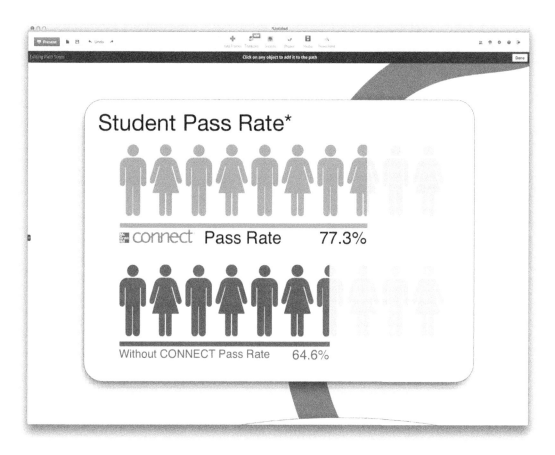

FIGURE 5-20: Prezi frame to zoom in to one section of the infographic during a presentation

The online version of Prezi is available for anyone to use for free, but there are additional paid licenses that provide more features, additional storage space online, and a separate desktop application. The desktop application enables you to keep your presentation in a local file instead of online, if that's a security concern. Also, using a file with the desktop application avoids any potential issues with Internet connectivity while you deliver your presentation because the entire presentation is saved locally on your computer.

Final Thoughts

It doesn't matter what business your company is in, you can benefit from visualizing your information. The business could be a local bakery, an online retailer, a government office, a venture capital firm, a private school, or a movie production company. Every company has valuable information that needs to be clearly communicated to employees, investors, and customers. Infographics and data visualization design practices can make your company information engaging and memorable.

Links

1. Bedford, TX Budget Poster, Randy Krum, InfoNewt:
   http://infonewt.com/portfolio/client-work/8781697

2. *BBC-o-Gram*, David McCandless, Information is Beautiful:
   http://www.informationisbeautiful.net/2010/the-bbc-o-gram/

3. Web Design Process, John Furness, Simple Square:
   http://www.simplesquare.com/a-website-designed

4. *How Affiliate Marketing Works*, Sugarrae.com:
   http://www.sugarrae.com/affiliate-marketing/how-affiliate-marketing-works/

5. *2011 Wisconsin Crash Calendar,* Joni Graves, University of Wisconsin-Madison:
   http://tic.engr.wisc.edu/viz

6. McGraw-Hill CONNECT Poster:
   http://create.mcgraw-hill.com/wordpress-mu/connectblog/
   files/2012/03/McGraw-Hill-Connect-Handout-WHITE-Small.jpg

Design matters. But design is not about decoration or about ornamentation. Design is about making communication as easy and clear for the viewer as possible.

—GARR REYNOLDS, *PRESENTATION ZEN*

6

Designing Infographics

If you have any interest in designing data visualizations and infographics, this chapter is for you. You might be ready to design one on your own, or you might work with a designer to put an infographic together. Either way, these design tips can help you create a cool infographic and avoid many of the common mistakes designers make.

Infographics are harder to design than you might think. There are thousands of "bad" infographic designs on the Internet because the designer ignored one, or many, of these rules. In a pattern similar to the millions of videos uploaded to YouTube, most of the infographics online are actually poor designs and get little traffic. The good designs rise to the top and are the designs that most often go viral in social networks.

This chapter doesn't point out and show any specific examples of bad designs that didn't follow these rules. Because I may have broken some of these rules in the past, I'm not here to criticize others, but to offer help to anyone that wants to get better at designing infographics. You can find thousands of examples of infographics online that break these rules on your own.

Following is a collection of top tips and tactics for designers that want to create better infographic designs. These will be tips focused on improving the content and structure of an infographic, and not software how-to tips. These best practices will apply no matter what software is used to put the infographic design together. It doesn't matter if you use Adobe Illustrator, Microsoft PowerPoint, or an online tool like Infogr.am. Specific software applications are covered in Chapter 7, "Design Resources."

Be Accurate

Accuracy is the most important aspect of an infographic design, and everything else is secondary. The data visualizations in your infographic must match the numbers.

The power of infographics works both ways and can hurt you if you get it wrong. The ability to communicate your information to your audience with a clear visualization can demonstrate your expertise in your subject area, build your credibility, and help your audience remember your message. Getting the data visualizations wrong can kill your credibility just as quickly and demonstrate your lack of expertise in your subject area. Your audience will assume that because you got one data visualization wrong, the rest of your message is also of questionable accuracy. One bad chart draws so much attention from the audience that it won't matter that the rest of the information is correct. The perception of bad information will have been set in the minds of the audience.

Figure 6-1 shows the most common mistake made in infographic designs: incorrect pie charts. The values in a pie chart MUST add up to 100 percent, but apparently many designers do not understand this basic fact. Pie charts should be used to show only how separate pieces are portions of a total amount. Percentages are portions of 100 percent.

The issue most often seen is that designers misuse pie charts and apply them to incompatible data. Even if the designer uses a charting program to create the pie chart, such as Excel, this can easily happen when the data is not clearly understood by the designer. This is the result of a concept called *Maslow's Hammer*[1], commonly phrased as, "When all you have is a hammer, everything looks like a nail.'

Designers overuse pie charts because they are so easy to create and mistakenly apply them to data sets that are not proportions of a whole.

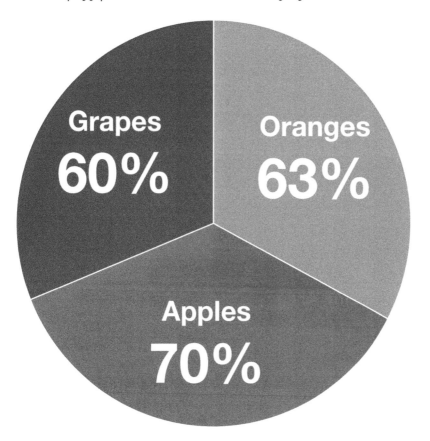

FIGURE 6-1:
WRONG! Pie charts MUST add up to 100 percent.

Many research survey questions enable the respondents to choose multiple answers. The results from this type of question yield frequency values for each available answer independently. For example, a hypothetical survey question might look like this:

Which types of fruit do you eat? [Check all that apply.]

- ▶ Apples

- ▶ Oranges

- ▶ Grapes

In this case, the resulting data would be better visualized in a bar chart because each fruit answer would represent a separate, independent frequency result. Figure 6-2 correctly visualizes the results as a stacked bar chart to show each percentage value separately as a portion of the maximum possible 100 percent. Combining them together into a pie chart would be an incorrect visualization of the data and demonstrates a complete lack of understanding of the data set.

If an infographic design visually shows the reader that you don't understand the data, you have used the power of data visualization against yourself. You will have effectively demonstrated your company's or client's lack of credibility. This can leave a powerful negative impression on your audience.

Be accurate and get the visualizations right!

Visualizing Area

It's key for data visualization designers to understand that we visually compare the sizes of objects based on their area (not their height). Numerical values are one-dimensional, but objects on a page or a screen are two-dimensional. This is where designers need to remember to use the math learned from high-school geometry class. If you didn't do well in geometry class, it's time to take another look.

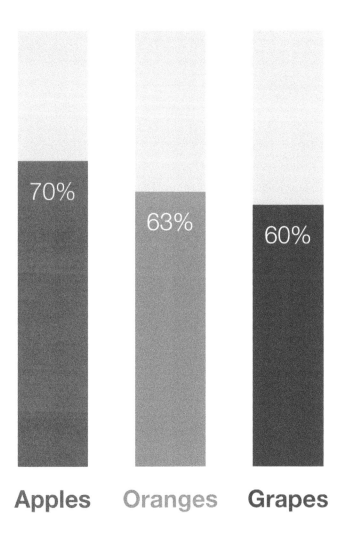

FIGURE 6-2:
The survey data is
correctly visualized
as a stacked bar
chart.

Some shapes are easy to size correctly because their area is directly proportional to one dimension. Now walk through a couple different ways to visualize comparisons of the following simple budget data.

DEPARTMENT	BUDGET
Marketing	$1,000,000
Sales	$3,000,000

Figure 6-3 demonstrates the math behind the easiest visualization, a bar chart. In a standard bar chart, the width of each rectangle remains constant, and only the height changes. If you change only the height, then the area changes in direct proportion.

FIGURE 6-3:
Dimensions of a bar chart to calculate area of the rectangles

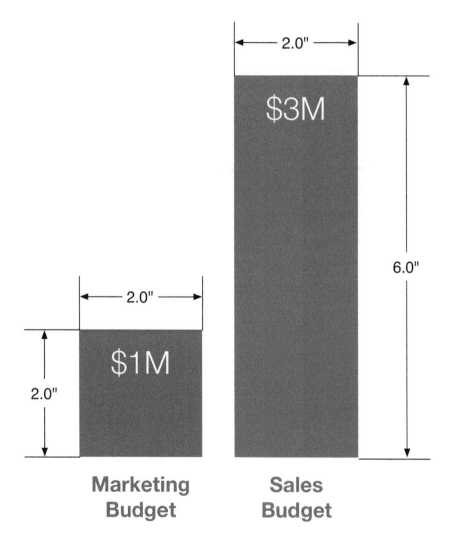

The area of a rectangle:

Width × Height = Area

The area of the Marketing bar:

2.0 in × 2.0 in = 4.0 in^2

The area of the Sales bar:

2.0 in × 6.0 in = 12.0 in^2

12.0 in^2 is three times the area of 4.0 in^2, and the Sales budget of $3 million is three times the value of the Marketing budget of $1 million. So, it correctly visualizes the data comparison with area by changing only the height of the bars. The math for rectangles is simple as long as you change only one dimension and the width remains constant.

The problem becomes more difficult when visualizing data by changing the sizes of nonstandard shapes: circles, icons, logos, and so on. This is where many designers mistakenly create data visualizations that don't actually match the data because they don't take the time to do the math required.

This issue is magnified when working with shapes in software because the design applications enable you to directly change only the width and height of an object, not the area. There's no input field where the designer can enter the area of an object because the software treats every object like a rectangle. So, designers need to do the mathematical calculations separately before sizing objects in the design software, but many make the mistake of simply changing both the width and height to match the data.

Now look at visualizing the same sample budget data with the size of circles.

π × radius^2 = Area of a circle

In Figure 6-4, you can see what happens when a designer mistakenly sizes circles by changing the diameter to match the data. If she incorrectly changes the diameter of the Sales circle in the software to be three times the diameter of the Marketing circle, the area of the Sales circle actually becomes 8.95 times larger.

The area of the Marketing circle:

$\pi \times 0.5$ in $\times 0.5$ in $= 0.79$ in^2

The area of the incorrect Sales circle:

$\pi \times 1.5$ in $\times 1.5$ in $= 7.07$ in^2

WRONG! Don't size circles by changing the diameter to match the data values.

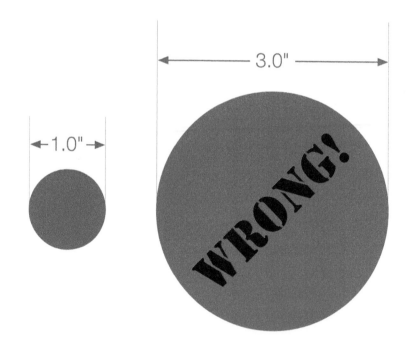

$1M
Marketing
Budget
Area = 0.79 in^2

$3M
Sales
Budget
Area = 7.07 in^2

This visualization doesn't match the data at all and becomes a false visual. The reason for this is that you are changing the size of two dimensions to represent one-dimensional data. Unlike rectangles, you can't keep the width constant and change only the height of a circle. It wouldn't be a circle anymore. This is also true for squares, icons, and logos where a designer wants to keep the aspect ratio constant so that the image looks correct in the design. You don't want to stretch or skew a company's logo by changing only one dimension.

To do this correctly, you have to start by calculating the area of the first circle, called the Master circle. Then, calculate the relative area of any additional circles in comparison to the Master circle by using the difference in values. In this case, the Sales budget is three times larger than the Marketing budget value, so the area of the Sales circle needs to be three times larger than the Marketing circle. It doesn't matter how many additional circles you create, but their areas all need to be calculated in comparison to the same Master circle.

Finally, use the area of each circle you just calculated to determine the diameter of the additional circles. The diameter is the numerical value you can use to enter that dimension in the design software. It doesn't matter which circle you choose to be the Master circle, but all the circles need to be sized proportional to the Master circle. If you started with the Sales circle as the Master circle, the area of the Marketing circle would be ⅓ the area of the Sales circle.

You can use a simple spreadsheet to show all the calculations. After you set up the spreadsheet, the only values you need to enter are the original data values you want to visualize and the diameter of the Master circle. The rest of the values are calculated automatically, and the designer can use all the calculated diameters to correctly size her design in the software application.

Table 6-1 shows the circle calculations for the sample budget data and uses the Marketing circle as the Master circle. If the budget data had more departments, they could be easily added as additional rows that all calculate in comparison to the Marketing department.

TABLE 6-1: Circle Calculations Spreadsheet

DEPARTMENT	VALUE	MASTER DIAMETER	MASTER RADIUS	AREA	RADIUS	DIAMETER
Marketing	$1M	1.0	0.5	0.7854		
Sales	$3M			2.3562	0.866	1.732

For reference, the equation to calculate the radius of a circle from the known area follows:

$$\text{Radius} = \sqrt{(\text{Area}/\pi)}$$

Diameter is then simply double the radius. Figure 6-5 shows the correct sizing of the circles based on the calculations from the spreadsheet, and the Sales circle is now correctly sized as three times the area of the Marketing circle.

FIGURE 6-5:
CORRECT circle siz-
ing based on area

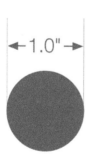

← 1.0" →

$1M
Marketing
Budget

Area = 0.79 in^2

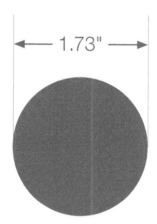

← 1.73" →

$3M
Sales
Budget

Area = 2.36 in^2

Pick a Good Topic

This might sound obvious, but many companies struggle with finding a good topic for an infographic design. A good infographic needs to be interesting because readers don't want to waste their time on boring, irrelevant topics. With information overload and thousands of infographics online, people have to choose which ones are worth reading.

Ideally, a good infographic topic focuses on some new piece of previously unknown information related to a subject the target audience is interested in. It would be even better if the information were something surprising to, and unexpected by, the audience. Topics that are counterintuitive or break expectations become sharable because people are surprised and want to share this new information they just learned with their friends.

There are two common topic areas that are worth a little more discussion: trending and controversial topics.

Trending Topics

There are some trending topics that are so popular that almost any infographic related to them generates a fairly decent amount of traffic and attention. However, the hot trending topics change over time. For example, currently any infographics released about social media, Star Wars, superheroes, or the iPhone seem to automatically draw in more traffic because these are the current, popular topics with the online, tech-savvy crowd.

Many companies release infographics based on a hot trending topic, which may or may not relate to their business, brand, or product. These can be successful with exploiting the trend and capitalizing on the attention they generate. This approach can be effective but can also be short-lived—just like the trends. Hot topics today are obsolete and out-of-date tomorrow.

Controversial Topics

Another popular approach is to focus on a controversial topic. If a company can connect with the audience on an emotional level about a topic it feels passionately about, the audience will be more likely to comment and share the infographic. The hope here is that "all links are good links." It doesn't matter if people post because they love the topic or they hate the topic. Their posts are creating backlinks that the search engines index, and their social network audiences also see the infographic—reaching a wider audience.

Controversial topics are a much riskier proposition because the audience may perceive that the company publishing the infographic is taking one side of the controversy. If it disagrees with the stance that it believes the infographic promotes, it can turn into an opposition to the company.

Search for Prior Art

As more and more infographics are published online, the more likely it is that a design related to your chosen topic already exists in the wild. Infographics published on the Internet never go away. They're all still out there somewhere, even if the original landing page on the company site is removed. Copies of them still exist on blogs, social networking sites, infographic gallery sites, and the Internet Archive (www.archive.org).

Going forward, the number of online infographics will continue to grow, so understanding the current state of existing prior art will continue to become more important as well. Use search engines and infographic gallery sites to gather any existing infographics related to your topic of choice.

The main purpose of a prior art search is to help make sure that your design doesn't repeat what has already been done. You don't want to replicate the same topic or use the same data visualizations in your design that were already used in another infographic. Your infographics should be unique, so you should also look to avoid any similar illustrations or color palettes used in prior designs.

The infographics you gather in a prior art search can also help identify potential data sources for your infographic. You may follow the source links and find more data to help build your own design.

From a promotional aspect, many mainstream media sites and publications will not post an infographic if the topic is exactly the same as a similar infographic they have already published in the past. Use the prior art search to help avoid duplicating an infographic topic that has already been done.

When you publish your infographic online, your prior art search can also help you build a list of sites to include in your outreach communication. Search for sites and authors that shared the previous infographics from your prior art search. Because your topic is similar (but not the same), these same people may also be interested in sharing your infographic with their audiences.

Focus on the Key Message

One of the first things I ask clients to do at the beginning of an infographic design project is to define the *key message* they want to communicate to the audience. The key message is the primary information you want the readers to understand and remember after reading your infographic. The challenge for designers that want to make their infographics easy to understand is to include the data and information needed to communicate and support the key message, but eliminate everything else.

Ideally, an infographic needs one clear message, and all the data visualizations and illustrations support that central message. Just because there is more data available doesn't mean you need to include it in the design. Many companies mistakenly believe that if they put several different data points into one infographic, it increases their credibility because it demonstrates how much data they have.

You wouldn't believe how many infographic designs struggle with this concept. If a design contains too much information, or doesn't have a clear story, it becomes confusing to the reader. When this happens, the readers usually give up and don't spend the time to figure out the message. By including too much information, you can actually communicate nothing to the readers.

The 5-second Rule

Why is the key message so important? It's a reader attention span problem similar to consumer product packaging on a crowded store shelf, articles in a newspaper, or a pile of job candidate resumes. Most readers are going to read an infographic for only a few seconds. They're skimming, and this is how the majority of readers will interact with your infographic. An infographic designer needs to approach the design process with this fact in mind.

A rule of thumb is that the design needs to clearly communicate the key message to the readers in less than five seconds. This is the 5-second rule, and comes from my own web analytics of millions of page views on the CoolInfographics.com site over the last five years. Most of the page view duration times are 5–10 seconds, and a good infographic design needs to successfully communicate its key message to the readers within that time. That way the infographic can communicate its main point to all the readers, even when they are skimming and they don't take the time to read the entire infographic.

Where's Google making its money? (as shown in Figure 6-6) is a great example of a design that succeeds within the 5-second window. Designed by NowSourcing for WordStream, this infographic was popular and heavily shared in social networks. Within 5 seconds, the reader understands that Google makes most of its money from advertising, and what a few of the top keyword categories are. Even if that's all readers understand before they move on to the next infographic, the design was successful in communicating its key message.

Listing all 20 top keyword categories in the pie chart design is interesting data and helps build WordStream's credibility for analyzing keywords. However, understanding the fine details that conference calls are the #11 keyword category is not necessary for the audience to understand the key message that Google makes its money from advertising. There's plenty of other data and information available about Google, but in this infographic it's all ignored, so the design can focus on passing its key message to readers quickly.

Readers appreciate infographics that get to the point quickly.

Tell One Story Really Well

Another way to approach this idea is to focus all the information in the infographic to tell one story really well. Don't try to tell a bunch of small stories. One of the secrets to any type of clear communication is to keep the information focused and eliminate any data that isn't directly related. Infographic designs that visualize data just because it's available become cluttered, and the readers don't know what data to focus on.

Figure 6-7 is one of my designs called *The Caffeine Poster*. The infographic focuses on visualizing the caffeine content of a bunch of different popular drinks so that readers can understand how much caffeine they would ingest if they choose a particular beverage. The design completely focuses on caffeine content, even though there is much more data available. Extra information about the parent companies of the brands, different sizes of the drinks, annual sales figures, geographic locations, and data about other ingredients were all eliminated to keep the design completely focused on caffeine content.

FIGURE 6-6:

Where's Google making its money?

Coolinfographics
.com/Figure-6-6

Source: How Does
Google Make Its Money:
The 20 Most Expensive
Keywords in Google
AdWords, *Wordstream*

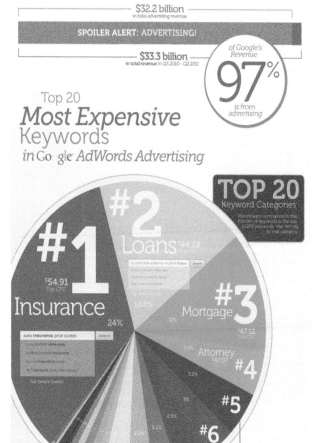

The Caffeine Poster

Discovered in 1819 by German chemist Friedrich Ferdinand Runge, caffeine is a crystalline xanthine alkaloid that is a psychoactive stimulant drug.

$C_8H_{10}N_4O_2$
(Caffeine)
1.23 g/cm³

Coffee

Caffeine Intoxication, also known as "the jitters", usually occurs after consuming 300mg of caffeine

Starbucks Tall Coffee, 12oz cup

SEP 29 September 29th is National Coffee Day

Einstein Bros. Coffee, 16oz cup

Caribou Small Coffee, 12oz cup

McDonald's Large Coffee, 16oz cup
Dunkin' Donuts Coffee, 16oz cup

Coffee (Brewed), 8oz cup

Coffee (Espresso), 1.5oz cup

Coffee (Instant), 8oz cup

Caffeine has a half-life (the time for the body to eliminate half of the caffeine) of approximately 4.9 hours

Coffee (Decaf), 8oz cup

Drinks

300

JOLT Energy, 12oz can

NOS Energy Drink 16oz can

250

Global consumption of caffeine has been estimated at 120,000 tons per year, making it the world's most popular psychoactive substance.

200

Monster or Rockstar, 16oz can

150

Starbucks Doubleshot + Coffee, 15oz can
Full Throttle, 16oz can

Starbucks Doubleshot, 6.5oz can

100

Red Bull Energy Drink, 8.3oz can
Amp Energy Drink, 8.4oz can

Mountain Dew, 12oz can

Diet Coke, 12oz can

50

Coca-Cola Classic, 12oz can

Sprite or 7-UP, 12oz can

mg of Caffeine

InfoNewt

FIGURE 6-7:

Focus on telling one story really well.
Coolinfographics.com/Figure-6-7
Source: The Caffeine Poster, *InfoNewt*

Visualize When Possible

In an infographic design, the more data you visualize, the better. You can use data visualizations, charts, graphs, icons, illustrations, and diagrams as design tools to help to make complex information easier to understand for the readers.

Visualizing the data helps with:

- Grabbing the attention of readers

- Reducing the amount of time it takes readers to understand the data

- Providing context to the data by showing a comparison

- Making the key message more memorable with the Picture Superiority Effect

- Making the information more accessible to readers who speak other languages

The whole point of designing an infographic is to make complex information easier to understand and interesting to the audience. To accomplish that, the infographic designer needs to visualize the data.

In contrast, infographic designs with a lot of text and numbers might appear at first glance to be complicated and intimidating to readers. If the infographic seems like it would take a long time to read through, most readers won't even try. They will move on to something else and leave the infographic behind without reading it.

Big Fonts Are NOT Data Visualizations

Using big fonts in an infographic to make the numbers stand out is not data visualization. This is a big pet peeve of mine, and it's done by designers in thousands of infographic designs and PowerPoint presentations. Displaying the number in a large font doesn't make it any easier for the audience to understand.

As mentioned in Chapter 1, "The Science of Infographics," data visualization is the language of context. One of the best ways to clearly communicate a new statistic with the audience is to show it in comparison to some information that it already understands. If the new information is shown as text alone, there's no context or frame of reference to help the reader to gain an understanding from the value.

Figure 6-8 shows an example of a statistic shown as text-only that might be included in an infographic. The common format is to show the data value in a large bold font and the associated description in a smaller font. The large font is intended to make the number stand out on the page and visually imply that the value is important.

64%

Parents look at the contents of their child's cell phone

FIGURE 6-8:
Big fonts are NOT data visualizations.

Reading is a slower process than pattern recognition, and this text doesn't give the reader any clues about whether the value should be interpreted as a large or small amount. The audience is left to understand this value based on its personal experiences and perspective. The readers will mentally make their own evaluation of this value based on some information they already know. In this way, the designer loses control of how the audience interprets the data because it has no idea what frame of reference each individual reader will use as a comparison.

Visuals Are Perceived as More Important

Another aspect of visualizing data is that the audience perceives any data shown as text alone as less important or irrelevant. In many infographic designs, there is a mix of visualized data and data shown as text alone. Figure 6-9 demonstrates the previous text-only data point shown next to a second data point that was visualized. With an icon, color, and a doughnut chart to visualize the percentage as a portion of the complete 100 percent, that statistic becomes easier to understand.

FIGURE 6-9:
Visualized data is perceived as more important.

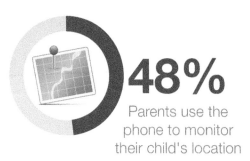

48%
Parents use the phone to monitor their child's location

64%
Parents look at the contents of their child's cell phone

The visualized data in an infographic pulls the reader's attention away from any other information shown only as text. This makes the text-only data points appear to be inferior or secondary information to the visualized data. When reading infographics, the text-only data is often skipped and ignored by the reader because it wasn't important enough to visualize.

It also goes back to the attention span issue as readers skim through infographics. They often focus only on the visuals and ignore the text because it's faster. Remember the 5-second rule. Most audiences skim the infographic and don't want to take the time to read all the text. They try to understand the message from the visuals alone and only a small portion of the audience will read the additional text.

If your data is important enough to be included in the infographic design, it's probably important enough to visualize.

Minimize Text

Nobody wants to read a text article that has been converted into a JPG image file and called an infographic. (Yes, I've seen this done). Readers look at your infographic with the expectation that with the use of visual design, the information will be simpler to understand and faster to read than a traditional text article or blog post.

Of course, chances are that you won't remove all the text from the design, but you should minimize it as much as possible. This is one of the biggest challenges when working with clients because they have so much information that they would like to communicate to readers. The temptation is that knowing you can get the audience's attention with a good info-graphic topic, companies want to throw all their related information into the design hoping that the readers will take the time to read everything.

The disconnect is that the infographic should focus on communicat-ing the key message and not try to be the ultimate guide to everything about your company or products. In general, people want to learn about the interesting topic and don't want to learn everything about the company that published the infographic.

Assuming you have an interesting topic to begin with, the reality is that the less text you include in your design, the more people you can reach. At first glance, the audience judges if an infographic is worthy of the time it needs to invest to read it. If it appears to be a lot of text, it is gen-erally regarded as too complex and "not worthy." Too much text implies that the design doesn't do a good job making the topic simple and easy to understand.

Figure 6-10 is a fun infographic design exercise in eliminating as much text as possible. Designer Marc Morera minimized each of the *Star Wars* movies down to visual diagrams of the character interactions throughout each movie. The fun for readers is to follow the different color-coded paths in the infographic and try to remember each related scene of the movie.

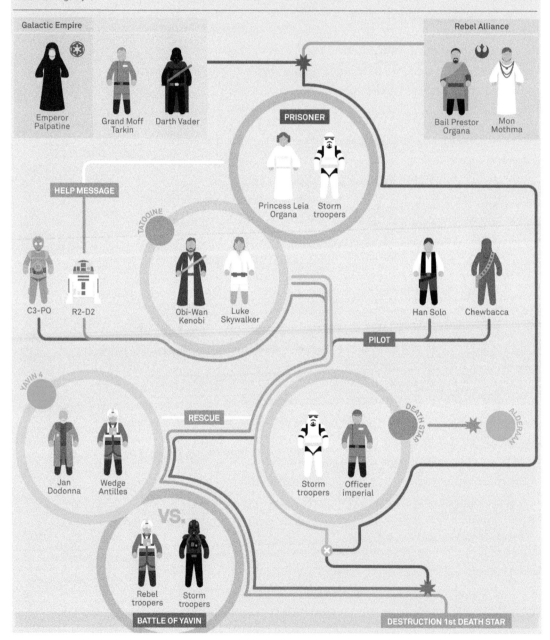

Episode IV
A NEW HOPE George Lucas 1977

0 bBY

It is a period of civil war.
Rebel spaceships, striking from a hidden base, have won their first victory against the evil Galactic Empire. During the battle, Rebel spies managed to steal secret plans to the Empire's ultimate weapon, the Death Star, an armored space station with enough power to destroy an entire planet.
Pursued by the Empire's sinister agents, Princess Leia races home aboard her starship, custodian of the stolen plans that can save her people and restore freedom to the galaxy....

Galactic Empire

Emperor Palpatine · Grand Moff Tarkin · Darth Vader

Rebel Alliance

Bail Prestor Organa · Mon Mothma

PRISONER

Princess Leia Organa · Storm troopers

HELP MESSAGE

TATOOINE

C3-PO · R2-D2 · Obi-Wan Kenobi · Luke Skywalker

Han Solo · Chewbacca

PILOT

YAVIN 4

Jan Dodonna · Wedge Antilles

RESCUE

DEATH STAR · ALDERAAN

Storm troopers · Officer imperial

VS.

Rebel troopers · Storm troopers

BATTLE OF YAVIN

DESTRUCTION 1st DEATH STAR

FIGURE 6-10: *Star Wars Episode IV* **infographic with minimal text.**
Coolinfographics.com/Figure-6-10
Source: Marc Morera Agusti

Some text is required to introduce the overall design and identify the characters, but there is little text throughout the design. In this case, less text actually encourages readers to engage with the design and interact longer as they take the time to follow the separate character paths.

Eliminate Chart Legends

Chart legends are evil. I find myself repeating this often to clients and designers.

Charts and graphs are a crucial data visualization element used in most infographics, and designers don't need to create all of them from scratch. They should use charting software such as Apple Keynote or Microsoft PowerPoint to create the charts and graphs included in the infographics designs whenever possible, but they also need to make them as easy to understand as possible.

In general, chart legends make readers work twice as hard to understand a particular chart because they have to look back and forth between the chart and the color key multiple times to understand the different sets of data represented in the chart. That's a lot of eye movement. As a part of cleaning up the chart designs, the designer should try to minimize the eye movements of the readers to make the charts easier to understand.

That means the responsibility is on the designer to improve the charts that the software applications create by default. This includes colors and spacing, but the primary change should be to eliminate the chart legends whenever possible. The readers still need some type of guide to the color-coding system in the chart, but if that guide is built right into the chart itself, there will no longer be a need for a separate chart legend.

Figure 6-11 shows the default bar chart created by PowerPoint. The data shown is the U.S. Census Population data from the 2012 Statistical Abstract[2] broken into common age groupings. By default, most charting software automatically includes the chart legend shown as a guide to the color-coding system. This is a simple example, but even here the reader will probably look back and forth a few times to understand what each bar in the chart represents.

PowerPoint automatically creates a chart legend by default.

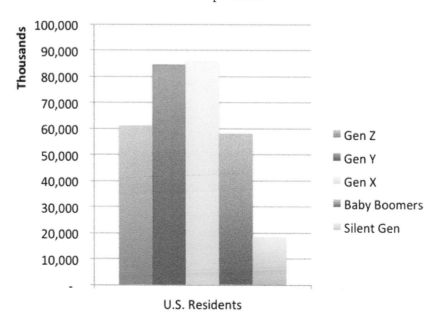

You should do a lot more to improve this chart design before including it in an infographic design, but this example will only focus on eliminating the chart legend. Figure 6-12 deletes the chart legend, and in its place you can see added icons and descriptions directly on the chart. This makes the color-coding much faster to understand because the reader can identify each data set with minimal eye motions. All the relevant information is within the reader's field of view, and the icons are also faster to understand than reading the text labels. As an additional benefit, the elimination of the chart legend also opens up more space on the page, so the chart can be increased in size or make room for additional information.

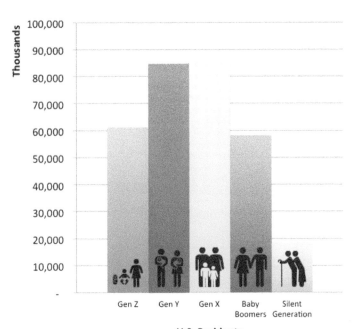

These types of design changes require some extra effort on the part of the chart designer. Adding separate text blocks or data labels is fairly easy within PowerPoint, but the icons are a little more difficult. Icons like these are not available natively from within PowerPoint, so designers must create or purchase their own. Then they can be placed manually to appear on top of the chart object in PowerPoint or whatever design program is used to put the infographic together. You can use stock vector art in infographics designs, and these particular icons were part of a set purchased from iStockPhoto[3].

Be Data Transparent

To be data transparent, the infographic needs to address the sources of the data included in the design in an open and honest manner. A large portion of the audience is initially going to be skeptical, so the design needs to get past the data integrity issue quickly. After you get the audience past the data believability issue, it can focus and engage mentally with the overall message the infographic is communicating.

Readers are initially looking to answer a handful of questions:

- Where does the data come from?
- How old is the data?
- Why should I believe the data?
- Is the infographic credible?

Credibility plays a huge part in the success of an infographic, both online and internal to companies. Readers won't share the infographic in social networks if they think the information is questionable.

Ignore data transparency at your own risk, and understand that designs that disregard data transparency are seen as not believable. Following are a few common mistakes made by infographic designers.

No Data Sources List

Surprisingly, a large number of infographics don't include any mention of where the data originated from. With no data sources to judge the credibility of an infographic, the readers quickly move from skeptics to unbelievers. As far as the audience can tell, the designer may have made up the numbers.

A frequent consequence of not listing any data sources in an infographic design is that all the comments, posts, and conversations about the infographic tend to focus on the unknown source of data. Accusations of false numbers, deception, and misleading information are quite common when this happens. This completely distracts the audience from the actual content of the infographic, and the infographic fails to inform readers or inspire conversation about its key message.

Obviously, this is not the outcome wanted by a company that has spent a lot of time and resources to create and publish the infographic.

Vague Data Sources

Almost as bad as not listing any data sources is listing vague sources of data that make it almost impossible for readers to find the cited numbers. Vague data sources are usually just the name of the host site that published the data, with no additional information about a specific report or article.

For example, an infographic about baby names in the United States might list a vague data source as only Data.gov. If readers want to see the original data, they would have to perform their own search within the referenced website in an attempt to find any data related to baby names. In addition, many sites do not have effective search functions. If the readers find any related information, they couldn't tell which specific data was used to support the infographic.

Sometimes, this method of listing vague data sources is used intentionally to leverage the existing credibility of the data source organizations without actually revealing the original data specifically.

An infographic design about household pets might cite The Humane Society as the source of the data used. Readers would have no recourse to find the original data. Was the data gathered from a printed flyer, a news article, a magazine, mentioned at a live event, or is it available on the website? The skeptical audience has no way of validating that the data actually came from The Humane Society, but many readers might believe the infographic simply because they believe The Humane Society is a credible organization.

Questionable Data Sources

The truth is that many, if not most, readers won't take the time or make the effort to check your data sources. The fact that the infographic has any sources listed at all is often good enough for many, many readers. The vast majority of readers are not going to follow the links and validate that the infographic designer interpreted the original data correctly. Similar to news articles, the readers are relying on their belief that the designer, author, or publishing company made sure the information was credible. The company publishing an infographic may also have an established credibility with the audience. If readers trust a specific company, they will probably trust an infographic published by that company.

However, there are some specific data sources that can automatically trigger a reader's skepticism. For many, Wikipedia and other blogs fall into this category even though the quality of content on Wikipedia has improved dramatically over the last few years. Honestly, there's nothing wrong with discovering data on Wikipedia, but your infographic will be much more credible if you use the reference links to track down the original source of the data to list as the citation in the infographic.

Any sites that aren't intended to be taken seriously are also regarded as questionable sources of data. Sites that focus on humorous content or personal blogs are not generally perceived as credible data sources.

Best Practices

An infographic design that is upfront about its data sources is instantly perceived to be more credible. There are a few best practices that are common to good infographics.

- ▶ Track down and cite the original source of the data, not the news article that quoted the data.

- ▶ List the data source references either inline with the data or in the footer at the bottom of the infographic.

- List the URL to the specific report or data set, not just the host site.

- Include the relevant date or year the data was published to establish relevancy.

In addition, one of the best practices is for an infographic author to make the source data available to readers online for download as a spreadsheet. This is often accomplished with Google Docs spreadsheets[4] that are accessible to the public. The infographic would include the URL directly to the data spreadsheet, which lists the data and shows any relevant sources or calculations made as part of the design. Readers can access the data directly and even use the data on their own.

The Fine Print

A handful of final things should be included at the end of every infographic design. Remember, after you release the infographic onto the wild Internet, it takes on a life of its own. It could be reposted by anyone and resized to fit into other site layouts (usually a reduction in size to fit onto a smaller web page).

Some designs are initially published in combination with other text content on the original landing page or part of a longer blog post. All that extra text is typically ignored when the infographic is reposted and shared on other sites. The infographic image is usually shared by itself, so all the relevant data needs to be included in the infographic image file. This ensures that the important, relevant information is always available to the audience.

Company Logo

Where does the infographic come from? This may seem like a no-brainer, but some infographics published online don't mention the company that published the infographic. Whoops—so much for creating links or building brand equity.

A brand or company logo at the bottom of the design works nicely as an indication that, "This infographic was brought to you by the good people at Company X." The URL to the company web page is also helpful and helps drive some additional traffic from interested readers.

Copyright License

As covered in Chapter 2, "Online Infographics," every infographic design is automatically protected by a standard copyright license in the United States. However, it's better to explicitly state either a copyright or a Creative Commons license on the infographic. That way your choices covering how you want the infographic to be treated by others is in the infographic when it gets shared on any other sites on the Internet.

This can be helpful if legal concerns arise. If people abuse your infographic design, posting a modified version or claiming it as their own design, you have a stronger legal position if the licensing restrictions were explicitly expressed on the original design.

Don't forget that a copyright statement also clearly identifies the copyright holder (a person or a company). If people want to contact the copyright holder to request additional permissions (such as including the infographic design in a book!) they need the ability to easily determine who owns the copyright.

Original Landing Page URL

As much as you would like them to, many people are not good about including a clickable HTML link back to your original infographic landing page when they repost the infographic on other sites.

You can always make contact and ask them to add the link to their post under the terms of your copyright license, but that assumes you're going to spend the time and effort to track down and verify every site that reposts the infographic. Even then, many sites will ignore your requests to add the link.

It's much easier to include the URL of the original infographic landing page in the infographic image. That way it's built in to the infographic when it gets shared on other sites. If readers want to find the full-size original version, they have the URL they can type into their browser.

Designer Credit

Whenever possible, you should credit the infographic designer that designed the infographic. It might be you, a designer from within the company, a freelance designer, or an outside design firm.

Readers appreciate infographic designs that come from an actual person as opposed to just a faceless company. They are more likely to comment, provide feedback, or share an infographic when they believe they are supporting (or criticizing) a specific individual. This sharing behavior is more frequent when they are sharing the visual story created by an individual as opposed to sharing a potential advertisement from a company. Infographics that list only the publishing company are often perceived as promotional material for the company, which can discourage people from sharing with their network of friends.

Separately, if the designer or design firm has built up their own brand equity, citing the designer on the infographic can also convey some of that expertise and credibility onto the infographic. An infographic may be perceived as more credible and become popular online based on the reputation of the designer. Followers of a particular designer are likely to find the design and share it on their own.

Of course, the credit listing also helps designers build their own credibility and helps to build the infographics design industry as a whole. Other companies that appreciate the design may follow the citation and contact the designer directly to discuss creating future designs. The reward for good work can be more work.

Putting It Together

You can see all these elements put together in the footer of an info-graphic design in Figure 6-13. This is a close-up of the bottom section from *Streamlining Your Digital Life with the iPad* from NextWorth (shown previously in Figure 3-7) and has all the relevant information included in the infographic JPG image file. In this way, all the important information travels with the infographic as it is shared on other websites across the Internet.

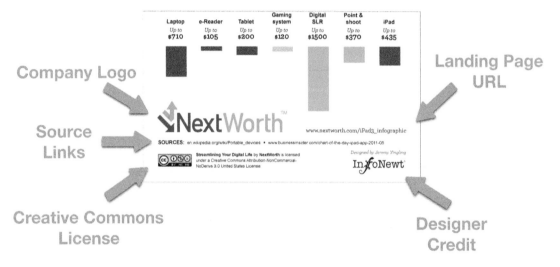

FIGURE 6-13:
Information in the footer stays with the infographic when shared on other websites.
Coolinfographics.com/Figure-6-13
Source: Streamlining Your Digital Life with the iPad, *NextWorth*

Final Thoughts

It doesn't matter if you are designing infographics yourself or working with a designer. Using these tips as guidelines can make a huge difference with how effective the final design will communicate to the audience, build the company brand equity, and is shared in social media.

Your next infographic design can avoid the most common design mistakes, and this will immediately make your design better than most of the other infographics published online.

References

1. Abraham H. Maslow, *The Psychology of Science*, (Richmond, CA: Maurice Bassett, 1966), p. 15. http://books.google.com/books?id=3_40fK8PW6QC&lpg=PP1&pg=PP1#v=onepage&q&f=false

2. 2012 Statistical Abstract, U.S. Census, http://www.census.gov/compendia/statab/cats/population.html

3. Family icons set, iStockPhoto, http://www.istockphoto.com/stock-illustration-11683088-family-icons-standard.php?st=4a39808

4. Google Docs spreadsheets, http://google.com/drive/apps.html#product=sheets

Links

1. *Where's Google making its money?*, WordStream and NowSourcing: http://www.wordstream.com/articles/most-expensive-keywords.

2. *The Caffeine Poster*, InfoNewt: http://www.coolinfographics.com/caffeine-poster/

3. *Star Wars* Infographics, Marc Morera: http://www.murera.com/starwars/

4. *Streamlining Your Digital Life* with the iPad, NextWorth: http://www.nextworth.com/ipad3_infographic

The art challenges the technology, and the technology inspires the art.

—John Lasseter

Design Resources

The question I get asked more than any other is, "What software do you use to design infographics?" Usually, the answer is, "It depends," because different projects need different data visualization applications based on the data the designer has to work with.

Along with the explosion of infographics online in the last couple of years, the number of new data visualization and infographic software applications and websites online has also grown dramatically. There is a huge variety of software, both free and paid, available to users—and the challenge is making a choice from all the options.

Many people are surprised to learn that the vast majority of the data visualizations created to be included in the infographics are designed manually. People seem to think that we load the data into a magic computer program, and *POOF!* it spits out an amazing infographic. Not true.

Desktop Software Tools

Most of the infographics that exist are put together with desktop application software. You can use these applications to visualize the data, edit the image of a logo, adjust a photo, or put the whole infographic design together. Desktop applications are the main tool of designers, but there are many more applications beyond those mentioned here.

Vector Graphics

All infographics designers need a core vector graphics software program they can depend on. No matter where you create the data visualizations or illustrations, the final product is usually put together in a vector graphics program.

For designers, the main advantage of a vector graphics program is that all the text, photos, illustrations, and data visualizations are treated as separate objects that can be easily moved, resized, overlapped, and rotated. This makes putting together the layout of the final infographic design much easier.

Any shapes or objects created in a vector graphics program are in a vector format (not a static bitmap or raster image), so they can be resized without losing any resolution or clarity. Vector images are actually mathematical equations that define how to display the shape on screen so the software can recreate the identical shape at any size with crisp, smooth edges.

Most vector graphic programs can also import static images (such as photographs) that are treated as moveable objects, but they have a fixed resolution. It's simple for a designer to move a static image and integrate it into the overall design, but resizing static images can be a problem. If a designer resizes a static image larger than its original resolution, it begins to look pixelated or blurry. This is why a designer will create objects as vectors whenever possible.

The circles shown in Figure 7-1 are a quick example of the difference between vector and static objects. If the original small circle shape was a vector object, you can see how it would retain the crisp, clean edges when enlarged. The software redraws a new edge for a circle with a larger diameter. Conversely, if the original circle is only a static image of a circle with a fixed resolution, the pixelated edges are magnified when the circle is enlarged.

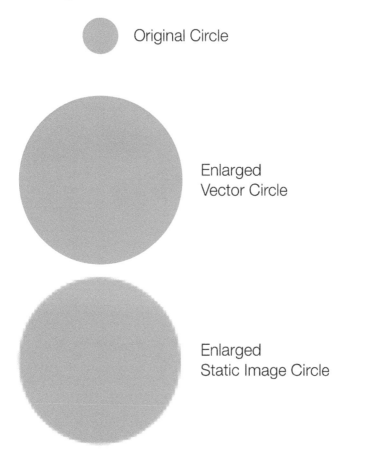

Original Circle

Enlarged
Vector Circle

Enlarged
Static Image Circle

FIGURE 7-1:
Differences when enlarging vector and static images

Ai Adobe Illustrator

Adobe Illustrator (Figure 7-2) is the premium vector graphics program on the market—and also the most expensive. As part of the Adobe Creative Suite, this is the package that most graphic designers rely on for any vector graphics work. It's big, it's complicated, and for any non-graphic designers that want to try to design their own infographics, the sheer complexity of learning Adobe Illustrator is intimidating. (www.adobe.com)

Original Image   High Color Trace   Silhouette Trace

FIGURE 7-2: Adobe Illustrator screen shot

Adobe InDesign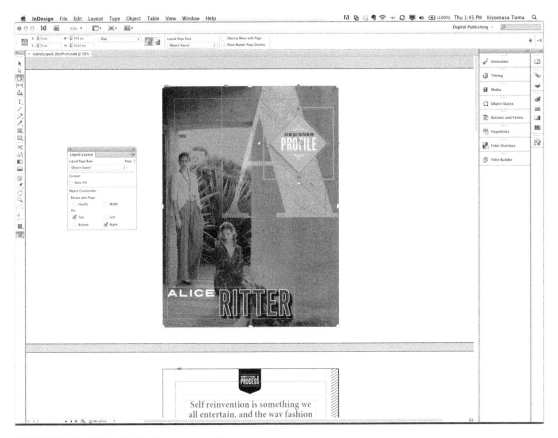

Another application from the Adobe Creative Suite, InDesign is the modern-day desktop publishing program (Figure 7-3). Meant for long-format print layouts, such as magazines and books, InDesign is also a great tool to put together many different pieces into a complete infographic. If your design has a lot of text, InDesign is especially useful for its text wrapping around images. (www.adobe.com)

FIGURE 7-3: Adobe InDesign screenshot

OmniGraffle

OmniGraffle (Figure 7-4) from the Omni Group is my personal application of choice when it comes to putting the final infographic designs together. I find it to be a much more lightweight and easier-to-use application than Adobe Illustrator, with most of the graphic functions required. Because it is primarily a diagramming tool, connecting objects together for flowcharts or network diagrams is easy. Although this program is Mac-only, there's also an OmniGraffle for iPad app that can also display and edit files created with the desktop application (Figure 7-5). (www.omnigroup.com/products/omnigraffle/)

FIGURE 7-4:
OmniGraffle
screenshot

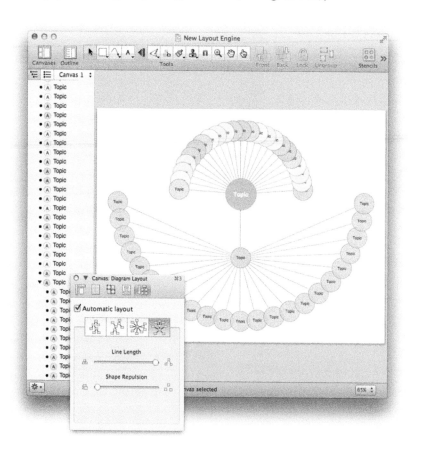

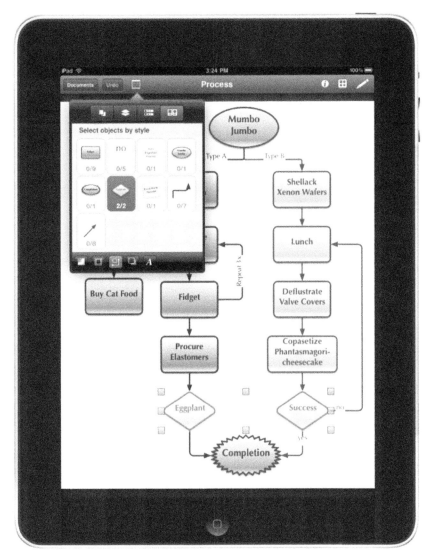

FIGURE 7-5:
OmniGraffle for
iPad

 ## Inkscape

Inkscape (Figure 7-6) is an open-source vector graphics editor that adds the use of Scalable Vector Graphics (SVG), an open XML-based W3C standard, as the native format. This is a powerful vector graphics program available for multiple platforms (Windows, Mac OSX, and Linux). The biggest advantage is that it's a free program for download. (www.inkscape.org)

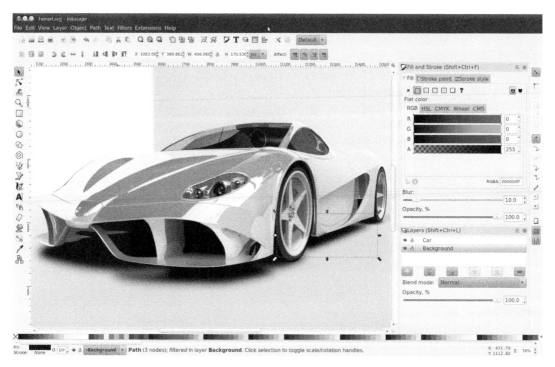

FIGURE 7-6: Inkscape screenshot

Microsoft PowerPoint

What? Microsoft PowerPoint? Yep. Although, it's obviously mainly used and marketed as a presentation application, at its heart PowerPoint (Figure 7-7) is a simple vector graphics program. The application allows users to create floating text blocks, insert vector object shapes and import images to arrange in an infographic design. The process should be familiar to people that design presentation slides since they are already comfortable moving objects around on the page.

PowerPoint also has the advantage that Microsoft Office is probably already on your computer, so it's a tool you or your company already owns. Designers can create custom paper sizes to layout a tall format infographic design instead of the standard presentation slides. If you use the built-in charts as part of the design, you can easily update the infographic with new data at a later date. (www.powerpoint.com)

FIGURE 7-7:

Microsoft Power-Point screenshot

Image Editing

Although some designers create entire infographic designs in an image editor application, these are primarily used to clean up images that are later imported into the vector graphics application. Image editors are a fantastic tool for changing colors, cropping images, and removing unwanted portions of images.

To make the background of a company logo transparent so that it blends into your infographic design, an image editor is the perfect tool. There are hundreds of image editing programs you can use, but these are the main ones used as part of an infographic design.

Ps Adobe Photoshop

Adobe Photoshop (Figure 7-8) is the dominant application for photo and image editing software. This is another application included as part of the Adobe Creative Suite. It has everything you need to clean up images for infographic designs, and way, way more. Similar to Illustrator, the high price point and overall complexity are major hurdles for many designers. (www.adobe.com)

Pixelmator

Pixelmator (Figure 7-9) is a much less expensive image-editing application on the Mac platform and is a popular tool of choice. This is a powerful, full-featured image editing application that is more than capable of handling the images used for infographic designs. (www.pixelmator.com)

FIGURE 7-8: Photoshop screenshot

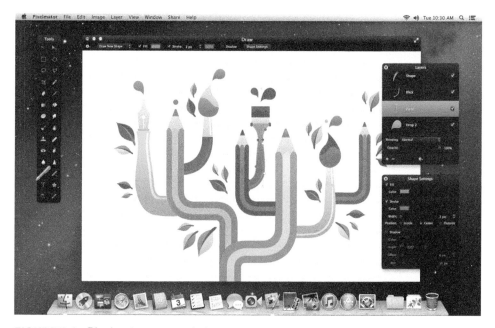

FIGURE 7-9: Pixelmator screenshot

 ## GIMP

GIMP (Figure 7-10) is a free image manipulation application used for photo retouching, image composition, and image authoring. GIMP has all the core image editing functions, but its main advantage is its cross-platform support for Windows, Mac, GNU/Linux, Sun OpenSo-laris, and FreeBSD. This is a great tool for those with a small budget. (www.gimp.org)

FIGURE 7-10: **GIMP screenshot**

Acorn

Acorn (Figure 7-11) by Flying Meat is an award-winning, low-cost image editing application, but this one is also Mac-only. Acorn is easy to use with some great design tools and filters. (www.flyingmeat.com/acorn)

FIGURE 7-11: **Acorn screenshot**

Online Data Visualization Tools

There are hundreds of websites can help create the different data visualizations that designers include in their infographic designs. It all depends on what type of information you have to work with and what story you want to tell. Do you need a map, a word cloud, a flowchart, a timeline, or a simple bar chart?

The incredible diversity of data visualizations is amazing to behold, and new visualization methods and styles are developed every day. Following are just a handful of the tools that have been helpful to designers.

Periodic Table of Visualization Methods

One tool that helps many designers determine which type of data visualization is appropriate for their data is the Periodic Table of Visualization Methods (shown in Figure 7-12) from Visual-Literacy.org. Sometimes designers need some inspiration to break out of the standard bar charts, pie charts, and line charts. In the table, the visualization methods are grouped by the different types of data being visualized (Strategy, Data, Concept, Metaphor, and more). When you hover your mouse pointer over any of the methods on the chart, it displays an example of that visualization for your reference. The examples are a few years old, so they may appear dated, but you'll still understand the visualization style that could be used to model your data. (www.visual-literacy.org/periodic_table/periodic_table.html)

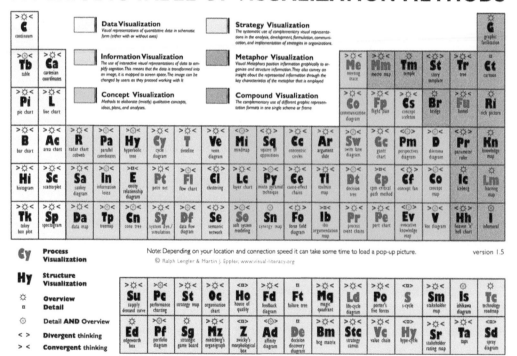

FIGURE 7-12: Periodic Table of Visualization Methods

Wordle.net

Wordle is a popular, free tool online for creating word clouds out of any text you have available. Word clouds size the font of each word based on its frequency in your text, so the largest words are the ones that appear most often. Figure 7-13 shows a word cloud of the entire Facebook Privacy Policy pasted directly from its website without any editing. After a word cloud has been created, you can edit the colors, layout, and fonts to your liking.

FIGURE 7-13: Facebook Privacy Policy on Wordle

Word clouds are usually used in situations in which your data is more qualitative than quantitative. The reader can get a general impression based on the word frequency, but no hard values are shown. There are also some advanced features to combine words in order to determine the frequency of phrases instead of just individual words. This is often used to separate positive and negative sentiment phrases, and the frequency difference between phrases such as "love" and "don't love." Without the phrases, only the raw frequency of "love" would be counted, regardless of its context. (www.wordle.net)

Chartle.net

Chartle is easy to use and free. In addition to the normal pie charts, line charts, and bar charts, Chartle has a number of other useful visualizations that are often used in infographics. Specifically, the maps, Venn diagrams, and gauges (Figure 7-14) are different and popular. (www.chartle.net)

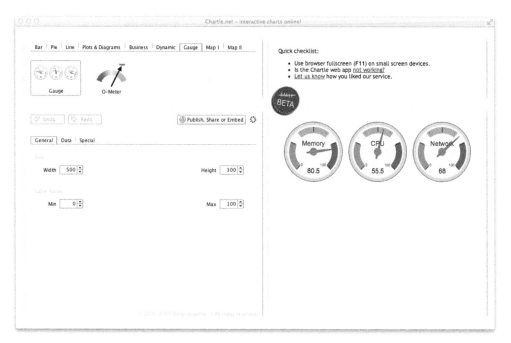

FIGURE 7-14: Chartle.net

ChartsBin

ChartsBin is an online, web-based visualization tool mainly used for visualizing data on a world map (Figure 7-15). You can enter your own data or browse the data sets in the gallery. The final visualizations can be downloaded as PNG image files to be placed into an infographic design. (www.chartsbin.com)

FIGURE 7-15: ChartsBin screen shot

DIY Chart

DIY Chart (Figure 7-16) has a number of chart templates that you can use as the data visualizations in an infographic design. You can create a handful of charts for free, and the $4.95/month fee for the Premium account gets you many more chart styles and removes the DIY Chart logo from your designs. You can save your chart images in BMP, PNG, Emf, or JPG formats to your local disk for use in infographic designs or even just as a chart in a blog post. (www.diychart.com)

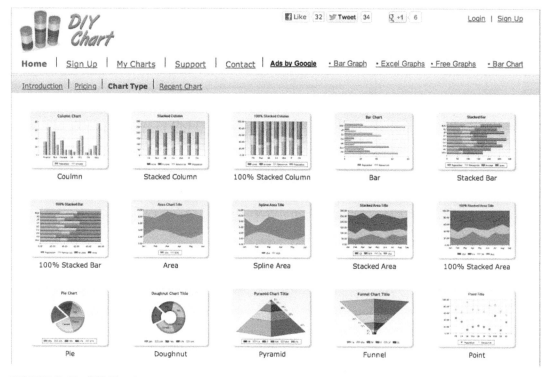

FIGURE 7-16: DIY Chart

Gephi

Gephi (Figure 7-17) is described as the Photoshop for data, and it's powerful for large, imported data sets of more than 50,000 nodes. After the visualization has been created, it can be exported to be included in an infographic design. (www.gephi.org)

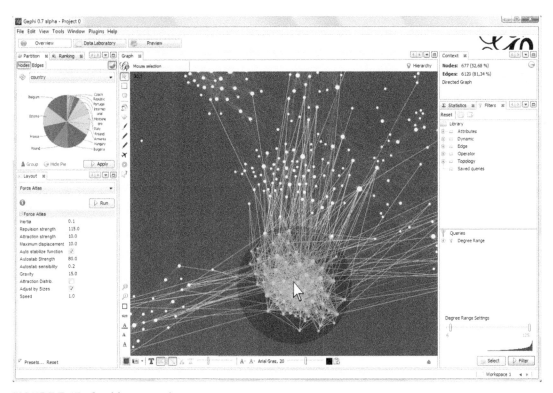

FIGURE 7-17: Gephi screen shot

Gliffy

Gliffy (Figure 7-18) is more for diagrams than traditional charts, such as flowcharts, Venn diagrams, network diagrams, and org charts. Diagrams can be saved as JPG, PNG, or SVG format files, which can then be included in an infographic design. (www.gliffy.com)

FIGURE 7-18: Gliffy diagramming application

iCharts

iCharts is a neat online tool for creating good charts. You can upload your data set and choose a chart type. A number of different chart types are available and you can customize all the chart attributes or use one of the chart design templates (Figure 7-19). When you finish, you can download your chart as a PNG image file for use in an infographic design. (www.icharts.net)

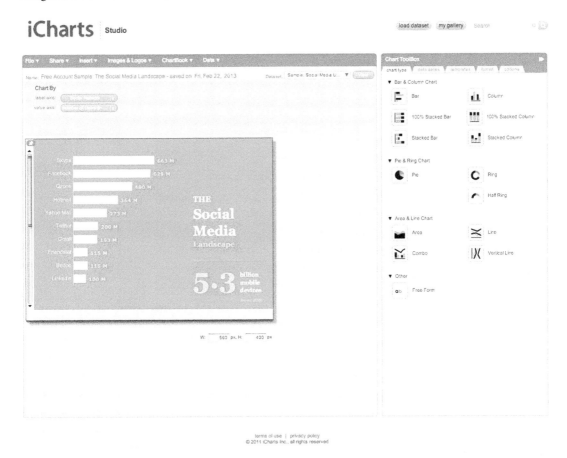

FIGURE 7-19: iCharts screen shot

Many Eyes

The Many Eyes project (Figure 7-20) is an ongoing experiment created by the teams at IBM Research and the IBM Cognos software group. The site enables you to create some more advanced data visualizations such as tree maps, bubble charts, word clouds, world maps, and network diagrams. Members can publish their visualizations online, and allow other members of the community to leave comments and view the raw data. (www-958.ibm.com/software/analytics/manyeyes/)

FIGURE 7-20:

Many Eyes visualization listing

The Noun Project

The Noun Project (Figure 7-21) is a fantastic resource to find icons related to the concepts you need to visualize in your infographic design. Most of the icons are free for use under a Creative Commons license as long as you give attribution to the designer in whatever design you include them in. Designers are always adding new icons to help build a broader visual language.

The Noun Project is built on donations and designs contributed by designers. If you can, consider contributing to the project. (www .thenounproject.com)

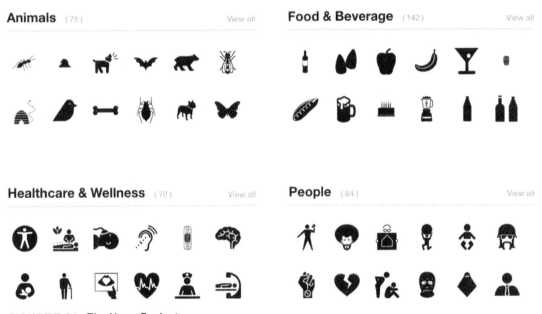

FIGURE 7-21: The Noun Project

Finding Data Online

One of the big challenges for infographics designers is finding the data they need to visualize as part of their infographic story. If you aren't using your own company data or research results, you will probably search online to find the data used to design your data visualizations.

Search engines (Google and Bing) can certainly help, but finding the perfect data for your infographic is tough if you have to look through millions of search results. Of course, the type of data you're looking for can help narrow down your search efforts.

Following are a number of data repository sites that host thousands of data sets. The intent of these sites is to make these data sets available to the public, but make sure you understand their terms of service.

Data.gov

The official data website of the U.S. Government, Data.gov is a project about transparency and the Open Government Initiative of the White House. As of this writing, the site currently boasts a total of 392,435 combined raw data sets, tools, and geo-data sets (www.data.gov).

DataMarket

DataMarket is a data repository site that enables users to view data visualizations of sets from around the world. Free access enables users to view and share the data, and Pro accounts ($59/month) enable access to premium tools to publish data and access to additional data sets, such as market research and financial market data. (www.datamarket.com)

FactBrowser

FactBrowser is self-described as a research discovery engine. It's a search engine dedicated to indexing the statistics quoted in news articles and press releases from companies and organizations. You can browse by category, company, source, consumer type, and regions of the world. (www.factbrowser.com)

Google Public Data

Google maintains a fantastic public directory with hundreds of data sets and metrics from many world governments and global organizations. Users can browse through the data sets and view the interactive data visualizations on the site. (www.google.com/publicdata/directory)

Internet World Stats

Internet World Stats has some great data based on Internet usage worldwide, population stats, and even some market research data. The site is often referenced in infographics as an indicator of the size and scale of the Internet. (internetworldstats.com)

Many Eyes

In addition to the data visualizations you can create on Many Eyes mentioned earlier, Many Eyes also hosts a huge repository of public data sets. There were 367,835 available data sets as of this writing, and members of the community add new sets all the time. The community also has the ability to comment on specific data sets to share thoughts or questions. (www-958.ibm.com/software/analytics/manyeyes/)

Quantcast

Quantcast measures, estimates, and forecasts site traffic for most sites on the web. For any designs that compare websites or site traffic, Quantcast is a great resource. Keep in mind that these are usually estimates and not actual data, but for comparison purposes, its numbers are usually in the ballpark. (www.quantcast.com)

Wikipedia

Of course many, many people use Wikipedia as a data source for infographics. There are lots of great HTML tables and individual statistics listed in the various entries. Always try to find the original source cited by Wikipedia (if available) so you get the raw data whenever possible. (www.wikipedia.org)

Wolfram Alpha

Wolfram Alpha probably has some statistics or data related to your topic and is always worth checking. It might be stats about the airplanes in the air over your location, information about caffeine, or demographics about a particular country. (www.wolframalpha.com)

Online Infographics Design Sites

A handful of new websites dedicated to designing infographics have launched recently. These sites enable you to input (or upload) your own data to create the charts and enable the user to choose from a collection of predesigned infographic templates for layout and style. These sites are mainly intended for the nondesigner audience that wants to create its own infographics without learning the software applications previously mentioned.

A handful of potential advantages for using these sites make them attractive:

▸ **Speed**—By using the templates and the online charting tools, you can create a complete infographic in less than an hour.

▸ **Hosting**—These sites host the final infographics online, so the user doesn't need to create a separate infographic landing page to host the final design.

▸ **SEO optimization**—For users that don't have the knowledge or skills to optimize the metadata on the infographic landing page, these sites can make the text in any infographic design available to the search engine crawlers to find your infographic.

▸ **Design style**—These templates enable the nondesigner users to break out of the PowerPoint-looking charts they would normally create. The design styles are fresh and new, which makes for a great looking infographic. Most of them also include data visualization styles not available in the MS Office suite.

Of course, there are a few potential disadvantages to using these design sites as well:

▸ **Templates**—Just like the presentation templates in PowerPoint, these templates will definitely be used by multiple people and may begin to look like stock designs. If your infographic design looks just like another design the audience has already seen, you're no longer unique and memorable.

▸ **Wrong chart**—Templates draw the user in with easy, predesigned charts, even if that chart isn't the right way to visualize the data you have to work with.

▸ **Dependency**—These are brand new companies and the websites may not be available 12 months from now. If this is where you host your infographic, you're dependent on the site to remain functional to keep your infographic live on the Internet.

- ▶ **Traffic and links**—If you host your infographic on these sites, and not on an infographic landing page on your own site, all the traffic and backlinks to your infographic design benefit the design site and not yours. Even using the embed-code to display the final infographic design on your own site is redirecting some of the traffic and PageRank to the design site.

- ▶ **Nonconfidentiality**—You may consider using an online design site to create an infographic of company data for internal use, but you may be inadvertently making your confidential company data public. Even if the site doesn't publish your infographic design publicly, you may be exposing your private data to the members of the design company. None of these sites claim that your data is encrypted or protected in any way, which may be in violation of your corporate policies.

These sites are a great way to start using data visualizations and infographics to communicate your message visually. If you design your own infographic using these tools, you should at least understand what you are sacrificing by not having complete control over your design.

Easel.ly

Easel.ly enables you to choose from a large library of templates, shapes, and objects to create and share an infographic design. Easel.ly doesn't have any advanced charting tools, so it's up to the designer to manually adjust the sizes of shapes to match the data values. The circles shown in Figure 7-22 would each need to be resized by the user to match the data. (www.easel.ly)

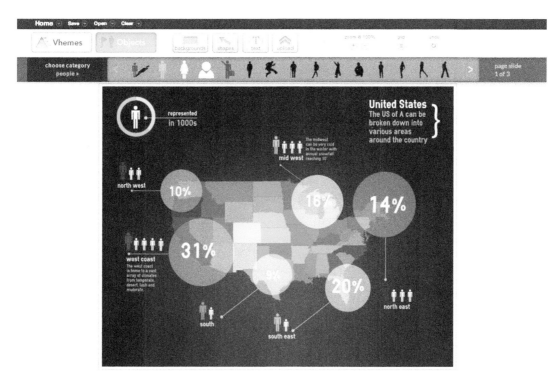

FIGURE 7-22: Easel.ly design interface

infogr.am

Infogr.am is an online tool for creating and sharing infographics and individual charts based on your own data. Shown in Figure 7-23, it has simplified and prepackaged the design process to four steps:

1. Choose a template.

2. Add your own data.

3. Customize the design.

4. Publish and share.

The charts are interactive, which adds some animation and changes the display based on decisions from the viewer. The tool also enables you to embed the final designs on your site or share on the major social media networks. (infogr.am)

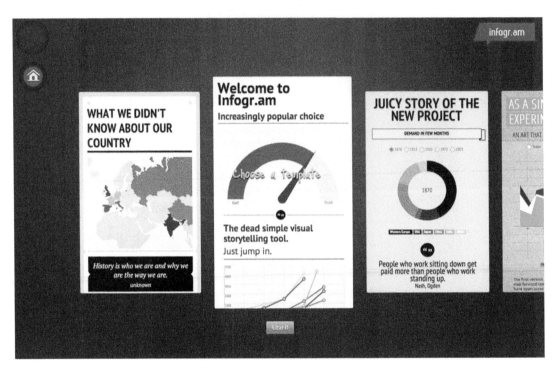

FIGURE 7-23: Infogr.am template chooser

Piktochart

Piktochart is a WYSIWYG editor for infographics online. The tool enables you to create infographics online with interactive charts, and claims they are optimized for SEO and social media sharing. Users may create an account for free and have access to a handful of templates (Figure 7-24). PRO users pay $9.99 per month and get access to approximately 100 more templates. It also claims to have more than 1,000 icons and graphics in its library of images for would-be designers to incorporate into their designs. (www.piktochart.com)

Venngage

Venngage is an online infographic creation site from the same people that developed the Vizualize.me infographic resume site mentioned in Chapter 4, "Infographic Resumes." Upload your data into one of the predesigned templates and then customize the final design to the colors that match your brand or style (Figure 7-25). There are both free and Pro accounts ($19/month) available. (venngage.com)

FIGURE 7-25:
Venngage design templates

Visual.ly

Visual.ly is primarily a gallery site for infographics, but it has recently launched the Visually Create! section of the website where users can create custom infographics based on a selection of predesigned templates (Figure 7-26). These are primarily social media-related designs that need access to connect with Facebook or Twitter to pull in the data used to create infographics (`create.visual.ly`).

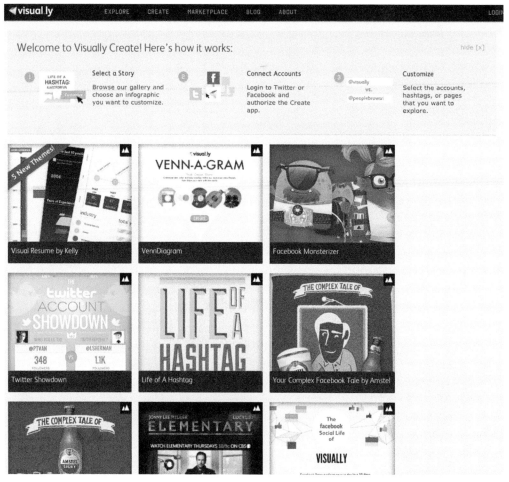

FIGURE 7-26: Visually Create!

Reading List

In addition to online resources, here are some of the other great books written about data visualization and infographics from my own reading shelf. Mostly focused on improving the data visualizations used in infographics, I highly recommend these books to anyone looking to learn more about using data to tell stories visually.

Visualize This: The FlowingData Guide to Design, Visualizations, and Statistics, Nathan Yau, (Wiley, 2011)

The Power of Infographics, Mark Smiciklas, (Que, 2012)

The Functional Art, Alberto Cairo, (New Riders, 2013)

Beautiful Visualization, Edited by Julie Steele and Noah Iliinsky, (O'Reilly, 2010)

The Visual Miscellaneum, David McCandless, (HarperCollins, 2009)

Beautiful Evidence, Edward Tufte, (Graphics Press, 2006)

Visual Complexity: Mapping Patterns of Information, Manuel Lima, (Princeton Architectural Press, 2011)

Infographics: The Power of Visual Storytelling, Jason Lankow, Josh Ritchie, and Ross Crooks, (Wiley, 2012)

Index

Credits

T0176783

EXECUTIVE EDITOR
Carol Long

SENIOR PROJECT EDITOR
Adaobi Obi Tulton

TECHNICAL EDITOR
Nancy Gage

PRODUCTION EDITOR
Christine Mugnolo

COPY EDITOR
San Dee Philips

EDITORIAL MANAGER
Mary Beth Wakefield

FREELANCER EDITORIAL MANAGER
Rosemarie Graham

ASSOCIATE DIRECTOR OF MARKETING
David Mayhew

MARKETING MANAGER
Ashley Zurcher

BUSINESS MANAGER
Amy Knies

VICE PRESIDENT AND EXECUTIVE GROUP PUBLISHER
Richard Swadley

VICE PRESIDENT AND EXECUTIVE PUBLISHER
Neil Edde

ASSOCIATE PUBLISHER
Jim Minatel

PROJECT COORDINATOR, COVER
Katie Crocker

COMPOSITOR
Maureen Forys,
Happenstance Type-O-Rama

PROOFREADER
Sarah Kaikini, Word One New York

INDEXER
Robert Swanson

COVER IMAGE
Courtesy of Ray Vella

COVER DESIGNER
Randy Krum